During good times Americans pay Uncle Sam their fair share in taxes. Uncle Sam is not reluctant about collecting from them.

Now with the alarming rate of unemployment, soaring inflation and rising taxes, it is your turn to collect from Uncle Sam.

This easy-to-understand book explains all of the benefits available from Uncle Sam which equal billions of dollars. So . . . don't wait. Get your fair share now!

HOW TO COLLECT BIG $$
FROM UNCLE SAM

THE COMPLETE HANDBOOK OF
U. S.
GOVERNMENT
BENEFITS

By
R. Emil Neuman

How To Collect Big $$ From Uncle Sam
THE COMPLETE HANDBOOK OF
U. S. GOVERNMENT BENEFITS

Revised 1989.

Publisher's note: The purpose of this book is to provide a concise, easy-to-understand explanation of benefits available under federal programs, and is not intended to give advice in specific matters relating to the laws and regulations about these programs. If specific questions or problems about eligibility or benefits available arise, contact the agency responsible for the program for advice.

ISBN 0-9614924-2-2

Published By
United Research Publishers
Box 2344
Leucadia, CA 92024

Printed in U.S.A

ACKNOWLEDGEMENTS

To my parents, Adolph and Ann Neuman, who made this book possible by bringing me into this world and encouraging me to finish college.

To Janet Gilliland for her continuing efforts in assuring this book is current, accurate and complete.

CONTENTS

How To Collect Big $$ From Uncle Sam

THE COMPLETE HANDBOOK OF
U. S. GOVERNMENT
BENEFITS

FOREWORD

Bureaucrats Made
This Book Necessary

This year $250 billion will be made available to Americans under a variety of federal programs. The benefits will range from hundreds of dollars a month to improve a family's diet to hundreds of thousands of dollars to start a business. Many people are unaware that these programs exist and are missing out on benefits that are rightfully theirs.

This book clearly explains how you can get your fair share of the billions of dollars that will be handed out, and it covers all the important aspects of the federal programs, including social security, business loans, unemployment compensation, legal assistance, housing and rent subsidies, job training, veterans benefits, education, health care, food stamps, and welfare. Also, the book tells you how to get valuable free information and services from the federal government.

We have taken great pains to make this the most concise, easy-to-read book available anywhere. The chapters include important information about federal programs and explain eligibility and benefits. We tell you where to go to apply for benefits and how to cut through governmental red tape. Toll-free trelephone numbers are provided in many cases to put you in direct contact with the government agency which can help you.

Hypothetical cases are used to help you better understand the programs and most chapters include a question-and-answer section dealing with many interesting facets of federal programs.

3

This book is of vital importance to every American because the vast majority have been kept ignorant of the variety of monetary benefits available through the federal government. Congress is appropriating billions of dollars a year in benefits to assist citizens. Those benefits are derived from the taxes you are paying. Uncle Sam is not embarrassed to hold out his hand to collect your hard-earned money in the form of taxes, and you should not be embarrassed to hold out yours to reclaim some of that money.

But how can you claim your fair share if you don't know what you have coming? The answer to this question is quite simple. This book fills the information void left by the federal government.

But why this void, you may ask. Again, simple — the bureauracy.

After Congress passes bills establishing these programs, they are turned over to federal agencies to be administered. It is the responsibility of these agencies to inform the public what benefits are available under each of the programs. But the agencies are not doing their jobs.

How often have you seen a spot on television explaining that you can get more than $400 a month to attend college. Or read in a magazine or newspaper that more than $800 a month in family support is available while you are unemployed. Probably never.

Most federal employees are dedicated and hard-working. But all too often people who work in the agencies—the bureaucrats—realize that the more people who find out what they have coming the more work they will have to do. Therefore, they have an incentive to keep the public in the dark. That incentive? A cushiony federal job with little actual work.

We believe the bureaucrats should start serving the public rather than perpetuating their own comfortable existence. The bureaucratic machinery probably will take a dim view of this book; it may have to start earning its salaries as more people avail themselves of benefits.

But we don't care what the bureaucrats think or say. We just want them to do a better job for you, especially during these hard times.

Chapter 1

How to Collect
Social Security at Any Age

As a working American, social security taxes are withheld
from your paycheck. You have no choice in the matter. You
can't tell your employer you don't want to be covered under
the Social Security Program because social security
deductions are required by law.

Social security probably is the least understood program
administered by the federal government. Even though social
security deductions represent a sizable sum of money over a
worker's productive years, few people worry about the Social
Security Program until they begin reaching retirement age.
But they are under the mistaken impression that only
Americans who have retired get monthly social security
checks.

Social security is much more than just a retirement
program. It can:

—provide monthly income to a worker and his family
  when the worker becomes disabled;

—provide monthly income to a worker's family when
  the worker dies, and

—provide medical benefits under the Medicare Program
  even before a worker retires.

How to Collect Big $$$ from Uncle Sam

Many years ago, Congress saw a need to establish the Social Security Program which provides for the material needs of workers and their families, and protects aged and disabled workers against the expense of illness that could otherwise exhaust their savings.

Congress saw the need, established the law and turned the administration of the Social Security Program over the federal employees. Congress expected the federal employees—the bureaucrats—to keep all Americans informed of the benefits available under the program.

Then why is there such a tremendous lack of public knowledge about such an important program which affects so many Americans? How often have you seen a spot on television or heard anything on the radio explaining your coverage under social security? Or, how often have you seen a social security benefit explained in a newspaper or magazine? More than likely, never.

The Social Security Administration does sell a handbook and it makes available brochures and pamphlets on social security benefits. But they're all too often difficult to read and hard to understand.

This chapter translates the federal bureaucrats' "mumbo jumbo" into a clean, easy-to-follow guide for people to understand. It covers the important aspects of social security eligibility and benefits. And it tells you where to go and how to cut through the bureaucratic red tape to get your benefits.

Here's What Social Security Is

Social security provides monthly income to retired individuals who have worked long enough to be eligible. It also offers checks to the individual's family, to a disabled worker who qualifies and to his family, and to a worker's family when an individual dies.

The cash benefit provisions of the Social Security Program are designed to partially replace the income that is lost when a worker retires, becomes severely disabled or dies. The program also provides partial protection against the high cost of health care under Medicare.

How to Collect Social Security At Any Age

The Social Security Program is aimed at preventing poverty and destitution rather than relieving these conditions after they occur, and revolves around five basic principles. They are:

—security for workers and their families grows out of their own work;

—benefits are an earned right;

—workers make contributions to help finance benefits;

—with minor exceptions, coverage is compulsory, and

—the amount of benefits are clearly defined under law.

Unlike other federal programs, such as welfare and food stamps, very few people are embarrassed about collecting social security. They realize that money is being taken directly out of their paychecks and they look upon social security as retirement insurance. Generally, the more an individual earns during his working years, the more he will receive under the Social Security Program.

Before an individual can collect benefits under social security, he must meet certain conditions. They are:

—possession of a social security number;

—deduction of money out of wages or payment of self-employment tax to be credited to a worker's social security record;

—accumulation of a sufficient number of calendar work credits, and

—completion of necessary application forms.

To meet the first condition under the Social Security Program, an individual should ask for Form SS-5 at the nearest Social Security Office. The form is an application for a social security number. An applicant must establish his age, identity and citizenship or alien status. He must give complete and accurate personal information to make sure that his earnings will be credited to his social security record.

If a person loses his social security card, he may apply for a duplicate by filling out another Form SS-5, giving the same identifying information he supplied for the first card. If a person wishes to correct the identifying information that he has given on the original application, the nearest Social Security Office will furnish him with Form 7003.

How to Collect Big $$$ from Uncle Sam

To meet the second condition under the Social Security Program, wages or self-employment income must have been earned and credited to the worker's social security record. Employee wages subject to social security deductions include:

—salary or hourly compensation;
—sales commissions;
—bonuses and wage dividends;
—vacation pay in lieu of vacations;
—dismissal pay;
—basic pay for active duty in the military service after 1956;
—cash tips totaling more than $20 in a calendar month.

Any type of work covered by social security earns credit. It doesn't matter if the work is full-time, part-time or temporary.

Employers are required to deduct social security taxes from employees' wages. The rate is 7.51 percent up to a maximum tax of $3,605. Employers are required to match your contribution on a dollar-for-dollar basis.

Self-employed persons are responsible for paying social security taxes on net annual earnings over $400. The tax is due when the self-employed person files his Federal Income Tax return. The present rate is 13.02 percent of net earnings up to a maximum tax of $6,249.60.

An individual may check his social security earnings record and estimated benefits by completing Form 7004, Request for Earnings and Benefit Estimate Statement and mailing it to the Social Security Administration. The best way to request Form 7004 is by calling the Social Security Administration toll free at 1-800-234-5772 or you can request Form 7004 by writing to: Social Security Administration, P.O. Box 57, Baltimore, MD 21203. If you are age 60 or over, a representative will give you earnings and estimated benefits information over the telephone.

On Form 7004 you will be asked to provide your name and social security number shown on your card. You will also be asked to provide other pertinent information such as your date of birth and other social security numbers or names you may have used. Even though you have used other social security numbers or names you may still get credit for those amounts paid into the social security system.

You will also be asked to provide your last year's earnings, this year's estimated earnings, your estimated future earnings and the age you plan to retire. It is important to provide the most accurate information possible because it will be used by the Social Security Administration to compile your Personal Earnings and Benefit Estimate Statement. This statement lists your earnings history, and gives you an estimate of the monthly benefits you and your family may qualify for now or in the future.

You will find several copies of Form 7004 on the last few pages of this book. As discussed later on in this book it is a good idea to periodically submit this form to the Social Security Administration to make sure your social security earnings are being properly recorded.

To meet the third condition under the Social Security Program, an individual must accumulate a sufficient number of calendar work credits.

For each $500 of wages paid or self-employment income earned, a person is credited with one quarter of coverage up to a maximum of four quarters in any calendar year. Your Personal Earnings and Benefit Estimate Statement will tell you how many calendar quarters of work credit you have earned.

To meet the last general condition under the Social Security Program, application forms must be completed for processing. An individual is responsible for submitting the necessary evidence to support his claim for social security benefits. However, the nearest Social Security Office has all the necessary forms and will assist by explaining what evidence is required to establish the claim.

Here's What Social Security Covers

The best way to explain the different types of benefits an individual can get from social security is to break the program down into the categories of people eligible. Those catagories include a retired worker and his family, explained under Retirement; a disabled worker and his family, explained under Disability; and the family of a worker who has died, explained under Death.

Retirement

A retired worker may get full monthly checks at age 65, or reduced payments may start as early as age 62. The worker considering retirement at the earlier age should note that if he retires at age 62, he will continue to get the reduced payment until he dies. Therefore, workers have an incentive of collecting larger monthly checks from social security by continuing to work until age 65.

Before a worker may get a social security retirement check, he needs to have credit for a certain amount of work under the Social Security Program. The work credit needed to become eligible for retirement benefits depends on when the worker reaches age 62. For those reaching 62 in:

—1980, 7¼ years of credit are needed;
—1981, 7½ years of credit are needed;
—1983, 8   years of credit are needed;
—1985, 8½ years of credit are needed;
—1987, 9   years of credit are needed;
—1989, 9½ years of credit are needed;
—1991 or later, 10 years of work credit are needed.

No one ever needs more than 10 years of work credit under the Social Security Program to get benefits. But if an individual stops working under social security before he has the necessary credit, as shown above, he can't get retirement benefits. Therefore, it is important for a worker to know how many work credits he has earned under social security.

If a worker finds out that he does not have the necessary work credits, he can return to work and add to those credits he already has. It is extremely important for an individual nearing retirement age to check into his work credit record to insure that he will receive full social security benefits. As discussed earlier, an individual can find out how many work credits he has earned by sending for his social security earnings record. But the Social Security Administration will provide that information only if a special note on the "Request for Statement of Earnings Form" is included. This is done by writing "QC" in the upper left hand corner of the request form.

Retirement Benefits

Once a worker finds out that he has enough work credits, he may wonder how much the monthly retirement benefit check will be.

A table which follows will provide a rough estimate of the monthly benefits an individual may expect to receive upon retirement. But keep in mind that the benefit rates automatically increase with the cost of living. So if you are a worker who is several years from retirement, you can expect to get more than the amount shown in the table.

The benefit rates in the table relate to an individual's retirement age, dependent status and average annual earnings. A word of explanation is needed here because the term average annual earnings may be a bit misleading. Only an individual's highest earnings subject to social security taxes over a number of years are used to compute average annual earnings.

Those earnings are based on an individual's actual taxable earnings up to a maximum amount established by the Social Security Administration. For example, the maximum wages subject to social security in 1951-54 were $3,600. The maximum wages subject to social security tax gradually increased over the years to the current $48,000 figure.

Average annual earnings are used to compute a worker's basic benefit. The basic benefit is the worker's full benefit he or she would receive if retiring at age 65. The worker's basic benefit in turn is used to compute other benefits payable to a worker's spouse and dependents. All benefits are computed as a percentage of the worker's basic benefit. For example, as shown in the table below, a spouse's retirement benefit is 50 percent of the retired worker's basic benefit, when retiring at age 65.

If an individual is a ways from retirement he will not be able to accurately calculate his average annual earnings. No one knows what future earnings will be nor do they know how much income will be subject to social security taxes. However, based on past and projected earnings, it may be possible for a worker to get a rough idea what his average annual earnings will be.

Included at the end of this chapter is a worksheet with instructions on how to compute your average annual earnings.

The following table will give you an idea of what a retired worker and spouse can expect to receive monthly when retiring at age 65.

Examples of Monthly Social Security Payments

Average Yearly Earnings	$3000	$4200	$5400	$6600	$7800	$9000	$10,200
Worker Retired at Age 65	344.00	420.00	494.00	570.00	650.00	700.00	750.00
Spouse (65 or older)	172.00	210.00	247.00	285.00	325.00	350.00	375.00

Here's a rough idea of what a retired worker and spouse can expect to receive monthly when retiring at age 62.

Examples of Monthly Social Security Payments

Average Yearly Earnings	$3000	$4200	$5400	$6600	$7800	$9000	$10,200
Worker Retired at Age 62	276.00	336.00	394.00	450.00	522.00	560.00	600.00
Spouse at 62 (No child)	130.00	158.00	186.00	214.00	243.00	262.00	281.00

It is important to note that if you retire at 62, your retirement checks will be permanently reduced. The amount of reduction in your monthly social security checks will depend on the number of months before you reach 65. For example, benefits will be reduced $5/9$ of 1% multiplied by the number of months before age 65. If you retire right at age 62 your benefit is reduced 20% ($5/9$ times 36 equals 20).

The reduction in your benefit due to early retirement won't affect payments to your spouse or eligible children. Their payments will still be based on your basic benefit (your full benefit if you had retired at age 65).

How to Collect Social Security At Any Age

Family Benefits

Social security is a family insurance program. When an insured worker begins to collect retirement benefits, certain family members also become eligible for benefits. Here are the principle benefits available to family members of a covered, retired worker.

The Wife

As shown in the chart on page 14, the wife is entitled to benefits equal to 50 percent of her husband's basic benefit if she starts collecting at age 65. At age 62, she can collect reduced benefits equal to 37½ percent of her husband's basic benefit. The wife will continue to receive this reduced benefit even when she turns 65. A wife can collect benefits at any age if she is caring for her husband's child who is under 16 (16 or over if disabled).

Divorced Wife

The former wife of a man eligible for retirement benefits is entitled to benefits on his record if she was married to him for at least 10 years and they have been divorced at least 2 years. The divorced wife's benefit is equal to 50 percent of her former husband's basic benefit if she starts collecting at age 65. At age 62, she can collect reduced benefits equal to 37½ percent of her former husband's basic benefit.

If the divorced woman remarries, she can no longer collect benefits based on her former husband's record. However, her remarriage won't affect benefits payable to her former husband's dependent children under her care.

The Husband (and Divorced Husband)

Under a March 1977 Supreme Court decision and a June 1977 Federal District Court decision, a husband can now collect benefits on his wife's work record, the same as what a wife can collect on her husband's record. Refer to The Wife and The Divorced Wife sections above. The exact same benefits are now available to a husband on the wife's work record.

How to Collect Big $$$ from Uncle Sam

These new rules could mean more benefits for many husbands. For example, the husband of a retired woman may now collect benefits under the wife's record if he is at least 62.

Dependent Children

The children of a retired, insured worker may be eligible to collect social security benefits. To collect benefits, a retired worker's child must be unmarried and younger than 18, or up to age 19 if still in high school. Unmarried children 18 or over can collect benefits if they become disabled before age 22 and continue to be disabled. The dependent child's benefit is equal to 50 percent of the worker's basic benefit.

A child is eligible for benefits on the record of the natural parents. A legally adopted child living with the stepparent (or receiving one-half support from the stepparent) can qualify for benefits under the stepparent's record. Thus, a child living with his real mother and stepfather can be eligible for social security benefits on the records of three people—his mother, real father and stepfather.

How Earnings Reduce Benefits

The retired worker's earnings from a job or self employment may reduce the monthly benefits payable to him and family members. The retired worker at age 65 to 70 may earn up to $8,880 without affecting monthly retirement benefits. However, for every $2 of earnings over these allowable limits, $1 in benefits will be subtracted from the benefit check of both the worker and each family member receiving benefits. If the retired worker is under age 65 the allowable earnings limit is $6,480. At age 70 or older the retired worker's earnings will not affect benefit checks, no matter what the amount.

The earnings of the worker's spouse and other dependents, over the allowable limit, will reduce only their benefit checks. The retired worker's benefit will not be affected. The earnings limit for a spouse and other dependents is the same as for the retired worker. How earnings affect benefit payments will be covered more thoroughly later on.

Maximum Family Benefits

There is a maximum monthly benefit that can be paid to a family. This provision is designed to prevent a family's benefits from exceeding the worker's recent earnings.

The present maximum family benefit is about 160 percent of the worker's basic benefit. The maximum family benefit is generally reached when a worker and 2 family members are collecting benefits. When several persons are collecting benefits on the same worker's record, each benefit (except the worker's) may be reduced to conform to the maximum family payment.

The maximum benefit provision also applies to disability and survivors benefits discussed later.

Questions and Answers

The preceding section provides an overview of retirement benefits under social security. The following questions and answers give more specific information. They are designed to answer the most frequently asked questions on social security retirement benefits.

Q. What is the main advantage and disadvantage of retiring at age 62?

A. The main advantage is that you can collect retirement benefits for a longer period of time. Life expectancy for a man age 65 is 13.7 years. For a woman, it is 17.7 years after reaching age 65.

Of course, the main disadvantage of retiring at age 62 is that benefits are permanently reduced to make up for the 3 extra years of additional payments. The reduction in your benefit because of early retirement, however, won't reduce payments to your spouse or children. They will still receive a percentage of your basic benefit (what you would have received had you retired at age 65).

Today many people are deciding to retire early at age 62. They recognize that life is too short to gamble on collecting the higher benefits at age 65. If you decide to retire before age 65, make sure you have adequate health insurance coverage. Medicare does not begin until you reach age 65.

How to Collect Big $$$ from Uncle Sam

Q. What are the advantages of postponing retirement past age 65?

A. If you choose to continue working past age 65 and do not collect social security benefits, you are entitled to increased benefits when you finally decide to retire. This increase amounts to 3 percent a year (up to a maximum of 15 percent) between the ages of 65 and 70, if you reach 65 after 1981.

Q. Under what conditions can reduced retirement benefits be increased?

A. If you become disabled after you retire at age 62 but before you reach age 65, you could collect disability benefits. Disability benefits would be higher than reduced retirement benefits.

Q. Can a wife retire on her husband's record at age 62 if her husband is over age 65 but not yet retired?

A. No. The husband must first retire before the wife can get benefits on his record. However, the wife could get reduced retirement benefits on her own record, even though her husband decides not to retire until after age 65.

Q. Can a divorced wife (wed for 10 years or more) retire on her former husband's record at age 62 if her husband is over age 65 but not yet retired?

A. Yes. Under a recent ruling she can collect when her ex-husband becomes *eligible* for benefits (whether or not he is actually receiving them) as long as they have been divorced 2 years.

Q. What happens when both a husband and wife are eligible for retirement benefits on their own work records. How much can they collect?

A. Each spouse can collect the higher of (1) the benefit available on their own record, or (2) a spouse's benefit available on the record of the husband or wife. For example, if a wife is entitled to $150 a month on her own record and $200 a month on the record of her husband, she will get the higher amount—$200 a month.

How to Collect Social Security At Any Age

Q. Can a retired couple get separate benefit checks?

A. Yes. The husband and wife can each get separate checks, or they can get a combined check. If they elect to get a combined retirement check, both must endorse the check before it can be legally cashed.

Q. Can a person collect retirement benefits even if they have never paid in a penny to social security?

A. Yes. A person who reached age 72 before 1968 may collect monthly benefits regardless of their past work record. Currently about 170,000 people are collecting such monthly benefit checks. People in this category who became 72 in 1968 or later needed at least 3 quarters of social security coverage to get these special benefits.

Q. Is there a minimum monthly social security benefit for a retired worker?

A. Yes. There is a special minimum benefit for some people 65 or over who worked under social security for over 10 years but who had very low earnings.

Q. What percentage of people in the United States who are age 65 or older are either collecting social security retirement benefits, or are entitled to collect benefits?

A. About 93 percent. This percentage is expected to increase to 97 percent by the year 2,000.

Q. Can a wife retire before her husband at age 62 on her own record, then get an increased spouse's benefit when her husband retires at age 65?

A. Yes. And, if the husband returns to work, she can still go back to collecting monthly benefits on her own record.

Q. Can a widow retire at age 60 on her deceased husband's record, then at age 62 switch to retirement benefits on her own record?

A. Yes. Also, a retired man can often switch to widower benefits and get a higher payment.

Q. How long does a spouse have to be married to a worker before he or she is eligible to collect retirement benefits on the worker's record?

A. Generally one year.

How to Collect Big $$$ from Uncle Sam

Q. Can a person collect social security and unemployment benefits at the same time?

A. No. States are now required to reduce unemployment benefit checks by the amount of a pension or other retirement benefit on a dollar-for-dollar basis during any week an individual was eligible for both types of benefits.

Disability

The possibility of disability hangs over everyone. When disability occurs, it may affect a family's financial security even more than the retirement or death of a worker.

The Social Security Program provides benefits to disabled workers under 65 and their families, persons disabled before age 22, disabled widows and dependents, and other individuals under special conditions.

It's important to understand what the Social Security Administration considers a disability. Disability is defined as "inability to engage in any substantial, gainful work by reason of any medically determinable physical or mental impairment which has lasted or can be expected to last for a continuous period of not less than 12 months or result in death".

The Social Security Administration makes a determination of disability on the basis of medical facts and an evaluation of the individual's remaining capacity for work. Age, education and work experience may also be considered.

If you are a worker and become disabled, you will be eligible for monthly benefits if you have worked under social security long enough. The amount of work you need depends on the age when you become disabled:

—before age 24, you need credit for 1½ years of work in the 3-year period ending when your disability begins;

—age 24 through 30, you need credit for having worked half the time between age 21 and the time you become disabled;

—age 31 or older, all workers disabled at 31 or older need credit for at least five years of work out of the ten years ending when they become disabled. Some workers may need additional credit depending on their age and when their disability began.

Disability Benefits

The amount of the monthly disability benefit is based on the average earnings under social security over a period of years. The exact amount of the benefit cannot be figured in advance because all earnings in a worker's social security record at the time of application must be considered, and an individual cannot forecast when he will become disabled. The Social Security Administration will, of course, figure the exact benefits at that time.

The table below can give you an idea of the monthly benefits a disabled worker under 65 and spouse can expect based on differing average annual earnings amounts.

Examples of Monthly Disability Payments

Average Yearly Earnings	$3000	$4200	$5400	$6600	$7800	$9000	$10,200
Worker under 65 and disabled	344.00	420.00	494.00	570.00	650.00	700.00	750.00
Spouse at 65 (No child)	172.00	210.00	247.00	285.00	325.00	350.00	375.00

Benefit rates automatically increase as the cost of living goes up.

The disabled worker and his family receive benefits after a waiting period of five full calendar months; the first payment is for the sixth full month. If a worker has been disabled more than six full months before he applies, back benefits may be paid, but not for the 5-month waiting period. It is important to apply soon after the disability starts because back payments are limited to the 12 months preceding the month you apply.

Moreover, after a person collects disability benefits for two consecutive years, he or she becomes eligible for hospital and medical coverage under medicare.

Family Benefits

Social security disability protection is designed to help make up the loss of income when a worker becomes disabled. This loss of income affects the worker's entire family. Therefore, once an insured worker collects disability, certain family members also become eligible for benefits.

21

How to Collect Big $$$ from Uncle Sam

Here are the principle benefits available to family members of a covered, disabled worker.

The Wife

As shown in the chart on page 21, the wife is entitled to benefits equal to 50 percent of her disabled husband's basic benefit if she starts collecting at age 65. At age 62, she can collect reduced benefits equal to 37½ percent of her husband's basic benefit. The wife can collect monthly benefits at any age if she is caring for the disabled worker's child under age 16 (16 or over if disabled).

The Divorced Wife

The former wife of a man receiving disability benefits is entitled to benefits on his record if she was married to him for at least 10 years. The divorced wife's benefit is equal to 50 percent of her former husband's basic benefit if she starts collecting at age 65. At age 62, she can collect reduced benefits equal to 37½ percent of her former husband's basic benefit.

If the divorced wife remarries, she can no longer collect benefits based on her former husband's record. However, her remarriage won't affect benefits payable to her former husband's dependent children under her care.

The Husband (and Divorced Husband)

As previously noted, under a March 1977 Supreme Court decision and a June 1977 Federal District Court decision, a husband can now collect benefits on his wife's record. The benefits are the same as what the wife can collect on the husband's record. Refer to The Wife and The Divorced Wife sections above. The exact same benefits are now available to a husband on the wife's work record.

These new rules will mean additional benefits for many husbands. For example, the husband of a wife receiving disability benefits can now stay home and care for the children while collecting monthly benefit checks.

Dependent Children

The children of a worker getting disability benefits may also be eligible to collect monthly checks. To collect benefits, a disabled worker's child must be unmarried and younger than 18, or up to age 19 if still in high school. Unmarried children 18 or over can collect benefits if they become disabled before age 22 and continue to be disabled. The dependent child's benefit is equal to 50 percent of the worker's basic benefit.

A child is eligible for benefits on the record of the natural parent. However, a legally adopted child living with the stepparent (or receiving one-half support from the stepparent) can qualify for benefits on the stepparent's record. Thus, a child living with his real mother and stepfather could be eligible for benefits on the records of three people—his mother, real father and stepfather.

How Earnings Reduce Benefits

The earnings of a spouse and children of a disabled worker may reduce their own monthly benefits. However, their earnings will not affect the disabled worker's benefits.

Who is Collecting Disability?

Presently about 3.5 million people are collecting monthly social security disability checks. However, the Social Security Administration estimates that as many as 7.7 million people may be eligible for disability benefits. Obviously, many disabled people who are legally entitled to benefits are not getting them.

The leading cause of disability under social security is heart disease and circulatory impairments. This accounts for about 30 percent of all disabilities. Other major causes of disability are:

—muscle and bone disorders (includes arthritis and back problems),

—mental disorders,

—cancer,

—respiratory problems, particularly emphysema, and

—accidents.

23

How to Collect Big $$$ from Uncle Sam

As for the age of disabled workers, over half are 50 or older. At this age most disabilities are due to heart trouble, muscle and bone problems, and cancer. In contrast, most disabled workers under 30 years of age suffer from a mental disorder, or were injured in an accident.

It is important to keep in mind that social security considers you disabled only if you have a medically determinable physical or mental disorder which prevents you from performing any substantial, gainful work and is expected to last for at least 12 months or result in death. So if your impairment prevents you from doing your regular work, you won't be eligible for benefits if you can still do some other kind of gainful work.

How Disability Determinations Are Made

Disability determinations are made by a team composed of a physician and disability examiner in the state where the applicant lives. This team makes disability decisions based on federal rules and regulations. To make disability decisions more uniform and objective, the Social Security Administration has developed standards for measuring the "level of severity" of a physical or mental disability. These standards are based on extensive research, experience and consultation with medical specialists. The standards cover the major parts of the body and consist of medically measurable factors which are used in deciding the seriousness of a physical or mental impairment. For example, in determining the disabling severity of a heart problem, the Social Security Administration would consider medically measurable factors such as the degree of heart enlargement, the extent to which circulation is impaired, etc. These factors can be measured and objectively evaluated. The Social Security Administration does not rely on a doctor's opinion; an opinion can't be measured.

In deciding on a disability claim, the Social Security Administration considers measurable medical evidence from both private physicians and government doctors. The key determination made is whether the evidence shows that an individual's physical or mental impairment prevents him or her from engaging in substantial, gainful employment.

To speed up processing the Social Security Administration now employs a broad "screening procedure" whereby cases having sufficient medical evidence of disability can be quickly approved for monthly benefit payments. Other cases are decided on an individual basis.

Unfortunately, the medical evidence necessary for speedy approval is not always available from the applicant or the Social Security Administration. Typically, family physicians do not keep good records nor are they interested in measuring the severity of a disability, and the process of gathering the needed medical evidence often is very time consuming.

Having the right kind of medical evidence that proves you are unable to engage in any substantial, gainful work will greatly speed up the time it takes to process your disability claim. Therefore, you may want to locate a physician who is an expert in measuring physical or mental impairments. This kind of medical authority will know what kind and quantity of evidence to submit with your application for disability benefits. Such an expert can often be found through local, state or county medical societies. Look in your telephone directory or call information and ask for the number of the medical society located in your county (or city). The local medical society will have a trained specialist available to help you. When calling, tell the information specialist specifically the kind of medical doctor you need. You might say something like this:

"I want to establish a social security (or SSI) disability claim for my lower back problem. To do this, I need measurable medical evidence of my back impairment. Please refer me to a doctor who is an expert in measuring the degree of impairment for my type of disability".

Most medical societies can refer you to a doctor who is an expert in this field. He will know what tests to perform on you, and how to prepare the results for submission to the Social Security Administration.

Determining the extent of disability in certain impairments can be troublesome. This is particulary true with mental disabilities. There is no problem if an individual is psychotic and completely out of touch with reality. But cases where a person is neurotic or suffering from a general nervous condition are more difficult to decide.

In the borderline cases, the Social Security Administration relies more heavily on the individual's age, training and work experience. Since medical judgments can vary substantially, the Social Security Administration also considers evidence presented by vocational and social authorities.

In recent years about 50 percent of the disability claims have been initially rejected because the medical evidence presented to the Social Security Administration did not demonstrate an inability to engage in substancial, gainful employment or that the disability was expected to last at least 12 months. This does not necessarily mean that an individual does not suffer from a disabling impairment. It only means that the medical evidence available to the Social Security Administration did not support a disability claim.

Having Enough Work Credits

All too often I get letters from disabled folks telling me they have been denied social security disability benefits because they did not pay into the system for 5 of the 10 years before they became disabled. Many folks do not know they must earn social security work credits for 5 of the last 10 years before they became disabled to get benefits. Many persons became disabled only to find out they are a few work credits short of qualifying for benfits. This is especially disheartening when a person has worked under social security their entire life except for the years just before their disability appeared.

There are a number of persons who are particulary vulnerable to a lapse in disability coverage. For example, mothers who stay home to care for a new baby may lose coverage if they're out of the workforce long enough. Also, men who leave jobs to return full-time to school may be in danger.

With a little ingenuity you can protect yourself against lapses in coverage. You need only $500 in wages or self-employment earnings to earn a quarter work credit. Only a small investment in time can continue your coverage. This coverage could mean hundreds of thousands of dollars to you and your family if you become disabled.

Women caring for small children are normally tied to the home. In this situation, self-employment income may be the best way to keep up with your coverage. Consider doing some kind of work at home on a free-lance basis. Often a former employer can provide work you can conveniently do at home while caring for small children. Many women even do occasional babysitting for friends or relatives to earn work credits.

Men with families should be concerned about a lapse in disability coverage. Men who take time off to attend school full-time should have a plan for continuing disability coverage. Since men are generally not tied to the home, they can usually find some minimal part-time employment to earn work credits. But if this is not possible, part-time self-employment should be considered. Many male students with a family do some type of part-time selling to generate self-employment income and earn work credits.

You should, of course, keep records on all self-employment income and expenses. You report your self-employment earnings when you file your Federal income tax return. Your income and expenses are reported on Schedule C (Profit and loss from business or profession). You complete your social security self-employment tax on Schedule SE.

You Can Appeal

If a disability claim is initially rejected, the applicant can ask for a re-examination by a separate reconsideration section of the Social Security Administration. Additional evidence is usually submitted at the time of the reconsideration. The reconsideration section reviews the previous evidence submitted, plus any newly developed evidence. The last step in the administrative appeals process is the appeals council. The applicant usually appears in person before the appeals council and presents witnesses and other expert testimony to help prove his disability case.

Rights to social security benefits are also enforceable in the federal courts after the claimant has exhausted the administrative appeals described above. A fairly large number of disability cases initially rejected by the Social Security Administration are finally reversed through administrative or federal court appeals.

Many lawyers are more than willing to take on the more promising disability cases on a contingency fee basis. If the case is won, they can deduct their fee from the back payments due the claimant. Of course, if the case is lost, the claimant does not owe the lawyer anything.

Sometimes local newspapers contain advertisements by lawyers who have been social security administrative law judges. They advertise that they will accept Social Security or Supplemental Security Income cases on a contingency fee basis. Finding a former administrative law judge willing to take your case would greatly increase your chances of success. You can often find a lawyer who has been a social security administrative law judge through your local lawyer referral service. This referral service is operated by county or city bar associations. You can find the number in your telephone book or by calling information. The lawyer referral service will have trained information specialists to help you. When calling, explain specifically the kind of lawyer you are looking for. You could say something like this:

> "I am appealing a social security (or SSI) disability
> claim decision. I want to locate a lawyer who has
> been a social security administrative law judge."

If a former administrative law judge is not available, ask for a lawyer who handles social security (or SSI) disability appeal cases. Either one will know the "ins and outs" of the appeal process. You'll be way ahead of the game.

Using the Privacy Act

Under the Privacy Act of 1974 you can obtain any records held by a federal agency that pertain to you. So if you have been turned down for disability benefits, you can request all medical records which show why you were turned down.

Obviously, these records could be of material value to you. How you can use the Privacy Act to help you collect benefits is fully explained in the chapter entitled "How to Use The Privacy Act To Get Documents the Government Has on You".

Many disability applicants pursue their claim right through to the federal courts. Why not? They have everything to gain and nothing to lose.

Getting Free Legal Advice

The Legal Services Corporation may be able to give you free legal advice on questions concerning your rights to social security benefits. The Legal Services staff can review the facts in your case and give you an independent opinion on whether you are rightfully eligible for social security benefits. If the Legal Services Corporation staff determines you are eligible for benefits, they can take your case before the Social Security Administration, or to the Federal Courts if necessary. The Legal Services Corporation has helped thousands of Americans collect benefits that were being denied them by the Social Security Administration.

The services offered by the Legal Services Corporation are discussed in detail in Chapter 6, How to Get Free Legal Assistance.

When Disability Benefits End

A disabled worker's eligibility for benefits ends if his condition improves so he is capable of doing substantial, gainful work. Eligibility also ends when there is a return to substantial, gainful work. If you return to work in spite of a severe impairment your eligibility may continue until you have completed a trial work period. Generaly, people who return to work before there has been medical improvement in their condition get a trial work period. During this period, they may work and still get disability checks. If you are eligible for a trial work period, you may test your ability to resume substantial work for as many as nine months. You will continue to receive your disability checks during this period no matter how high your earnings are. The trial work period ends after you have done some work in nine different months or when you recover from your disability, whichever occurs first. Since the trial work provision is intended to give a disabled person the opportunity to test his or her ability to work and hold a job, minor work activity in the trial work period may be disregarded. As a general rule, when you are working in the trial period, only months in which you are employed and earn more than $50 will count as a month of trial work. If you are self-employed, only months in which your net earnings are more than $50 or you devote more than 15 hours to the business will count as months of trial work. The nine different work months may be consecutive or they may be separated by months or even years in which you do not work at all. At the end of the trial work period, your case is reviewed to see whether you are able to engage in substantial, gainful work. If you are, your benefits will continue for three additional months before being stopped. If, on the other hand, the Social Security Administration finds at the end of the trial work period that you are still unable to do substantial, gainful work, your disability benefits will continue.

Questions and Answers

The preceding section provides an overview of disability benefits under social security. The following questions and answers give more specific information. They are designed to answer the most frequently asked questions on social security disability benefits.

Q. What happens when a person collecting disability benefits turns 65?

A. At age 65 persons collecting disability benefits are transferred to the retirement category. Benefits stay the same. However, all conditions affecting retirement apply. For example, the person could work and earn up to the exempt amount without a reduction in benefits.

Q. Does the Social Security Administration have a rehabilitation program for disabled workers?

A. Yes. The Social Security Administration is required to refer disabled persons to a state rehabilitation program to determine the feasibility of getting the person a job. However, only a very small number of disabled persons ever get jobs as a result of rehabilitation training.

Q. How long does a spouse have to be married to a disabled worker before he or she can collect benefits on the disabled worker's record?

A. Generally 1 year.

Q. Is there any overlap between worker's compensation and social security disability?

A. All states now have worker's compensation programs paying benefits to disabled workers. But these programs pay benefits only if an injury or illness is work-related. Only about 5 percent of total disabilities fall within this category. Therefore, there is very little overlap between the two programs.

Q. Can a person collect social security disability benefits and worker's compensation at the same time?

A. Yes, but the combined benefits can't exceed 80 percent of a person's earnings for any year out of the 5 years prior to when the worker became disabled.

Q. Can a person legally collect Veteran's disability benefits and social security disability benefits at the same time?

A. Yes. The Social Security Act does not prohibit such dual payments. However, many private pension plans do adjust their disability payments when a person also collects social security disability.

Q. Can a disabled person not covered for regular social security benefits qualify for benefits under Supplemental Security Income?

A. Yes. Under Supplemental Security Income, a person who has not worked long enough to earn coverage under regular social security may be eligible under Supplemental Security Income if the individual's asset value and income are low enough. The determination of disability is the same as under the regular social security program. Supplemental Security Income is covered later on in this chapter.

How to Collect Big $$$ from Uncle Sam

Q. Can a person collecting regular social security disability also collect under Supplemental Security Income disability?

A. Yes. Over one-third of the disabled persons receiving regular social security benefits also receive Supplemental Security Income payments. Refer to the section of Supplemental Security Income for more information.

Q. What are some examples of the kinds of medical evidence usually submitted in connection with a claim for disability benefits?

A. —a report signed by a licensed physician;
   —a copy of the medical records, if any, of a hospital, clinic, institution, sanitarium, or public or private agency, and
   —other medical evidence including reports of clinical findings, laboratory findings, diagnosis and treatment prescribed.

Q. When is it necessary for the Social Security Administration to verify a claimant's medical evidence?

A. Examinations at government expense may be necessary for one or more of the following reasons:
   —To clarify the clinical findings and diagnosis.
   —To obtain highly technical or specialized medical data not otherwise available.
   —To resolve a material conflict or inconsistency in the evidence.
   —To resolve the issue of medical improvement in continuing disability cases.

Death

If a worker dies, checks can go to certain members of his family. A lump-sum payment also can be made to the widow or widower. But before survivors can get social security benefits the deceased worker must have a certain amount of work credits under social security. The table below shows how much credit is needed:

Born after 1929, die at	Born before 1930, die before age 62	Years you need
28 or younger		1½
30		2
32		2½
34		3
36		3½
38		4
40		4½
42		5
44	1973	5½
45	1974	5¾
46	1975	6
48	1977	6½
50	1979	7
52	1981	7½
54	1983	8
56	1985	8½
58	1987	9
60	1989	9½
62 or older	1991 or later	10

Survivor's benefits can also be paid upon the death of a worker who does not meet the above requirements but who worked at least a year-and-a-half in the three years before death.

Death Benefits

The table which follows provides an estimate of the benefits available to the surviving spouse of a deceased worker. Benefit rates are based on the deceased worker's average annual earnings and the age of the worker's surviving spouse at the time of the worker's death. Keep in mind that the worker's annual earnings are the highest earnings over a period of years based on a maximum amount set by the Social Security Administration.

If a principle worker in your family dies it is important to contact the nearest Social Security Office to determine the amount of your monthly benefit check. However, if you want a rough idea of what the monthly benefit may be upon the death of a principle worker, submit Form 7004, as discussed earlier in this chapter to get a statement of earnings record.

The following table will give you an idea what benefits are paid to a surviving spouse.

Examples of Monthly Death Benefit Payments

Average Yearly Earnings	$3000	$4200	$5400	$6600	$7800	$9000	$10,200
Widow or Widower at Age 65	344.00	420.00	494.00	570.00	650.00	700.00	750.00
Widow or Widower at age 62	286.00	348.00	410.00	472.00	538.00	580.00	622.00
Widow or Widower at age 60	246.00	300.00	354.00	408.00	464.00	500.00	536.00

Family Benefits

Almost everybody knows about social security retirement benefits. Fewer people know of the life insurance coverage under social security. However, this life insurance coverage could be worth hundreds of thousands of dollars to the family of a deceased worker. It is often the most valuable "asset" that a young family has.

Here are the principal benefits available to family members of an insured, deceased worker.

The Widow or Widower

The widow or widower of a deceased worker is entitled to monthly benefits. As shown in the chart on page 34, the amount which can be collected depends on the age of the widow or widower at the time of application for survivor's benefits. At age 65, the widow or widower can collect 100 percent of the deceased worker's basic benefit; at age 62, 82.9

percent; and at age 60, 71.5 percent. Monthly benefits can be collected at age 50 if the widow or widower becomes disabled within 7 years of the worker's death. In this case, the benefit rate is 71.5 percent of the deceased worker's basic benefit. The widow or widower can collect benefits at any age if caring for the deceased worker's child who is under 16 (16 or over if disabled). In this case, the benefit rate is 75 percent of a deceased worker's basic benefit.

A widow or widower who remarries before age 60 can no longer collect benefits based on the former spouse's record. (An exception: If the subsequent spouse is collecting benefits on someone else's record.) However, if that marriage ends, previous benefits will be reinstated upon application. A widow or widower who remarries at age 60 or older can continue to collect survivor's benefits on the former spouse's record.

Divorced Widow

The divorced wife of a deceased worker is entitled to survivor's beneifts if she was married to the worker for at least 10 years. The amount she can collect depends on her age at the time she files for survivor's benefits. At age 65 she can collect 100 percent of the deceased worker's basic benefit. At age 62 she can collect 82.9 percent; and at age 60 she can collect 71.5 percent. Monthly benefits can be collected at age 50 if the divorced widow becomes disabled within 7 years of the worker's death. In this situation, the benfit rate is 71.5 percent of the deceased worker's basic benefit.

A divorced widow can collect monthly benefits at any age if she is caring for the deceased worker's child who is under 16 (16 or older if disabled). The benefit rate in this situation is 75 percent of the deceased worker's basic benefit. Generally, a divorced wife must be unmarried at the time she applies for benefits. If she remarries before age 60 she can no longer collect benefits based on her former deceased husband's record. If she remarries after age 60 she can continue to collect benefits on her former deceased husband's record. A disabled widow can continue to collect benefits on her deceased husband's record if she remarries after age 50.

Dependent Children

The children of a deceased worker may be eligible to collect monthly social security benefits. To collect benefits a deceased worker's child must be unmarried and younger than 18, or up to age 19 if still in high school. Unmarried children 18 or over can collect benefits if they became disabled before age 22 and continue to be disabled. The eligible child's benefit is 75 percent of the deceased worker's basic benefit.

A child is normally eligible for benefits on the record of the natural parent. However, a legally adopted child living with the stepparent (or receiving one-half support from the stepparent) can qualify for benefits on the stepparent's record. Thus, a child living with his real mother and stepfather can be eligible for benefits on the records of three people—his mother, real father and stepfather.

Parents

The dependent parents of a deceased worker can collect benefits under certain conditions. The parent must be at least 62 years old and be able to prove that the deceased child was providing at least one-half of his or her support. A stepparent is also eligible for benefits if the child was legally adopted before age 16.

Lump Sum Payments

A lump sum payment can be paid upon the death of an insured worker. The amount is low—$255. The lump sum payment can be paid only to a survivng spouse or to a child entitled to benefits.

NOTE: If the deceased is a veteran, an addtional payment of up to $450 may be available through the Veterans Administration. See page 179 for further information.

How Earnings Reduce Benefits

The widow's or widower's earnings from a job or self-employment may reduce their monthly survivor's benefits. However, their earnings, regardless of the amount, will not affect monthly benefits payable to the deceased worker's children. The widow or widower at age 65 to 70 may earn up to $8,880 without a reduction in monthly survivor's benefits. However, for every $2 of earnings over the limit, $1 in benefits will be subtracted from the monthly check going to the widow or widower. If the widow or widower is under age 65 the allowable earnings limit is $6,480. At age 70 or older the widow or widower's earnings, regardless of the amount, will not reduce benefit payments.

As mentioned above, earnings of a widow or widower affect only their benefits checks. Monthly benefits going to the deceased worker's chidren are not affected. For example, a widowed mother who works full-time may lose part of her benefits, but the children will continue to collect their full benefits. The earnings of the children, over the allowable limit, will reduce only their benefits. The widow's or widower's benefits will not be affected.

Questions and Answers

The preceding section provides an overview of survivor's benefits under social security. The following questions and answers give more specific information. They are designed to answer the most frequently asked questions on social security survivor's benefits.

Q. About how many mothers and children in the U.S. are eligible for monthly survivor's benefits in case of the death of a father?

A. About 95 percent of all mothers and children in the U.S. are now eligible for monthly benefits.

Q. How many people are now collecting survivor's benefits?

A. About 4 million.

Q. Why is the lump sum payment so low—$255—when burial costs are so high? Why hasn't it gone up like the other social security benefits?

A. The Congress has not raised the lump sum payment because of the fear it would encourge further increases in the costs of funerals.

Q. How long after the death of a worker can an application for a lump-sum death payment be filed?

How to Collect Big $$$ from Uncle Sam

A. Application for the lump-sum death payment must be filed within a 2-year period of the insured person's death. The filing period may, however, be extended under certain conditions.

Q. How long must a spouse have been married to a worker before he or she can collect survivor's benfits?

A. Generally, at least 9 months.

Q. What happens if a widow outlives 2 or more husbands—whose records can she collect on?

A. She can collect survivor's benfits on the husband's record which yields the highest benefit payment.

Q. Can a widow collect survivor's benefits at age 60, then switch to retirement benefits on her own record at age 62?

A. Yes, but a new application will have to be filed. The conversion is not automatic.

How to Protect Your Social Security Investment

Your investment in social security is very valuable to you and your family; and, like any investment, you have to check on it from time to time. You have to check to make sure the Social Security Administration has accurately credited your account with all your earnings. You also have to make sure your account has been credited with all the quarters of work credit you have earned.

Many different people are involved in keeping track of your social security account. Here's what happens. Social security taxes are deducted from your pay. Your employer matches that amount and mails the total taxes into the Internal Revenue Service (IRS). The IRS then sends a report of your earnings to the Social Security Administration. They enter this information into the computer and hopefuly credit your account.

As you can see, there is a lot of room for human and machine error. For example, if one of the digits in your social security number is transposed by an employee, your earnings will be credited to someone's else's record. It could happen and it does, occasionally. A government bureaucrat can have a bad day, or a trainee could be handling your records.

You should check the accuracy of your social security record at least every three years, maybe more. According to the law, an earnings record can't be corrected beyond 3 years, 3 months and 15 days after wages were paid or self-employment income earned. You can still have errors or omissions corrected after that time, but it is much more difficult. You might have to take your case to court.

In one case, only $9.62 stood between a worker and a lifetime of disability benefits. A polio victim applied for disability benefits but she needed only one additional quarter of earnings to qualify for benefits. The records showed she was paid $40.38 in one quarter, but at that time $50 was needed to earn a quarter of coverage. Later she was able to show that she was actually paid more than $50 in the period in question. However, the court ruled against her and benefits were denied. (Dorothy Evans vs Richardson U.S.D.C. Western District of Michigan 9/9/74).

As discussed earlier, a person can check on their social security earnings record by mailing a compelted Form 7004, Request for Statement of Earnings in to the Social Security Administration. It should be mailed to: Social Security Administration, P.O. Box 57, Baltimore, MD 21203. Extra copies of Form 7004 are included on the last few pages of this book. Additional forms can be obtained from the Social Security Administration. Don't forget to write "QC" in the upper left-hand corner of the form. The forms available, from the Social Security Administration, don't say, "QC" in the corner. If "QC" is not on the form, they will only send you your statement of earnings, not your quarters of credit earned.

Combining Work With Social Security Checks

Many people work while collecting social security benefits. Some work because they want to while others must work to supplement their social security checks. This section tells you (1) what earnings are counted by the Social Security Administration in determining the maximum allowable earnings, and (2) how to get the maximum dollars back from your earnings.

Income That Counts

When figuring what income may affect your social security checks you must count earnings from work of any kind, whether or not covered by social security, except tips amounting to less than $20 in a month. Total wages and net self-employment earnings must be added together in arriving at total income.

Earnings From a Job

The gross wages or salary, before payroll deductions, are counted. This includes bonuses, commissions, fees, vacation pay, and any severance pay. If you receive any pay in a form other than cash (such as lodging or meals) include its cash value in figuring earnings.

Some payments from an employer are not counted as earnings. These include payments for moving and travel expenses and certain types of sick pay.

Earnings From Self-Employment

The net profit (revenue minus business expenses) from your business or partnership is counted. The amount of time you devote to the business is not considered, only the income. However, during the first year of retirement you can earn any amount and still get benefits if your services are not "substantial". In deciding whether services are substantial the Social Security Administration considers such things as time devoted to the business (less than 15 hours per month is not substantial), the kind of work done, and the value of your services.

Income Earned Abroad

Earnings from employment or self-employment outside the United States that is covered by the social security system (where social security taxes are withheld) are subject to the same earnings tests as if earned inside the U.S.

A different test is applied to work outside the U.S. that is not covered by the social security system (where social security taxes are not withheld). If the person works 7 days or more either full or part-time in any month, social security benefits for that month will be forfeited for the worker and his family.

Unearned Income

Generally, income which is not earned from a job or self-employment doesn't count. The following types of income do not count as earnings for social security purposes:
—Investment income in the form of dividends from stock you own, unless you are a dealer in securities.
—Interest on savings accounts.
—Income from social security benefits, pensions, other retirement pay or veteran's benefits.
—Income from annuities.
—Gain or loss from the sale of capital assets.
—Gifts or inheritances.
—Rental income from real estate you own, unless you are a real estate dealer.
—Royalties you receive in or after the year you became 65 from patents or copyrights that were obtained before that year.
—Retirement payments to you (if you're a retired partner) from a partnership.

Other types of payments do not count as wages under certain conditions. These include sick pay under a plan or system, payments from certain trust funds, payments from certain annuity plans, sick pay more than 6 months after the employee last worked, loans from employers, moving expenses, travel expenses and pay for jury duty. Special rules apply to some of the payments listed above. If you receive payment from any of the situations above, contact your social security office to find out if the payment counts as income.

Is Working Worth It?

Before pursuing any type of work, you should stop and figure out if working is worth your time. Consider how much you will earn versus your overall expenses. When you work you'll have to pay social security taxes on your earnings. That's right. You'll have to pay social security taxes even though you're already collecting social security benefits. Of course, you'll have to pay income taxes. Then there are work related expenses such as transportation, food, clothing. Lastly, if you earn more than the allowable limit, you'll have to forfeit $1 in benefits for every $2 of "excess" earnings. These are factors you should carefully think out before deciding to return to work.

Part of Your Social Security Benefits May Be Taxable

Most people do not pay taxes on their social security benefits. But if in addition to your social security benefits you have substantial income, up to half of your benefits may be subject to Federal income tax.

The amount of your social security benefits subject to tax is the smaller of:
1. One-half of your annual social security benefits, or
2. One-half of the amount by which your adjusted gross income (*plus* tax exempt interest *plus* one-half of your gross social security benefits) exceeds $25,000 if you're a single taxpayer, $32,000 if you're filing jointly or zero if you're married and live with your spouse and file separate returns.

The Social Security Administration should send you a statement showing the benefits you received during the year. The IRS can provide a form which helps you figure out whether any of your social security benefits are taxable.

A Word of Caution

One last word, the Social Security Administration has established a procedure for identifying persons collecting social security benefits while earning over the maximum allowable wages. Under this procedure, the social security numbers of people collecting benefit checks are compared by use of a computer with earnings data reported to the Internal Revenue Service. Those social security numbers showing "excess" earnings are printed out by the computer. The Social Security Administration can use this information as the basis for reducing benefit checks.

Why You Should Apply for Social Security Benefits

Whenever you think you may be eligible for social security beneifts, but you are not sure, go ahead and file an application. That's right. Go ahead and file even if you called the Social Security Administration and were told you were not eligible. Get the rejection in writing.

The following actual case example shows why you should file a written application whenever you are in doubt about your eligibility.

Clayton Woolley died in 1959 due to injuries suffered while on the job. His widow and three children started collecting workmen's compensation. Mrs. Woolley telephoned the Social Security Administration to ask whether she could also collect social security benefits. She was told no (in error). Mrs. Woolley accepted that answer as fact.

However, in 1971, Mrs. Woolley filed an application for survivor's benefits on behalf of her 2 children, under 18 years old. She was awarded benefits going back only 12 months. She then sued to get the benefits due from 1959, claiming that the telephone call to the Social Security Administration back in 1959 was an intent to file. She lost the case. The judge ruled that she had not filed a written application for benefits.

Had Mrs. Woolley filed a written application—even though the Social Security Administration said she was not eligible for benefits—she would have received thousands of dollars additional benefits due her and her family.

Again, the moral: When in doubt, file a formal application for benefits. It is your right. You have nothing to lose. You have everything to gain.

How to Collect Social Security Checks While Living Outside the U.S.

If you are a U.S. citizen or a citizen of any of the following

43

countries: Argentina, Austria, Barbados, Belguim, Bolivia, Brazil, Bulgaria, Canada, Chile, Columbia, Costa Rica, Cyprus, Czechoslovakia, Denmark, Ecuador, El Salvadore, Finland, France, Gabon, Greece, Guyana, Ireland Israel, Italy, Ivory Coast, Jamaica, Japan, Leichtenstein, Luxembourg, Malta, Mexico, Monaco, The Netherlands, Nicaragua, Norway, Panama, Peru, Philippines, Poland, Portugal, San Marino, Spain, Sweden, Switzerland, Turkey, United Kingdom, Upper Volta, West Germany, Yugoslavia, or Zaire your checks will keep coming even though you live outside the U.S. Checks will not be sent to: Albania, Cuba, East Berlin, East Germany, Cambodia, North Korea, People's Republic of China, or Vietnam.

It usally takes longer to deliver checks outside the U.S. because of the longer distances and extra handling needed. Your social security check is usually dated the 3rd of the month. It is payment for the month before. For example, a check dated September 3, is payment for August. Delivery times may vary from country to country, and your check will not arrive the same day each month. Occasionally, something will happen to cause an extra delay. If you don't get your check after a reasonable waiting period, contact the nearest foreign service post or write directly to the Social Security Administration.

Foreign governments can, and often do, tax your social security. If you are planning to go abroad you can find out about taxes in a foreign country at that country's embassy in Washington, D.C. Social Security benefits are calculated in U.S. Dollars and there is no provision for increasing or decreasing them because of changes in the international exchange rates.

Advantages of Direct Deposit of Social Security Checks

You can have your social security checks deposited in your checking or savings acount at a bank, savings and loan association, or similar institution, or federal or state chartered credit union. Direct deposit of checks has several advantages. For example:

—You don't have to stand in line to cash or deposit your check.
—If you're away from home your money is available in your account instead of sitting in your mail box.
—You don't have any problem cashing your check because it goes directly into your account.
—You don't have to worry about losing your check or having it stolen.

If you want to arrange for direct deposit of your checks, contact the financial organization of your choice and ask for a direct deposit form, SF-1199.

You May Be Eligible For a Refund of Excess Social Security Contributions

When you pay social security tax on wages more than $48,000 for 1989, you are entitled to a refund on the excess tax paid. If you worked for more than one employer during the year you can claim a refund of your excess contribution on your federal income tax return for that year. If you worked for only one employer during the year, you should apply to that employer for a refund.

Each employer is required to give you a receipt for the social security taxes deducted from your pay. This receipt is usually your W-2 form, but it can also be in the form of pay stubs which itemize deductions. Each employer is required to give you a receipt at the end of the year, or when you terminate your employment.

Where to Go

To obtain information or to apply for monthly social security benefits, get in touch with the Social Security Office in your area. If you are unable to visit that office because you are hospitalized or unable to leave your home, a social security representative can come to see you. Or you may call or write or have someone do it for you.

To find the address of the Social Security Administration nearest your home, call your local Federal Information Center. A complete list of Federal Information Centers is included at the back of this book. Ask the information specialist for the address of the Social Security office nearest you.

How To Cut Red Tape

Before you visit your Social Security Office to apply for benefits, you should become familiar with the eligiblity requirements and the benefits you may be entitled to. Probably the best way to do this is to carefully read this chapter.

Before you or your family can get benefits under social security, you must first apply for them. It is important to contact the Social Security office if:

—you or your spouse are unable to work because of an illness or injury that is expected to last a year or more;

—you are within three months of reaching age 62;

—You are within two or three months of age 65, even if you don't plan to retire, or

—someone in your family dies.

When you visit the Social Security Office you will need certain papers to demonstrate that you are eligible for benefits. The types of proof needed will vary depending on the nature of the claim.

Records Needed for Retirement or Disability Claims

The records needed depend on the circumstances as shown below:

—Insured worker: Social security card (or record of number); proof of age; copy of W-2 for the previous year, or, if self-employed, last federal income tax return.

—Spouse 62 or older: Social security number; proof of age, proof of marriage.

—Spouse under 62 (caring for a child): Social security number; proof of marriage; child's birth record.

—Child: Social security number; proof of age; if adopted, proof of adoption; if stepchild, marriage certificate of child's natural parent and stepparent.

—Divorced wife: Social security number; proof of age; proof of marriage; proof of divorce.

Records Needed for Survivor's Claims

The social security number of the deceased is needed in addition to a death certificate. Other records needed depend on the circumstances as shown below:

—Widow or widower 60 or older (50 if disabled): Social security number; proof of age; proof of marriage.

—Widow or widower under 62 (caring for child): Social security number; proof of marriage; child's birth record.

—Child: Social security number; proof of age; if adopted, proof of adoption; if stepchild, marriage certificate of natural parent and stepparent.

—Divorced wife 60 or older (50 if disabled): Social security number; proof of age; proof of marriage; proof of divorce.

—Divorced wife under 62 (caring for child): Social security number; proof of marrige; proof of divorce; child's birth record.

—Parent of deceased: Social security number; proof of age; proof of parental relationship with the deceased person (such as the latter's birth certificate).

—Person other than widow or widower claiming $255 lump-sum payment: Statement of burial expenses from funeral home.

What Records Will the Social Security Administration Accept

Generally, documents submitted to the Social Security Administration in establishing a claim must be certified by the issuing agency. A birth record from a state department of health agency must bear its official seal. However, a religious record of birth is acceptable if made before the person's fifth birthday. Proof of marriage must be the original marriage certificate or a certified copy of a religious record of marriage. Proof of divorce must be a certified copy of the divorce decree.

How To Save Time

Take all necessary papers with you when you go to the Social Security Administration to file a claim. However, do not delay filing a claim because you do not have all the necessary documentation. Get the application on record as soon as possible.

Before going to the social security office, call first to make sure you are bringing all the necessary information needed for your circumstances. This is particularly true with a disability claim. Also, ask the social security representative the best time to go to the office to avoid crowded conditions. Generally, early in the month and early in the week are the most congested.

Estimating Your Monthly Social Security Benefits

As discussed earlier you can obtain your Personal Earnings and Benefit Estimate Statement by mailing in a completed Form 7004 to the Social Security Administration. (If you are age 60 or over you can get the information over the telephone). This statement lists your social security earnings history, and gives you an estimate of the monthly benefits you and your family may qualify for now or sometime in the future.

The statement also shows the maximum yearly earnings subject to social security tax, your actual social security taxed earnings, and the social security taxes you paid. The statement also shows the quarters of work credits you have earned. You must have 40 social security credits to be fully insured for retirement benefits.

Be sure to review the social security earnings part of the statement carefully to identify any discrepancies in the social security taxes you paid and taxes actually credited to your personal account. Report any differences to the toll free telephone number shown on the statement.

An example of a Personal Earnings and Benefit Estimate Statement is shown on the following two pages.

How to Collect Social Security At Any Age

FACTS ABOUT YOUR SOCIAL SECURITY

THE FACTS YOU GAVE US

Your Name ....
Your Social Security Number ....
Your Date of Birth ....June 7, 1941
1988 Earnings ....Over $43,800
1989 Earnings ....Over $45,000
Your Estimated Future Average Yearly Earnings ....Over $45,000
The Age You Plan To Retire 65

We used these facts and the information already on our records to prepare this statement for you. When we estimated your benefits, we included any 1988 and 1989 earnings you told us about. We also included any future estimated earnings up to the age you told us you plan to retire.

If you did not estimate your future earnings, we did not project any future earnings for you.

YOUR SOCIAL SECURITY EARNINGS

The chart below shows the earnings on your Social Security record. It also estimates the amount of Social Security taxes you paid each year to finance benefits under Social Security and Medicare. We show earnings only up to the maximum amount of yearly earnings covered by Social Security. These maximum amounts are also shown on the chart. The chart may not include some or all of your earnings from last year because they may not have been posted to your record yet.

Years	Maximum Yearly Earnings Subject To Social Security Tax	Your Social Security Taxed Earnings	Estimated Social Security Taxes You Paid	Years	Maximum Yearly Earnings Subject To Social Security Tax	Your Social Security Taxed Earnings	Estimated Social Security Taxes You Paid
1937-1950	$ 3,000	$ 0	$ 0	1970	$ 7,800	$ 0	$ 0
1951	3,600	0	0	1971	7,800	0	0
1952	3,600	0	0	1972	9,000	0	0
1953	3,600	0	0	1973	10,800	0	0
1954	3,600	0	0	1974	13,200	0	0
1955	4,200	0	0	1975	14,100	0	0
1956	4,200	0	0	1976	15,300	0	0
1957	4,200	226	5	1977	16,500	1,500	87
1958	4,200	0	0	1978	17,700	5,716	345
1959	4,800	253	6	1979	22,900	22,900	1,403
1960	4,800	1,107	33	1980	25,900	25,900	1,587
1961	4,800	1,257	37	1981	29,700	29,700	1,975
1962	4,800	3,770	117	1982	32,400	32,400	2,170
1963	4,800	28	1	1983	35,700	32,385	2,169
1964	4,800	0	0	1984	37,800	33,020	2,212
1965	4,800	1,748	63	1985	39,600	30,480	2,148
1966	6,600	237	9	1986	42,000	35,963	2,571
1967	6,600	0	0	1987	43,800	43,800	3,131
1968	7,800	0	0	1988	45,000	Not Yet Posted	
1969	7,800	0	0	1989	48,000		

YOUR SOCIAL SECURITY CREDITS

To qualify for benefits, you need credit for a certain amount of work covered by Social Security. (See "How You Earn Social Security Credits" on the reverse side.) The number of credits you need will vary with the type of benefit. **Under current law, you do not need more than 40 credits to be fully insured for any benefit.**

Our review of your earnings, including any 1988 and 1989 earnings you told us about, shows that you now have **at least 40 Social Security credits**.

How to Collect Big $$$ from Uncle Sam

ESTIMATED BENEFITS

RETIREMENT   You must have **40** Social Security credits to be fully insured for retirement benefits. Assuming that you meet all the requirements, here are estimates of your retirement benefits based on your past and any projected earnings. The estimates are in today's dollars, but adjusted to account for average wage growth in the national economy.

The earliest age at which you can receive an unreduced retirement benefit is **65 and 8 months**. We call this your full retirement age. If you work until that age and then retire, your monthly benefit in today's dollars will be about **$1,150**

If you continue to work and wait until you are 70 to receive benefits, your monthly benefit in today's dollars will be about **$1,620**

SURVIVORS   If you have a family, you must have **26** Social Security credits for certain family members to receive benefits if you were to die this year. They may also qualify if you earn 6 credits in the 3 years before your death.   The number of credits a person needs to be insured for survivors benefits increases each year until age 62, up to a maximum of 40 credits.
Here is an estimate of the benefits your family could receive if you had enough credits to be insured, they qualified for benefits, and you died this year:

Your child could receive a monthly benefit of about . . . . **$ 610**

If your child and your surviving spouse who is caring for your child both qualify, they could each receive a monthly benefit of about . . . . **$ 610**

When your surviving spouse reaches full retirement age, he or she could receive a monthly benefit of about . . . . **$ 815**

The total amount that we could pay your family each month is about **$1,435**

We may also be able to pay your surviving spouse or children a one-time death benefit of . . . . **$ 255**

DISABILITY   Right now, you must have **26** Social Security credits to be insured for disability benefits. And, **20 of these** credits had to be earned in the **10 year period immediately before you became disabled**.   If you are blind or received disability benefits in the past, you may need fewer credits.   The number of credits a person needs to be insured for disability benefits increases each year until age 62, up to a maximum of 40 credits.

If you were disabled, had enough credits, and met the other requirements for disability benefits, here is an estimate of the benefits you could receive right now:

Your monthly benefit would be about . . . . **$ 755**

You and your eligible family members could receive up to a monthly total of about. **$1,135**

IF YOU HAVE QUESTIONS   If you have any questions about this statement, please read the information on the reverse side. If you still have questions, please call **1-800-937-7005**.

3499520

50

How to Collect
Supplemental Security Income

Many needy people are not eligible for regular social security benefits because of an insufficient work history. Other people who are collecting regular social security benefits are not getting enough to meet their needs. To help these peple the Congress created the Supplemental Security Income program. Through monthly payments this program provides a minimum income to eligible people who have little or no income or resources. Over 4 million Americans now collect over $6 billion a year in SSI benefits.

Here's How You Can Qualify For Supplemental Security Income

Supplemental Security Income (SSI) covers needy people age 65 or older and people of any age who are disabled or blind. The disability criteria under SSI are the same as under regular social security. That is, a person must have a physical or mental impairment that (1) prevents him from doing any substantial, gainful work, and (2) is expected to last for at least 12 months or result in death. A blind person must have vision no better than 20/200 with glasses, or tunnel vision with a limited visual field of 20 degrees or less.

If you are 65 or older, disabled, or blind the decision as to whether you can get supplemental security income payments generally depends on (1) the value of the things you own, and (2) how much income you have.

Things You Can Own

An individual may have resources (assets) up to $2,000 and a couple may have resources up to $3,000. The following resources are not counted in determining the amount of a claimant's resources:

—A home and the land adjacent to it, regardless of value.
—Personal effects or household goods with a total market value of $2,000 or less.
—A car which has a retail value of $4,500 or less, or a

car of any value used by the household for transportation to a job or to a place for treatment of a specific medical problem.
—Life insurance policies with a total face value of $1,500 or less per person.

Also excluded are property essential to self-support and certain community stocks held by natives of Alaska. If a person's countable resources exceed the limit by a small amount, the person may still qualify for supplemental security income if he or she agrees to sell the excess assets within a specified time.

In determining the eligibility of a disabled child under 18 (or 21 if a student), the resources of the parents are considered. However, once the child reaches 18 (or 21 if in school), only his or her resources—not the parent's—are considered in determining eligibility for SSI payments. The resources of relatives are never considered in determining eligibility.

Income You Have

An individual may be eligible with income of less than $793 a month or a couple with less than $1,149 a month. If a couple has been separated for over 6 months, each person is treated as an individual. Under the Supplemental Security Income program, income means more than just cash or checks a person receives. It includes many items which would not be considered income for federal or other tax purposes. Some examples of the kinds of income that would be counted include:
—Social security checks,
—Other federal benefits (railroad retirement, veteran's compensation),
—Private pensions or annuities,
—Worker's compensation,
—Inheritance or gifts,
—Support payments,
—Rents,
—Interest, dividends.

Although many items are counted as income for

supplemental security income purposes, a number of other items are not counted in determining your income. The following items are not counted in determining the amount of income:

- —$20 a month of unearned income such as social security benefits, or veteran's compensation, rent or interest,
- —$65 a month of earned income (wages and/or net earnings from self-employment) plus ½ of the earned income over $65.
- —Refund of taxes paid on real property.
- —Assistance by a state or local political subdivision which is based on need (Welfare).
- —Grants, scholarships, and fellowships.
- —Home grown produce consumed by the individual and his or her family.
- —Irregular or infrequent earned income if it totals no more than $30 in a calendar quarter.
- —Foster care payments for a child who is not receiving supplemental security income payments.
- —One-third of child support payments received by an eligible child from an absent parent.
- —Earnings up to $400 a quarter but not more than $1,620 a year of an unmarried student under 22 years of age.
- —Income necessary for fulfillment of an approved plan to achieve self-support established for a blind or disabled person.

Supplemental security income payments can be paid only to people who live in one of the 50 states or District of Columbia and who are either U.S. citizens, immigrants lawfully admitted for permanent residence, or immigrants who are permanent residents in accordance with rules established under the Immigration and Nationality Act.

In determining the eligibility of a disabled child under 18 (or 21 if a student), the income of the parents is considered. However, once the child reaches 18 (or 21 if in school), only his or her own income is considered in determining eligibility for SSI benefit payments. The income of relatives is never considered in determining eligibility.

SSI Benefits

SSI benefit payments vary from state to state. This is because each state may supplement the Federal Government's basic SSI benefit. The Federal benefit can range up to $358 a month for an individual and $553 for a couple. However, a state's contribution can boost SSI benefits to over $400 a month for an individual and over $750 for a couple.

States may also provide other benefits to SSI recipients. These include money for:
—replacement of personal possessions such as household furniture or clothing lost or damaged by a catastrophe;
—moving expenses;
—housing repair;
—certain housing modifications and additions;
—assistance to prevent foreclosure.

California provides eligible SSI recipients extra money each month as a restaurant allowance in cases where home cooking facilities are not available.

A person or couple receiving SSI benefits—but living in a household where support and maintenance is being provided—will have benefits reduced by one-third. For example, if a widow is living with a son or daughter who support her, the monthly SSI check will be reduced.

In most states persons receiving SSI are also eligible for Medicaid. This can be a great help because Medicaid provides more coverage than Medicare in many cases. For example, Medicaid pays for such things as prescription drugs, eye examinations, eye glasses and hearing aids—Medicare does not normally cover these costs.

Greater Benefits

Couples receiving both SSI and VA pensions (see page 173) can sometimes receive greater benefits if the Veteran's spouse files for SSI on her own rather than filing as a couple. Why? Because the Social Security Administration does not consider the veteran's pension benefits when determining SSI eligibility for a veteran's spouse.

How to Collect Social Security At Any Age

For example, let's say Mr. and Mrs. Smith are married and have no income except his VA monthly pension of $300 and their monthly SSI benefits of $100 for a total income of $400 a month. The Smiths can terminate their SSI application as a couple and Mrs. Smith can file as an individual. She is then eligible for the full SSI benefit of $200. The Smiths combined income is then $500 a month—an increase of $100.

How To Apply

Your application for Supplemental Security Income benefits must be filed at the local social security office. For persons already collecting regular social security benefits, the procedure is very simple. The Social Security office merely has to verify the financial data on your application. In some cases, benefits can be paid for three months during the verification process. Also, the Social Security Administration can give a needy couple up to $200 in case of an emergency.

More Questions and Answers

If you have read this far, you should know more about social security benefits than 98 percent of the American population. I hope you have enjoyed reading about social security and I hope the material will help you now or sometime in the future.

Here are some final questions and answers about social security benefits you may find interesting.

Q. Who is benefiting more from social security in relation to what is paid into the system—Women or Men?

A. Women are getting much more in benefits compared to men when the amounts paid into the system are considered. This is true because so many women who have never worked get wife's and widow's benefits on their husband's records without ever having paid in a penny to the system.

Q. Does a married working woman receive more benefits than a married woman who has never worked?

A. Yes. A married working woman can retire on her own record at age 62, whereas a married non-working woman can't get retirement benefits until her husband retires. Also, survivor's benfits would be payable on the working wife's record. Whereas, these benefits would not be payable upon the death of a non-working wife. Also, an insured working wife could get disability benefits on her own record while a non-working wife could not. Finally, benefit rights of a working wife are not affected by divorce or remarriage. However, a divorced non-working wife, married less than 10 years,is not entitled to benefits on her former husband's record. She's left with no protection.

Q. Of the millions of women collecting social security retirement benefits today, how many are collecting on their own work record?

A. About one-half are collecting on their own work record.

Q. Dollar for dollar, does an unmarried worker get less overall protection than a married worker?

A. Yes. A married worker pays the same amount into the system as a single person. However, the married worker gets much more coverage for his money. A married worker gets coverage for himself plus his wife and children. But a single worker only gets coverage for himself. A single worker could probably get greater coverage from a private plan for less money.

Q. How many children are now collecting social security benefits?

A. About 3 million.

Q. Does a separation short of a divorce have any effect on a spouse's benefits?

A. No. Only a legal divorce affects benefits.

Q. About how many people are collecting both from social security and welfare (AFDC)?

A. Only about 4 percent of the AFDC caseload is also collecting benefits under social security.

Q. Does the Social Security Administration recognize a common law marriage in establishing eligibility for benefits?

How to Collect Social Security At Any Age

A. A common law marriage may be considered the same as a legal marriage if also recognized by state law. The Social Security Administration generally accepts statements from relatives as proof of common law marriage.

Q. Can a person collect Social Security while in jail?

A. Yes. Incarceration of any kind does not affect benefit payments under social security. As discussed in this Chapter, social security benefits are an earned right growing out of a person's own work.

Q. How many convicts are collecting social security retirement benefits?

A. According to Federal estimates, about 4,500 convicts are receiving $30 million a year in social security benefits. Convicts collecting social security get an average of over $350 each month.

Q. Can a person collect Supplemental Security Income while in jail?

A. No. Upon incarceration Supplemental Security Income payments should stop. Unlike social security benefits, Supplemental Security Income is not an earned right growing out a person's own work and can be cut off at any time at the discretion of the Social Security Administration.

Q. What are some examples of countable resources for SSI purposes?

A. Resources include checking accounts, savings accounts, stocks, bonds, jewelry and other things of value.

Chapter 2

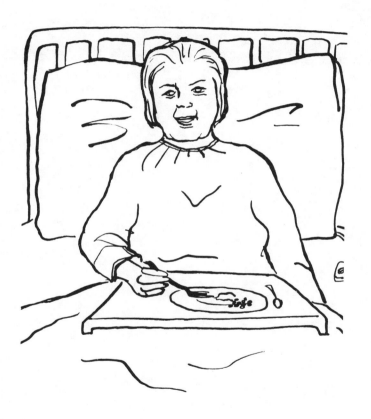

How to Collect
Medicare $$$

When Congress was debating the national health insurance program for the aged and disabled, called Medicare, doctors through the American Medical Association bitterly opposed it. Doctors felt that it was a step toward socialized medicine. More important, they were concerned that the limits placed on payments to doctors for services would reduce their profits.

Medicare, however, has made many doctors rich. Although limits are placed on the charges for treatment under Medicare, there is no limit on the number of times a doctor can see a patient. The result is that doctors develop streamline techniques for herding elderly people in and out of offices on a production line basis. Some doctors see 50 or more Medicare patients per day.

Payments to doctors under Medicare are handled by private insurance companies such as Blue Cross and Blue Shield under contract with the federal government. These private firms, which are dominated by the medical profession, seldom question charges for services made by doctors under

Medicare. Medicare often is referred to as nothing more than a collection agency for doctors paid for by the taxpayers.

Despite the many problems associated with Medicare, overall it is a good program. In the absence of a total national health insurance program, Medicare does provide help for elderly and disabled people in paying medical bills. More than 29 million Americans are covered under Medicare at a cost of $62 billion annually.

Medicare contains two parts — hospital and medical insurance.

Medicare hospital insurance helps pay for the care a patient receives in a hospital and for certain follow-up care after the patient returns home.

Medicare medical insurance helps pay for doctor's services, outpatient hospital services and many other medical items and services not covered under hospital insurance.

Probably the best way to explain Medicare is to separate the program into its two parts to discuss eligibility and benefits.

Medicare Hospital Insurance

Everyone 65 years of age or older who is entitled to monthly social security retirement benefits gets hospital insurance automatically. But a worker doesn't actually have to retire to get hospital insurance protection under Medicare. An individual who reaches age 65 but decides to keep working is eligible for hospital insurance protection if he has worked long enough under the Social Security Program.

Disabled workers under age 65 who have been getting social security disability benefits for two consecutive years or more and people insured under social security who need dialysis treatment or a kidney transplant because of chronic kidney disease are eligible for coverage. Wives, husbands or children of insured workers also may be eligible if they need kidney dialysis or a transplant.

People age 65 or older who are not automatically entitled to hospital insurance can buy this protection. The premium is $156 a month. To buy hospital insurance, an individual also will have to enroll and pay a low premium for medical insurance.

How to Collect Medicare $$$

Medicare hospital insurance helps pay for three kinds of care: (1) in-patient hospital care; (2) in-patient care in a skilled nursing facility, when medically necessary after a hospital stay; and (3) home health care. Medicare hospital insurance can help pay for in-patient care if all of the following four conditions are met:

—A doctor prescribes in-patient hospital care for treatment of your illness or injury,

—You require the kind of care that can only be provided in a hospital,

—The hospital is participating in Medicare,

—The Utilization Review Committee of the hospital or a Professional Standards Review Organization does not disapprove your stay,

When all four conditions are met, hospital insurance pays for covered services in a participating hospital for an unlimited number of days except for the first $560. This is called the hospital insurance deductible. So after you pay the first $560 Medicare hospital insurance pays for all other covered expenses regardless of the cost or number of days spent in the hospital. This is a significant improvement in hospital coverage compared to previous years.

When you are in a skilled nursing facility, you pay $25.50 a day for the first 8 days. Medicare pays any additional covered costs. From the 9th through 150th day Medicare pays for 100 percent of covered costs. After the 150th day Medicare hospital insurance pays nothing for care in a skilled nursing facility. Since Medicare hospital insurance pays nothing after the 150th day, it may be a good idea to consider private supplemental insurance as discussed later. Medicare hospital insurance can pay for these services:

—A semi-private room (2-4 beds in a room) plus all your meals, including special diets,

—Regular nursing services,

—Rehabilitation services such as physical, occupational and speech therapy,

—Drugs furnished by the facility plus medical supplies such as splints and casts,

—Use of appliances such as a wheelchair,

—Operating and recovery room costs,

—Intensive care unit costs,

—Lab tests, X-rays and radiation therapy.

Medicare Medical Insurance

Medicare *medical* insurance can help pay for medically necessary doctor's services, out-patient hospital services, out-patient physical therapy, and speech pathology services and a number of other medical services that are not covered by the hospital insurance part of Medicare. Medical insurance can also help pay for necessary home health services when hospital insurance cannot pay for them.

Medicare medical insurance is a voluntary program open to persons eligible for hospital insurance coverage. The cost of medical insurance is $31.90 a month. Nearly everyone eligible for Medicare signs up for medical insurance. The cost of comparable private coverage would be much more.

After you have incurred $75 in reasonable charges for covered services, medical insurance pays 80% of the reasonable charges for all additional covered services during the rest of the calendar year.

During a hospital stay covered by hospital insurance, you may also receive services from doctors who are responsible for radiology and pathology services provided by the hospital. Charges for these services are paid by medical insurance without your having to meet the $75 annual deductible. For these services medical insurance pays 100% rather than 80% of the reasonable charges.

Medicare medical insurance can help pay for these services:

—Medical and surgical services,

—Diagnostic tests and procedures that are part of your treatment,

—Other services which are ordinarily furnished in the doctor's office and included in his or her bill, such as X-rays you receive as part of your treatment, drugs and biologicals that cannot be self-administered, physical therapy and speech pathology services, services in an emergency room or out-patient clinic, laboratory tests billed by the hospital,

—Treatment of mental illness outside a hospital up to $250 a year,

—Podiatrist services for non-routine foot care,

—Ambulance service, under certain conditions,

—Blood, except for the first three pints in a calendar year.

Medicare Cannot Pay For These Services

The services listed below are not covered by either Medicare's hospital or medical insurance plans.

—Routine physical examinations and tests directly related to such examinations,

—Routine foot care,

—Eye or hearing examinations for prescribing or fitting eye glasses or hearing aids,

—Immunizations (unless required because of an injury or immediate risk of infection),

—Cosmetic surgery unless it is needed because of accidental injury or to improve the functioning of a malformed part of the body,

—Routine dental work or dentures,

—Private-duty nursing care,

—Christian Science practitioners,

—Personal comfort services such as massages,

—Extra charges for a private room, unless needed for medical reasons,

—Personal convenience items such as radio and T.V.

Should You Get More Insurance Coverage?

The Medicare program does not cover all medical costs. In fact, it pays only about 40 percent of the medical bills of a typical beneficiary. This leaves a huge gap that must be filled by you or private insurance coverage.

A person needing extensive medical care could very quickly run up a 5-figure bill. For example, some of the costs not covered under Medicare *hospital* insurance include:

—$560 deductible upon entering a hospital.

—100 percent of the costs in a skilled nursing facility after the 150th day.

These costs are in addition to the many medical services not covered under *hospital* insurance. Then *medical* insurance pays only 80 percent of covered costs after a $75 yearly deductible.

Several things should be considered in deciding whether to purchase additional insurance coverage. These include your age, physical condition, and your financial condition. The weaker your physical and financial condition, the more you need insurance to suplement medicare coverage.

Above all, don't wait until you reach 65 to apply for private supplemental insurance coverage. Why? Because many large private insurance companies won't accept new subscribers who are 65 or older.

Factors to Consider in Deciding on
Private Insurance Coverage

As mentioned earlier, elderly Americans are paying about 60 percent of their medical bills despite Medicare insurance. These medical bills represent money that elderly persons can ill afford.

The answer to this problem in many cases is private insurance coverage. There are many different kinds of plans offered. Some of these plans are very good and inexpensive. Others leave much to be desired and are costly.

When considering private insurance, you should consider the following factors before you buy:

—To what extent does the policy plug the gaps in Medicare coverage. Some of the major gaps are private nursing care and outpatient drug costs. The more gaps filled, the better.
—To what extent does the policy limit payment for pre-existing illnesses. You don't want a policy that will not pay for treatment for a heart attack because you had the condition before you got the policy. The less restrictions, the better.
—Does the policy pay for services provided or does it

pay by the day? If the policy pays you a flat amount such as $40 or $50 a day, make sure the rate will increase with inflation.

Above all, keep in mind that your best insurance is keeping yourself healthy by following a program of eating properly and exercising regularly.

Your Right To Appeal

If you disagree with a decision on the amount Medicare will pay on a claim or whether services you receive are covered by Medicare you always have the right to ask for a review of the decision.

Under Medicare hospital insurance the health facility that provides the services submits the claim for payment but Medicare will send you a notice of the decision made on the claim. If you feel that the decision is incorrect, you can ask for a review of the claim. Any social security office can help you request a review. If you are still not satisfied after the review and if the amount Medicare would pay if the claim were fully allowed is $100 or more, you can ask for a formal hearing. Cases that involve $1000 or more can eventually be appealed to a Federal court.

Under Medicare medical insurance, whether you or the doctor or supplier submits the claim for payment, Medicare will send you a notice of the decision made on the claim. If you disagree with the decision you can ask the Medicare carrier that handles the claim to review it. Then, if you still disagree with the decision, and if the amount Medicare would pay if the claim were fully allowed is $100 or more, you can request a hearing by the carrier. To reach the $100 mark, you may combine claims if they are all within the 6 month limit for appeal. The notice you receive from Medicare which tells you of the decision made on your claim will also tell you exactly what appeal steps you can take.

Where To Go

To obtain information or to apply for Medicare, get in touch with the local Social Security Administration office. To find the telephone number of the local office, call the Federal

Information Center nearest your home. A complete list of Federal Information Centers is included in the back of this book. Ask the information specialist for the number of the Social Security Administration office nearest your home.

If you are unable to visit the office because you are hospitalized or unable to leave home, a social security representative will come to see you. Or you may call or write or have someone else do it for you.

How to Cut Red Tape

Before you visit your Social Security Office to apply for Medicare you should become familiar with the eligibility requirements discussed in this chapter.

In applying for Medicare, you will need certain information to demonstrate your eligibility. You will need the following information:

—your social security card or a record of your social security number, and

—your birth certificate.

Before visiting the Social Security Office, give them a call to find out the specific information to bring along.

Questions and Answers

Q. Where can someone find out if a hospital, skilled nursing facility, or home health agency is participating in Medicare?

A. Your doctor, or someone at the institution or agency, can tell you.

Q. Does hospital insurance pay for services in a foreign hospital?

A. Yes, but only under certain conditions. Hospital insurance can help pay for emergency in-patient hospital care in a foreign hospital if you are living in the United States when an emergency occurs and a foreign hospital is closer than the nearest U.S. hospital.

Q. Will hospital insurance pay for cosmetic surgery?

A. No—except when furnished in connection with prompt repair of accidental injury or for the improvement of the functioning of a malformed body member.

Q. Can hospital insurance pay anything toward the cost of care in a Christian Science sanatorium?

A. Yes. Hospital insurance can cover certain hospital and extended care services furnished to in-patients of a sanatorium operated, or listed and certified, by the First Church of Christ, Scientist, in Boston.

Q. What if someone cannot pay the amounts that the hospital insurance does not cover?

A. He may want to ask at the local public assistance office about help under a state program such as Medicaid.

Q. Will medical insurance pay for services of a chiropractor?

A. Medical insurance helps pay for only one kind of treatment furnished by a licensed and Medicare-certified chiropractor. The only treatment that can be covered is manual manipulation of the spine to correct a subluxation that can be demonstrated by X-ray. Medical insurance does not pay for the X-ray or for any other diagnostic or therapeutic services furnished by a chiropractor.

Q. Who makes the decision whether to rent or purchase durable medical equipment a doctor has prescribed for use at home?

A. The patient does. When considering purchase, particularly of expensive equipment, you should keep in mind that the Medicare payments are made over a period of time based on the reasonable rental rate for the equipment, and that these payments stop when your need for the equipment ends. So, in deciding whether to purchase equipment, you may wish to talk to your doctor about how long you may need it.

Q. Once I turn 65 and become eligible for Medicare insurance, will my wife automatically become eligible even though she is under 65?

A. No. Your spouse and other dependents do not get Medicare coverage just because you do. Your wife must wait until she is 65 to be eligible for coverage (unless she meets the disability requirements).

How to Collect Big $$$ from Uncle Sam

Q. Do Medicare payments go to me or my doctor?

A. Medicare can pay you or it can pay your doctor direct. When Medicare pays your doctor, it is called an assignment. The assignment method of payment can be used only when you and your doctor agree to it. When your doctor agrees to an assignment, he must also agree to accept what Medicare decides is a reasonable charge for services. Medicare then pays the doctor for 80 percent of the reasonable charge and you are responsible for the remaining 20 percent.

Q. Generally, will doctors accept the assignment method of payment?

A. Many doctors are reluctant to take Medicare assignments because they normally charge considerably more than what Medicare considers a reasonable charge. If this is the case with your doctor, you could end up with hefty Medicare bills.

Q. Why doesn't Congress increase Medicare insurance coverage and save older persons millions of dollars in medical bills?

A. Because the Congress would also have to raise taxes to pay for the increased cost of Medicare coverage. Tax increases are almost never popular with the American public.

Chapter 3

How to Collect
Business Loan $$$

• For the past seven years Eddie Burger has worked as the manager of the local branch of a national restaurant chain, but being very independent and resourceful he feels he is going no place. He has reached the highest salary offered and he knows that he could make much more by purchasing the franchise to one of the chain restaurants. He only has a few thousand dollars saved, not near enough to buy his own business, and he's not quite sure what to do.

• Sally Curl has worked all her life as a beauty operator in someone else's salon and now she has a chance to buy the shop. But she doesn't have enough money to buy the business and supplies the shop needs. She feels very frustrated because she doesn't know where to go and her local banker denied her application for a loan.

Ed and Sally, like most Americans, don't know that they may get a business loan from the federal government's Small Business Administration (SBA). And, they may be able to get a loan for up to $500,000.

The problem is not that money isn't available to help people get started in business. This year Congress has made more than $3 billion available for small business loans.

The problem, like with other federal programs, is bureaucracy. SBA is not doing enough to properly inform the public of the availability of business loans. SBA, as a matter of policy, does not publicize the business loan service it provides. Nor does it tell people how easy it is to get a loan.

If SBA did its job, thousands of more small businesses could get started every year. So if you have ever dreamed of owning a business, this chapter may help make your dreams come true.

Some Facts on SBA Loans

Congress created the Small Business Administration in 1953 to encourage, assist and protect the interests of small business. One main goal of the SBA is to help Americans get started in their own small business. Congress has appropriated billions of dollars for the sole purpose of getting small businesses off the ground. And Congress has directed the SBA to help every qualified American who desires a small business regardless of their past experience or financial status.

To carry out this Congressional mandate, the SBA has opened up loan offices throughout the United States. And applying for a loan at these local offices is no more difficult than applying for a commercial loan. The typical application for an SBA loan takes about 4-6 weeks.

The important factor is knowing what to do and how to do it. Not knowing the steps involved in getting SBA financing can only result in frustration and delay. Knowing how to go about getting a loan will put you in a business of your own in the fastest possible time.

Why Uncle Sam Wants to Help
You Start a Small Business

Small business is important to the health of the economy. There are almost 12 million small businesses in America. These small businesses employ nearly 60 percent of the nation's work force. That's a larger percentage than large corporations and government put together. So if the small business sector is not healthy, the entire economy suffers. Likewise, when new small businesses do not start up in sufficient numbers the entire economy suffers.

The Federal government is dedicated to making as many job opportunities available as possible. Uncle Sam knows the more people in the work force, the more tax revenue will be realized. What's more, less unemployment compensation will have to be paid out. Small business is the key to creating job opportunities and keeping the economy healthy.

Uncle Sam knows that many commercial lenders consider new small business ventures poor risks. New small businesses are usually supported by weak collateral and have no established track record. To help small businesses get started, Uncle Sam has directed the SBA to encourage these riskier business loans by guaranteeing private lenders against loss due to nonpayment. Sure, some losses will be incurred through loan non payment. But these losses are more than offset by the overall contribution small business makes to the economy as a whole.

SBA Organization

SBA operates about 96 local offices throughout the United States which are authorized to make business loans. Most of these local offices are district offices which report to one of the 10 SBA regional offices. The regional offices in turn report to SBA headquarters, Washington, D.C., where overall policy is set.

Each SBA district office contains a financing division, a portfolio management division, and a management assistance division. The duties of each of these divisions are as follows:

—The *financing division* processes and approves (or declines) loan applications.

—The *portfolio management division* services loans, monitors borrowers' payments and business status and when necessary, liquidates defaulted loans.

—The *management assistance division* sponsors classes on business management and provides individual counseling through various programs.

What is a Small Business?

For business loan purposes, SBA defines a small business as one that is independently owned and operated, not dominant in its field and meets employment or sales standards developed by the Agency. For most industries, these standards are as follows:

Manufacturing — Number of employees may range up to 1,500, depending on the industry in which the applicant is engaged.

Wholesaling — Maximum number of employees not to exceed 500.

Services — Annual receipts not exceeding $3.5 to $13.5 million, depending on the industry.

Retailing — Annual sales or receipts not over $3.5 to $13.5 million, depending on the industry.

Construction — General construction: average annual receipts not exceeding $17 million for the three most recently completed fiscal years.

Agriculture — Annual receipts not exceeding $3.5 million.

Here's How to Qualify for a Loan

By far, most financing for businesses in America comes from private lenders through commercial banks and savings and loan institutions. If a bank will loan you the needed money for a business, you don't need Uncle Sam. But if banks turn down your loan application, then the SBA may be able to help you.

The SBA operates two basic programs to help Americans own a business. These programs are:

—the 7(a) Lending Program which is the principal source of business loans for most Americans.

—the Economic Opportunity Loan (EOL)program for low income and disadvantaged people.

Most small independent businesses qualify for financing under one of these loan programs except speculative firms, newspapers, television or radio stations and other forms of media and gambling establishments.

Each of the SBA loan programs are discussed below.

The SBA 7(a) Lending Program

The "better qualified" loan applicants are assigned to this program. Generally, to be eligible for loan assistance, you must meet the following requirements.

—be of good character,

—show ability to operate the business successfully,

—show the proposed loan is of sound value,

—show that the past earnings record and future prospects of the business indicate ability to repay the loan out of profits, and

—be able to provide from your own resources sufficient funds to withstand possible losses, particularly during early stages, if the venture is a new business.

In addition, applicants for loans must agree to comply with SBA regulations that there will be no discrimination in employment or services to the public, based on race, color or national origin.

SBA's Economic Opportunity Loan (EOL) Program

The EOL program is for persons who cannot qualify for SBA's regular loan program due to lack of capital and other financial reasons. This program is tailored to the special needs of persons having little or no money and experience in business. Under this program normal SBA credit standards are relaxed, and normal capital investment requirements are more flexible.

To be eligible for an Economic Opportunity loan under SBA regulations a business must be 50 percent owned by a person(s) who either (1) have low income, or (2) have been denied access to adequate financing through private lending channels because of social or economic disadvantage.

The SBA defines low income as the inability to meet basic family needs. As for social and economic disadvantage, SBA's standard operating procedures state this can result from a number of factors including:

—Being an honorably discharged Vietnam-era veteran. Each SBA office has one or more special loan officers for veterans. Their job is to give special attention to

77

veterans seeking loan assistance. Veterans' loan applications are assured prompt processing.

—Physical handicaps. The SBA gives special attention to handicapped persons. To be eligible, applicants must provide adequate medical proof of a permanent physical impairment. The SBA assists in working out special problems related to the running of a small business by a handicapped person. A borderline loan application has a good chance of being decided in favor of the handicapped person.

—Inner-city resident. Being a resident in an urban area with high concentrations of unemployment or low income persons.

—Business in depressed area. The business is located in an economically depressed area where local banks are unable or unwilling to provide small business loans.

Congress intended the Economic Opportunity Loan program to be a "last resort" source of loan funds for qualified disadvantaged persons. Accordingly, the SBA is prepared to take greater risks in providing loans under this program.

How to Apply

The SBA is not in business to compete with private lending institutions. So, the SBA will not provide financial assistance for a business if you can get a loan from private sources. Therefore, before you can get SBA loan help you must first be turned down for a loan by at least two different banks. (If you live in a city with population under 200,000, you only need to be turned down by your own bank.) Only after you have been refused a regular bank loan can you apply for SBA loan assistance.

Getting Turned Down

You must apply for your business loan with your regular bank where you have an account, plus one other bank which is capable of handling your loan. Both banks must refuse you.

How to Collect Business Loan $$$

At each bank you must submit a bonafide application. You can't just call up a bank and ask if it would loan you money for an egg farm. You must provide the bank with the necessary information on which to make an intelligent decision on your loan application. You'll have to provide the bank with information about yourself and about the business.

Here is the minimum information you should provide the bank when applying for a loan.

DESCRIPTION OF BUSINESS: Prepare a written description of your existing or proposed business. Include information on the following: Type of business, date of information, location, product or service, brief history of business or proposed future operation, area serviced, competition, customers, and suppliers.

MANAGEMENT'S EXPERIENCE: Prepare resumes on each owner and key management personnel. Resumes should stress experience and management capability.

PERSONAL FINANCIAL STATEMENTS: Prepare financial statements for all principal owners (20% or more). Statements should be current (not older than 60 days).

FINANCIAL DATA (BUSINESS):

Existing Business: Prepare a balance sheet and profit and loss statement for the past 3 years. A schedule showing aging of accounts payable and accounts receivable should be included. Balance sheet items of significant dollar amounts should be explained.

Proposed Business: Provide a pro forma balance sheet reflecting sources and uses of your capital and borrowed funds.

PROJECTIONS: Prepare a projection of future operations for at least one year or until positive cash flow can be shown. How much money do you expect to take in, what will the expenses be, and what is your basis for these estimates. These projections should be in Profit and Loss Statement format.

MONEY REPAYMENT: Prepare a brief statement on how the loan will be repaid. Include repayment sources and time required.

How to Collect Big $$$ from Uncle Sam

OTHER ITEMS AS THEY APPLY:

a. Leases (copy of proposal)

b. Franchise agreement

c. Purchase agreement

d. Plans, specifications and cost breakdown

e. Copy of licenses

f. Letters of reference

g. Letters of intent, contracts and purchase orders.

h. Partnership agreement

i. Articles of incorporation

After being refused, ask your banker to make you the loan under SBA's loan guarantee plan or to participate with SBA in a loan. If the banker is interested, ask him to contact the SBA for a discussion of your application. In most cases, the SBA will deal directly with your bank.

If the banks won't grant you a business loan under any circumstances, then you'll have to apply directly to SBA for a loan. If this happens to you, don't panic. About 60 percent of all SBA Economic Opportunity loans are obtained directly from SBA without any bank involvement whatsoever.

Applying for SBA Assistance

At this point you either have (1) found a bank willing to go along with an SBA financing plan, or (2) decided to apply for a loan directly from SBA. In either case, you'll now have to convince the SBA of the worthiness of your planned business venture. You'll be required to fill out an SBA loan application plus a number of other forms designed to help SBA assess the soundness of the business. As a minimum, you'll have to complete an Application for Loan, Statement of Personal History and Monthly Cash Flow Projection. Each is discussed below:

Application For Loan (SBA Form 4)

The application requires basic information on the business and its owners and management. You'll have to list the names of all officers or partners together with their annual compensation. You'll also have to state how you plan to use the loan money. A copy of the Application for Loan is included in the back of this Chapter.

80

Statement of Personal History

This form requires general information on your personal background. You'll have to give your place of birth and past and present addresses. You'll also have to state whether you have a criminal record. A copy of the Statement of Personal History is included in the back of this Chapter.

Monthly Cash Flow Projection

This form requires information on all monthly sources and application of money for the business. You'll have to estimate the revenue you expect to take in and all anticipated expenses.

Other forms will be required depending on individual circumstances. If you need help in completing the forms, someone at SBA should be available to help you. Remember, improperly prepared forms will be kicked back to you, causing delay in getting your money. So make sure things are done right before submitting anything for SBA's approval.

Evaluating Your Loan Application

Your bank (or other private lender) makes the initial review of your loan application. Your bank then sends your application and supporting documents to the SBA. Make sure your bank includes the certification that the loan is not available elsewhere at reasonable terms and the loan will not be made without an SBA guarantee.

Your loan application package will include the lender's evaluation of the merits of your loan. This will include an assessment of your ability to repay the loan, the adequacy of your collateral and other pertinent comments.

The SBA has the final say on whether your loan will be approved. They will evaluate your loan application to determine your chances of success in your own business. You must establish that you have (or can obtain) the necessary knowledge and experience to operate and manage your business on a profitable basis

An important factor is whether you plan to devote your full attention to the business. If you plan to operate the business yourself and manage the day-to-day activities, that's an important plus in your favor. If the business is your sole source of income, that's also good. The SBA figures that you'll work hard at the business when you and your family's livelihood depends on it.

You must also have a reasonable investment in the business. As a general rule, 30 to 50 percent of the total cost is considered reasonable. Here again the SBA figures you'll work hard at the business when you have a relatively large investment at stake.

The SBA will look closely at the size of the market for your product or service. You'll have to pinpoint your market and show how you plan to successfully sell to that market. This is often the easiest element for the loan applicant to demonstrate.

The SBA will establish your ability to repay the loan. They will look at your credit history, especially with a new business venture. Special attention will be given to such things as whether you ever filed for bankruptcy or defaulted on a loan.

Having a criminal record will not necessarily disqualify you for loan assistance. However, if you deny having a record and then the SBA finds out otherwise, your application will be rejected.

Finally, the SBA will look at your ability to pledge something as collateral to protect the interest of the government. Loans will not be declined because of lack of collateral if other factors are favorable.

Keep in mind that under the Economic Opportunity Loan program SBA is prepared to take greater risks to get you started in a business of your own. That means SBA can accept minimal capital investment and minimal collateral from you. So, don't count yourself out no mater how weak your financial conditions seems. SBA procedures state that a business loan cannot be refused because of inadequate collateral as long as the loan applicant is willing to pledge whatever collateral is available. Of course, SBA must have a reasonable assurance that the loan will be repaid.

Reasons Why a Loan May Be Denied

The SBA will not approve a loan application if:
—the funds are otherwise available from private sources
   at reasonable terms;

—the loan is to (a) pay off a loan to a creditor; (b) provide funds for distribution or payment to the principals of the applicant, or (c) replenish funds previously used for such purposes;

—the applicant is a non-profit enterprise;

—the loan allows specualtion in any kind of property;

—the applicant is a newspaper, magazine, book publishing company or similar enterprise;

—any of the gross income of the applicant is derived from gambling activities;

—the loan provides funds to an enterprise primarily engaged in lending or investing;

—the loan finances real property that is held for investment purposes;

—the loan encourages monopoly or is inconsistent with the accepted standards of the American system of free enterprise;

—the loan is used to relocate a business for other than sound business purposes.

Here's What You Can Collect

There are three types of loan assistance available through the SBA to help finance your business. These are: guaranteed loans, participation loans, and direct loans. Each type of loan assistance is discussed below.

Guaranteed Loans

SBA guarantees your bank that if you don't repay the loan the SBA will pay it back. The SBA guarantees up to 90 percent of the loan. The maximum loan amount is $500,000. The SBA loan guarantee is the most common type of SBA loan assistance. Your bank should favor this kind of arrangement because it is risk free for them. The interest rate on the loan is established by the private lender. The SBA won't allow an interest rate higher than one-half percent above the prime rate as quoted in the Wall Street Journal on the day of the loan application. Guaranteed loans account for over 60 percent of all loans made under SBA's regular 7(a) loan program.

Participation Loans

Under this arrangement the SBA puts up loan money in conjunction with a private lending firm. The SBA can contribute a maximum of $150,000 or up to 75 percent of the loan while the lending institution contributes not less than 25 percent. According to SBA regulations, a participation loan cannot be made if a guaranteed loan is available.

Direct Loans

The SBA can loan money directly to you without the involvement of a bank or other lending institution. However, under SBA regulations, a direct loan cannot be made if a guaranteed or participation loan is available.

SBA business loans can be made for up to 20 years if funds involve the acquisition or construction of real property. Other business loans are made for up to 10 years. Loans to provide working capital are usually limited to 6 years. The rate of interest on loans is regulated by the SBA and varies depending on economic conditions.

The demand for direct loans sometimes exceeds the funds available at certain SBA loan offices. To fairly allocate the available loan money, SBA makes direct loans on a first come, first served basis. Direct loan applicants are placed on a waiting list. Then, applicants receive loans in accordance with their position on the waiting list as loan funds become available.

Management Assistance

In addition to providing business loans, the SBA offers management assistance. Since money alone can't solve all business problems, the SBA considers management assistance to be a very important part of its overall program. This is especially true in cases where the loan recipient has little or no prior business experience.

SBA provides management assistance and counseling in five basic ways:

Service Corps of Retired Executives is an organization of retired business executives who volunteer their services to help small business owners solve problems.

How to Collect Business Loan $$$

Active Corps of Executives is an organization of volunteers drawn from the ranks of active executives in industry, trade associations, educational institutions, and the professions.

The Call Contract Program employs consultants to provide management and technical assistance to socially and economically disadvantaged small business owners.

Small Business Institute is a program which provides faculty-supervised management counseling to small businesses by university graduate and undergraduate students.

SBA employees known as business management specialists advise small businesses and may call upon the assistance of volunteers and paid consultants.

Franchising

The SBA has helped finance a large number of franchise businesses. The first franchise loan was granted in 1959. Since then SBA has made or guaranteed roughly 20,000 loans totaling well over $1 billion to franchise businesses. Some of these franchise businesses include recognizable names such as McDonalds, Dairy Queen, Baskin Robbins, Aamco Transmissions and Radio Shack Corporation.

The Federal Trade Commission defines a franchise as follows:

> "A system used by a company (franchisor) which grants to others (franchisees) the right and license (franchise) to market a product or service and engage in a business developed by it under the franchisor's trade names, trademarks, service marks, know-how and method of doing business."

Franchising in the United States is a dynamic and growing method of business activity. For example, accoridng to the Department of Commerce, franchise sales of goods and services are expected to reach almost $300 billion. Of this amount, about 90 percent is expected to come from retail sales.

And, not all franchise businesses sell fast food. About 80 percent of all retail franchise sales come from auto and truck dealers and gasoline stations, and soft drink bottlers.

The loan refusal rate for franchise loan applications is lower than for other businesses according to a report by the General

Accounting Office (GAO). The GAO said the loan refusal rate for franchises was less than 11 percent based on a limited survey. This means that almost 90 percent of applicants got loans. That doesn't sound bad.

Most franchise loans are guaranteed loans made under SBA's regular 7(a) program. Guaranteed loans account for about 65 percent of all franchise loans. The SBA can still grant franchise loans under the Economic Opportunity Loan program. But, less than 5 percent of EOL funds are used to finance franchises.

If you are considering various kinds of business opportunities, you might investigate the advantages of a franchised business.

Where to Go

To find the telephone number of your local SBA office, call the Federal Information Center nearest your home. A complete list of Federal Information Centers is included in the back of this book. Ask the information specialist for the number of the Small Business Administration office nearest your home.

How to Cut Red Tape

As a first step, make sure you understand the principles covered in this chapter. Then, as you go along, call the SBA as questions or problems arise. It is always a good idea to deal with one specific SBA official. Some SBA officials will bend over backwards to help you. Others could care less. Finding the right contact can really help expedite approval of your loan request.

Questions and Answers

Q. What happens when a borrower is temporarily unable to make a loan payment?

A. The SBA may defer payments of the loan principal. Such grace periods are allowed to assure the successful establishment of a business.

Q. What percent of the SBA's Economic Opportunity Loans have gone to minority groups?

How to Collect Business Loan $$$

A. About 70 percent.

Q. Can an SBA loan be paid off before it is due?
A. Yes, in most cases.

Q. Why do most small business fail?
A. The two main reasons why a business fails are insufficient capital, especially when the business starts up, and poor management.

Q. Who determines the value of a borrower's collateral?
A. The SBA normally relies on a commercial bank to establish collateral value.

Q. What kind of collateral will the SBA accept?
A. Security for a loan may consist of one or more of the following:
   —A mortgage on land, a building and/or equipment.
   —Assignment of warehouse receipts for marketable merchandise.
   —A mortgage on chattels.
   —Guarantees or personal endorsements, and in some instances, assignment of current receivables.

   A pledge or mortgage on inventories usually is not satisfactory collateral, unless the inventories are stored in a bonded or otherwise acceptable warehouse.

Q. Generally, does the SBA provide business loans for amounts greater or lessor than non-SBA loans?
A. SBA business loan amounts are generally twice that of non-SBA loans. This is because private lenders are willing to loan more when the government guarantees them against loss.

Q. What are the typical interest rates for SBA loans?
A. Unlike other Federal programs, the SBA does not have fixed loan rates established by legislation. Instead, SBA allows lenders to charge interest at the prevailing market rate.

Q. What percentage of SBA business loans go into default?
A. Default rates have been steadily increasing with these hard economic times from 4% to a forecast 10% in future years.

How to Collect Big $$$ from Uncle Sam

SBA Form 4
Loan Number

U.S. Small Business Administration

APPLICATION FOR LOAN

I. Applicant/Information About You

Name

(1)

Street Address

City, State, Zip Code

Telephone

II. Information About Your Business

Name of Business

(2)

Address of Business

City, State, Zip Code

County | Telephone

Type of Business | Date Established

(3)

Number of Employees | IRS Employer I.D. Number

(4)Present: (4A) After Approval | (5)

Bank Where Your Business Has An Account

(6)

III. Information About Management: List the name of all owners (having 20% or greater interest), officers, directors, and/or partners. Provide the percent of ownership and the annual compensation.

Name and Title | % of Ownership

(7) | (8)

Address | Annual Compensation

| (8A)

Name and Title | % of Ownership

(7) |

Address | Annual Compensation

Name and Title | % of Ownership

(7) |

Address | Annual Compensation

Name and Title | % of Ownership

(7) |

Address | Annual Compensation

IV. How You Plan to Use the Loan Money

Building

(9) ☐ New ☐ Purchase ☐ Renovate | Amount for Building | Amount for Land

| $ | $

Amount for New Equipment | Amount for Notes Payable

$(10) | $(11)

Amount for Working Capital | Amount for Equipment Repair

$ (12) | $(10)

Amount for Accounts Payable | Other (See Instructions)

$ (11) | $(12)

(13) **Total Loan Requested** ➡ | $

(14) **Term of Loan** ➡ Years: | Months:

(15)V. Summary of Collateral

	Present Market Value	Present Mortage Balance	Cost Less Depreciation
A. Land and Building			
B. Inventory			
C. Accounts Receivable			
D. Machinery and Equipment			
E. Furniture and Fixtures			
F. Other			
Total Collateral $			

SBA Form 4 (9-78) Previous Editions Are Obsolete

VI. Assistance

(16) List the names of attorneys, accountants, appraisers, agents, or other persons rendering assistance in preparation of this form.

Name and Occupation | Total Fees Paid

Address | Fees Due

Name and Occupation | Total Fees Paid

Address | Fees Due

INSTRUCTIONS FOR APPLICATION FORM

Sections I, II, III. Please provide the information requested. "You" refers to the proprietor, general partner or corporate officer signing this form.

(17) **Section IV.** Use of the loan money; if your use of the loan fits one of the categories listed on the application form, please fill out this section. If you use "other" submit a list on a separate sheet of paper and label the list Exhibit A.

(18) **Section V.** Summary of collateral: if your collateral consists of (A) Land and Building, (B) Inventory, and/or (C) Accounts Receivable, fill in the appropriate blanks. If you are using (D) Machinery and Equipment, (E) Furniture and Fixtures, and/or (F) Other, please provide an itemized list (labeled Exhibit B) that contains serial and identification numbers for all articles that had an original value greater than $500.

(19) **Section VI.** Provide the information requested for all professional services used while preparing the application. You will be asked to complete another form **after loan closing** that will itemize compensation actually paid for services rendered in connection with this application.

Yes	No	CHECKLIST FOR APPLICATION PACKAGE
(20) ☐	☐	All Exhibits must be signed and dated by person signing this form.
(33) ☐ to (48A)	☐	1. Have you submitted **SBA Form 912** (Personal History Statement) for each person e.g. owners, partners, major stock holders, etc.; the instructions are on **SBA Form 912**?
(49) ☐	☐	2. Have you filled out a personal balance sheet (**SBA Form 413** may be used for this purpose) for each stockholder (with **20%** or greater ownership), partner, officer, and owner. Label this Exhibit C.
(53) ☐	☐	3. Have you included the statements listed below: 1,2,3 for the last three years; 1,2,3,4 dated within **90 days** of filing the application; and statement 5? This is Exhibit D. (Management (49) Assistance has **Aids** that help in the preparation of financial Statements.) (50) 1. Balance Sheet 2. Profit and Loss Statement 3. Reconciliation of Net Worth (51) 4. Aging of Accounts Receivable and Payable (49) 5. Earnings projections for at least one year (52) (If Profit and Loss Statement is not available, explain why and substitute Federal Income Tax Forms.)
☐	☐	4. Have you completed a list which contains the original date and amount, present balance owed, interest rate, monthly payment, maturity and security for each loan or debt that your business currently has? Please indicate whether the loan is current or delinquent. An asterisk (*) should be placed by any of these debts that will be paid off with the SBA loan. This should be labeled Exhibit E. *(over)* ↓

How to Collect Business Loan $$$

Yes No

□ □ (54) **5.** Have you provided a brief history of your company and a paragraph describing the expected benefits it will receive from the loan? If not, you must do so. Label it Exhibit F.

□ □ (55) **6.** Have you provided a brief description of the educational, technical and business background for all the people listed in **Section III** under management? If not, you must do so. Please mark it Exhibit G.

□ □ (56) **7.** Do you have any co-signers and/or guarantors for this loan? If so, please submit their names, addresses and personal balance sheets as Exhibit H.

□ □ (57) **8.** Are you buying machinery or equipment with your loan money? If so, you must include a list of the equipment and the cost. This is Exhibit J.

□ □ (58) **9.** Have you or any officers of your company ever been involved in bankruptcy or insolvency proceedings? If so, please provide the details as Exhibit K.

□ □ (59) **10.** Are you or your business involved in any pending lawsuits? If yes, provide the details as Exhibit L.

□ □ (60) **11.** Do you or your spouse or any member of your household, or anyone who owns, manages, or directs your business or their spouses or members of their households work for the **Small Business Administration**, Small Business Advisory Council, SCORE or ACE? If so, please provide the name and address of the person and the office where employed. Label this Exhibit M.

□ □ (61) **12.** Does your business have any subsidiaries or affiliates? If yes, please provide their names and the relationship with your company along with a current balance sheet and operating statement for each. This should be Exhibit N.

□ □ (62) **13.** Do you buy from, sell to, or use the services of any concern in which someone in your company has a significant financial interest? If yes, provide details on a separate sheet of paper labeled Exhibit P.

□ □ (63) **14.** If your business is a franchise, have you included a copy of the franchise agreement? Please include it as Exhibit R.

□ □ (64) **15.** If you or any principals or affiliates have ever requested government financing, list the name of the agency (including **SBA**), the amount requested or approved, date of request or approval, present balance, and status (i.e. current, delinquent). This should be Exhibit S.

CONSTRUCTION LOANS ONLY

□ □ (65) **16.** Have you included in a separate exhibit (Exhibit T) the estimated cost of the project and a statement of the source of any additional funds? If not, please do so.

□ □ (66) **17.** Have you filed all the necessary compliance documents (**SBA Form Series 601**)? If not, loan officer will advise which forms are necessary.

□ □ (67) **18.** Have you provided copies of preliminary construction plans and specifications? If not, include them as Exhibit U. Final plans will be required prior to disbursement.

DIRECT LOANS ONLY

□ □ (68) **19.** Have you included two bank declination letters with your application? These letters should include the name and telephone number of the persons contacted at the banks, the dates and terms of the loan, the reason for decline and whether or not the bank will participate with **SBA**. In towns with 200,000 people or less, one letter will be sufficient.

SBA Form 4 (9-78) Previous Editions Are Obsolete

---

(69) **AGREEMENTS AND CERTIFICATIONS**

Agreement of Nonemployment of SBA Personnel: I/We agree that if **SBA** approves this loan application **I/We** will not, for at least two years, hire as an employee or consultant anyone that was employed by the **SBA** during the one year period prior to the disbursement of the loan.

Certification: I/We certify: (a) **I/We** have not paid anyone connected with the Federal Government for help in getting this loan. **I/We** also agree to report to the SBA **Office of Security and Investigations, 1441 L Street N.W., Washington, D.C., 20416** any Federal Government employee who offers, in return for any type of compensation, to help get this loan approved.
(b) All information in this application and the Exhibits is true and complete to the best of my/our knowledge and is submitted to **SBA** so **SBA** can decide whether to grant a loan or participate with a lending institution in a loan to me/us. **I/We** agree to pay for or reimburse **SBA** for the cost of any surveys, title or mortage examinations, appraisals etc., performed by non-**SBA** personnel provided **I/We** have given my/our consent.
(c) **I/We** give the assurance that we will comply with sections 112 and 113 of volume 13 of the Code of Federal Regulations. These Code sections prohibit discrimination on the grounds of race, color, sex, religion, martial status, handicap, age, or national origin by recipients of Federal financial assistance and require appropriate reports and access to books and records. These requirements are applicable to anyone who buys or takes control of the business. **I/We** realize that if **I/We** do not comply with these non-discrimination requirements **SBA** can, call, terminate, or accelerate repayment of my/our loan.

Authority to Collect Personal Information: This information is provided pursuant to Public Law 93-579 (Privacy Act of 1974). **Effects of Nondisclosure:** Omission of an item means your application might not receive full consideration.

I/We authorize disclosure of all information sumitted in connection with this application to the financial institution agreeing to participate in the loan.

As consideration for any Management and Technical Assistance that may be provided, **I/We** waive all claims against **SBA** and its consultants.

I/We understand that **I/We** need not pay anybody to deal with **SBA**. **I/We** have read and understand Form 394 which explains **SBA** policy on representatives and their fees.

For Guaranty Loans please provide an original and one copy (Photocopy is Acceptable) of the Application Form, and all Exhibits to the participating lender. For Direct Loans submit one original copy of application and Exhibits to **SBA**.

It is against SBA regulations to charge the applicant a percentage of the loan proceeds as a fee for preparing this application.

If you make a statement that you know to be false or if you over value a security in order to help obtain a loan under the provisions of the Small Business Act you can be fined up to $5,000 or be put in jail for up to two years, or both.

_____
Signature of Preparer if Other Than Applicant

_____
Print or Type Name of Preparer

_____
Address of Preparer

If Applicant is a proprietor or general partner, sign below:

By: _____ Date
If Applicant is a corporation, sign below:

Corporate Seal   Date

By: _____
                Signature of President

Attested by: _____
                Signature of Corporate Secretary

89

How to Collect Big $$$ from Uncle Sam

Please Read Carefully - Print or Type

Each member of the small business concern requesting assistance or the development company must submit this form in TRIPLICATE for filing with the SBA application. This form must be filled out and submitted:

1. If a sole proprietorship, by the proprietor;
2. If a partnership, by each partner;
3. If a corporation or a development company, by each officer, director, and additionally, by each holder of 20% or more of the voting stock;
4. Any other person, including a hired manager, who has authority to speak for and commit the borrower in the management of the business.

United States of America

SMALL BUSINESS ADMINISTRATION

STATEMENT OF PERSONAL HISTORY

Name and Address of Applicant (Firm Name)(Street, City, State and ZIP Code)	SBA District Office and City
	Amount Applied for:
(20)	(23)

1. Personal Statement of: (State name in full, if no middle name, state (NMN), or if initial only, indicate initial). List all former names used, and dates each name was used. Use separate sheet if necessary.	2. Date of Birth: (Month, day and year) (24)
	3. Place of Birth: (City & State or Foreign Country) (25)
(21) First Middle Last	U.S. Citizen? ☐ yes ☐ no If no, give alien registration number: (26) #

| 4. Give the percentage of ownership or stock owned or to be owned in the (22) small business concern or the Development Company. | Social Security No. (27) |

5. Present residence address	City	State
From To Address (28)		
Immediate past residence address		
From To Address (29)		

BE SURE TO ANSWER THE NEXT 3 QUESTIONS CORRECTLY BECAUSE THEY ARE IMPORTANT.

THE FACT THAT YOU HAVE AN ARREST OR CONVICTION RECORD WILL NOT NECESSARILY DISQUALIFY YOU. BUT AN INCORRECT ANSWER WILL PROBABLY CAUSE YOUR APPLICATION TO BE TURNED DOWN.

6. Are you presently under indictment, on parole or probation?

(30) ☐ Yes ☐ No   If yes, furnish details in a separate exhibit. List name(s) under which held, if applicable.

7. Have you ever been charged with or arrested for any criminal offense other than a minor motor vehicle violation?

(30) ☐ Yes ☐ No   If yes, furnish details in a separate exhibit. List name(s) under which charged, if applicable.

8. Have you ever been convicted of any criminal offense other than a minor motor vehicle violation?

(30) ☐ Yes ☐ No   If yes, furnish details, in a separate exhibit. List name(s) under which convicted, if applicable.

9. Name and address of participating bank

(31)

The information on this form will be used in connection with an investigation of your character. Any information you wish to submit, that you feel will expedite this investigation should be set forth.

Whoever makes any statement knowing it to be false, for the purpose of obtaining for himself or for any applicant, any loan, or loan extension by renewal, deferment or otherwise, or for the purpose of obtaining, or influencing SBA toward, anything of value under the Small Business Act, as amended, shall be punished under Section 16(a) of that Act, by a fine of not more than $5000, or by imprisonment for not more than 2 years, or both.

Signature (32)	Title	Date

It is against SBA's policy to provide assistance to persons not of good character and therefore consideration is given to the qualities and personality traits of a person, favorable and unfavorable, relating thereto, including behavior, integrity, candor and disposition toward criminal actions. It is also against SBA's policy to provide assistance not in the best interests of the United States, for example, if there is reason to believe that the effect of such assistance will be to encourage or support, directly or indirectly, activities inimical to the Security of the United States. Anyone concerned with the collection of this information, as to its voluntariness, disclosure or routine uses may contact the FOIA Office, 1441 "L" Street, N.W., and a copy of 59 "Agency Collection of Information" from SOP 40 04 will be provided.

SBA FORM 912 (5-78) SOP 50 10 1 EDITION OF 4-75 WILL BE USED UNTIL STOCK IS EXHAUSTED

1. SBA FILE COPY

Chapter 4

How To Collect
Unemployment Compensation $$$

Each week almost 3 million Americans collect unemployment benefit checks. Most people know that you can collect unemployment benefits if you are laid off. However, a fewer number of people know that you can collect weekly unemployment checks in some cases even if you:

—quit your last job,

—were fired from your last job,

—leave work to go to another state, or

—are going to school.

The unemployment insurance program began during the depression days. The program was authorized under the Social Security Act of 1935. Back then, its primary purpose was to replace spending power to those who lost their jobs. Thus, when an individual spent unemployment compensation money it created a demand for goods and services which also created a demand for new jobs and alleviated the unemployment problem.

Unemployment could hit any of us at any time. And, unemployment compensation is not welfare. It is not charity. While you are working, your employer pays a certain amount of money into an unemployment insurance fund. These funds are used to pay unemployment benefits to workers who have lost their jobs. In a few states the worker also pays a small amount into the unemployment insurance fund. The Federal government pays a large part of the unemployment program amounting to about $13 billion a year.

The unemployment insurance program covers workers in all 50 states, Puerto Rico and the Virgin Islands. Unemployment benefits are paid through about 1,700 local unemployment insurance offices.

Here's How You Qualify for Unemployment Benefits

In order to be eligible to receive unemployment compensation, you must have worked in a job where your employer paid into the unemployment compensation fund. However, in times of high unemployment, many workers may still be covered for compensation even though their employers did not pay into the unemployment fund. You must also have worked a long enough period of time to receive unemployment benefit checks. The amount of time that you have to work in order to be eligible for benefits varies from state to state. You must have lost your job through no fault of your own or quit because of a "good cause". Most people who lose their jobs can collect benefits. You must be physically able to work and available to accept suitable employment. Lastly, you must be actively seeking work.

Covered Employment

In order to collect unemployment benefits you must have worked at a job where your employer paid into the unemployment insurance fund. Most employers are required to pay into the fund by law. But if you worked at a job where your employer did not pay into the unemployment insurance fund, but should have, you may still be eligible to collect benefits. The unemployment office will track down your former employer and request back payment of the unemployment taxes due. Your former employer may object and even refuse to pay. But this should not effect your entitlement to benefits. The important question is: Was your employer legally required to pay into the fund? If the answer is "yes", you're probably entitled to benefits whether or not he actually paid in.

In periods of high unemployment the federal government may loosen eligibility requirements. During these periods (like in 1975, 1976) unemployed workers may be eligible for benefits whether or not an employer was required to pay into the unemployment insurance fund.

Length of Employment

In determining whether you have worked long enough to receive benefits, states determine what is called your base period, which is usually 52 weeks. You do not have to work during the entire base period. You only have to work as long as your state requires. Some states require that within your base period you must have worked a certain number of weeks. Other states require that you earn a certain amount of money—$1,100 for example—during the 52-week base period. While other states have a combination of earnings and weeks worked requirements.

A word of explanation is in order for the term "base period". Your base period is determined by the date you apply for benefits. Some states consider your base period to be the 12 months preceding the day you apply for unemployment compensation. For example, if you apply for benefits on December 31 of a year, your base period will be from January 1 to December 31, the day you apply. Other states calculate your base period in another way. Some states disregard several months before the date you apply for benefits. For example, in California, the first 4-7 months before the date you apply for benefits are not counted in determining your base period. Why do states calculate your base period that way? This is to prevent a person from working a short period of time and then quitting his job to collect unemployment compensation benefits.

Employee vs. Being Self-Employed

The basic purpose of the unemployment insurance program is to provide benefits to employees who are out of work through no fault of their own. The program was never designed to provide benefits to self-employed persons. Hence, it is very important to make the distinction between an employee and a self-employed person (independent contractor). Basically, if you work for someone else you are an employee. Conversely, if you work *only* for yourself, you are considered self-employed.

Very often an employer will classify a worker as contract labor instead of an employee. The employer will do this to get around paying the unemployment insurance tax and withholding federal and state income taxes from the worker's wages.

Even though an employer classifies you as an independent contractor (self-employed person) you may actually be an employee in the eyes of the unemployment office. This may be true even though you signed a contract stating that you were an independent contractor.

The unemployment office considers specific factors in deciding whether you are an employee or independent contractor. Some of these factors are:

Did you have a supervisor?
> *An employee has a supervisor.*
> *A self-employed person does not.*

Could you be fired?
> *An employee can be fired.*
> *A self-employed person cannot.*

Who determined your hours?
> *An employee is told when to work.*
> *A self-employed person sets his or her own hours.*

Who supplied work tools?
> *An employee is given tools.*
> *A self-employed person generally supplies his or her own tools.*

How often did you get paid?
> *An employee normally gets paid by the hour.*
> *A self-employed person normally gets paid by the job.*

How to Collect Unemployment Compensation $$$

If these factors point in the direction of an employee, there's a good chance of being classified as an employee by the unemployment office. Remember, it is the unemployment office's classification that counts, not your employer's.

Owning Your Own Business

If you own a business as a sole proprietor or partnership, you're probably not eligible to collect unemployment benefits. This is because you are considered a self-employed person.

But if your business is a corporation, you can probably collect benefits if you are "laid off". This is because the corporation is legally considered to be a separate entity, independent of you or any other person. In other words, the corporation is your employer, just as if you worked for a giant corporation like General Motors. One thing that could hurt your chances of collecting is if the corporation had not been paying unemployment insurance taxes on your wages. This would be especially detrimental if you owned 100 percent of the corporate stock. But if the corporation had been paying the required unemployment insurance tax, you should be entitled to collect just like any other corporate employee.

Federal Employees

Former federal government employees and military service persons are entitled to collect unemployment benefits. Service persons must be discharged under conditions other than dishonorable. Benefit payments are determined by their pay-grade at the time of separation from the service.

Persons employed in a foreign country can apply for unemployment benefits in the state in which they are a resident. Benefits will be paid in accordance with that state's payment rates.

Why Are You Unemployed

Of course, if you were laid off, there is no problem in collecting unemployment compensation—you are out of work through no fault of your own. However, this does not mean that you cannot collect compensation if you quit your job or were fired.

When You Are Fired

If you are fired from a job, some kind of misconduct must generally be demonstrated by your former employer before your unemployment claim can be rejected. However, if you are simply "incompetent" or even "negligent" you are still eligible for benefits (some states may disqualify you because of negligence). Often, there is a very fine line between misconduct and competence.

Usually, misconduct must be specifically related to your work. You must do something that is obviously harmful to your employer's business, such as:

—attacking a fellow employee or seriously interfering with the work activities of other employees,

—stealing cash or other items from your employer or intentionally damaging an employer's property,

—refusing to perform a reasonable work order that is obviously within the scope of your job duties.

Notice that all of the above are related to a disruption of the employer's business. This is the key element that is necessary to show misconduct.

Many people get fired because they can't get along with a supervisor and find themselves continually arguing about something. Arguing, in itself, is not justification for disallowing an unemployment compensation claim as long as "misconduct" cannot be shown.

If you are fired for a non job-related reason you may still be eligible to collect benefits. For example, if you are convicted of a crime that is not related to your employment, but you're fired because of it, you may still be eligible for benefits.

This is a good time to point out that if you start collecting unemployment benefits your former employer must pay a higher unemployment tax. Therefore, your employer has an incentive to keep you off the unemployment rolls. When you apply for benefits, the unemployment office sends certain forms to your former employer to be filled out. The forms ask your employer to explain the reason behind your job termination. He has about 10 days to respond. If you were fired, your employer may try to show that he was justified in firing you. If he can show this, he will not have to pay the higher tax. Some employers contest all unemployment benefit claims of former employees. They designate a special company official whose job is to dispute unemployment claims.

Don't let this worry you. You are going to know the rules of the game. No matter how hard your former employer disputes, you will have the edge.

How Misconduct Affects Benefits

Generally the seriousness of the misconduct determines what the penalty will be. Some states make a person wait several weeks before benefit payments start. Other states reduce benefits or disallow benefits altogether because of misconduct.

What To Do If You're Fired

Let's say you're fired. Your employer calls it misconduct. But you don't agree. In this case, you should find a witness or two to show there was no conduct on your part. Maybe the witnesses (along with your statements) could show you are just not suited for the type of work you were doing (incompetence).

If you are fired for a long list of things, you can still collect unemployment compensation if misconduct is not evident in any of the employer's complaints.

Let's say you quit. You were convinced your employer was going to fire you anyway. In this case, you could probably still collect benefits in most states. However, there must be compelling evidence that you were on the verge of losing your job.

Keep in mind that your story should always be consistent. This is especially true in the forms you fill out. Serious inconsistencies can harm your chances for benefits.

Quitting Work—Job Related Reasons

All states allow payment of unemployment compensation

benefits if you leave work because of a "good cause". The definition of good cause varies from state to state. Generally, a wide range of reasons are considered "good cause" for leaving a job.

Your Health

A large number of job-related things could affect your health and force you to leave a job. Many people quit because of: poor lighting, noxious fumes, dust which makes you choke. Your work hours could give you insomnia. Lifting heavy objects strains your back or neck. Some people can't cope with job pressures. They become nervous and irritable. The job strains become so great they simply can't take it any longer. They quit.

Having a doctor's note advising you to quit is helpful, but not absolutely necessary. The important thing is to have a list of documented reasons why you had "good cause" to leave the job. As long as you are still available to do another kind of more suitable work, you'll still be able to collect benefits.

Your Safety

Often an employer does not provide a safe working environment for its employees. In other cases, getting to work may be unsafe. Leaving a job because of safety reasons can constitute "good cause" for quitting a job.

By not providing enough safeguards to assure the safety and welfare of employees, many smaller employers unknowingly violate the law. Not providing adequate safety equipment, not keeping floors and work areas clean, leaving combustible materials laying around, may all violate certain federal, state and local laws and ordinances. If it can be shown that working conditions are violating existing laws, you have a powerful case for "good cause".

Getting to work may be dangerous. Let's say you're a female who has to walk or ride through a rough, high-crime area, especially late at night. You're afraid of being mugged or raped. This may be a very "good cause" for quitting a job.

False Promises

When a person is hired for a job, promises are often made.

There could be promises of fast promotions, training programs, travel, etc. Then as time goes on, these promises are not kept. Or, maybe a rosy description was given about the nature of the work. Later, you find out the work is not so rosy. All these reasons may be considered "good cause" for leaving a job. However, keep in mind that the reasons for leaving must be work related. A false promise must be about some aspect of the job.

Your Wages

The unreasonable lowering of wages may be "good cause" for leaving a job. Generally, if your employer lowers your wages 10 percent or more but requires that you do the same work you can collect unemployment compensation. Even if your wages aren't cut, you can still collect if you quit because your wages were substantially less than those of others in your community who are doing the same type of work.

Having your hours drastically cut may also be considered "good cause". If you were hired as a full-time employee, but end up as part-time, you can probably collect benefits if you quit. This is especially true if your income needs call for a full-time job.

Other Reasons For Quitting

You can collect unemployment benefits if you quit a job because it violated your religious morals. An example would be if you are required to work on Sundays or on religious holidays. Other aspects of a job may also go against a person's religious beliefs. Examples would be if you're required to wear scanty clothing or sell something that could be considered a "rip off".

The Supreme Court recently ruled in favor of an Indiana man who quit a job because of his religious beliefs. Eddie Thomas worked in an Indiana plant that manufactured tank parts. He quit the job because he believed his religious beliefs forbade him from manufacturing war materials. He was denied unemployment benefits. But, the Supreme Court ruled that workers who quit jobs that are in conflict with their religious beliefs may not be denied unemployment benefits.

How to Collect Big $$$ from Uncle Sam

Keep in mind that your employer pays more tax if you start collecting unemployment compensation. So don't be surprised if your employer tells the unemployment compensation office that you did not have "good cause" for quitting. Your employer has a money incentive to keep you off the unemployment compensation rolls. Be prepared to argue your case, using witnesses and other evidence, if necessary.

Quitting Work—Non Job Reasons

Many states allow you to collect unemployment benefits even if you quit work for non job-related reasons. Examples are leaving a job because a spouse has been transferred or quitting to care for a family member who is seriously ill. Note that these reasons are beyond the control of the worker. If the situation is within your control, your claim for benefits may be in trouble.

Having a Baby

Most states do not pay unemployment benefits for leaving work to have a baby. Benefits are usually denied for the duration of the pregnancy plus a period of time after birth. But, if your family doctor advises you to quit and you are still available to do other kinds of work, you are eligible to collect in many states.

What happens if you're fired because you are pregnant? (Yes, this happens every day!) You can collect benefits in most states as long as you are still available for work.

Quitting For Other Reasons

Some states are very liberal in allowing benefits while others are more strict. It is important that you find out what the requirements are in your particular state. Most states will not allow benefit payments when you quit work for the following reasons:

—to attend school full-time (you're usually not available for work while in a classroom),
—personal reasons like getting married or divorced,
—to travel.

Remember, even if you quit for one of the above reasons, still apply for benefits. Get an official rejection. You may be surprised by getting a regular unemployment check.

How Quitting Without "Good Cause" Affects Benefits

What happens if the unemployment compensation office determines that you left work without good cause? Answer: All states will penalize you. But, the penalty varies greatly from state to state. You may have to wait a number of weeks before you can start collecting, or you could be denied benefits altogether.

In the states which make you wait before you can start collecting benefits, the wait is often between 5 and 8 weeks. The reasoning is that if you haven't been able to find work after the waiting period, it's no fault of your own. It's probably the fault of the economy. There's a slump, and jobs are hard to come by.

The stricter states allow no benefits to be paid during the entire period of unemployment. Before benefits will be paid, most states require that you work at another job for a certain period of time and earn a specified amount of money. In effect you are being made to qualify for benefits based on the new job; not the previous one which was left without "good cause".

Able To Work

To be eligible to collect unemployment compensation benefits, you must be mentally and physically able to work. This does not mean you must be able to do any kind of work. It only means that you must be available to do some kind of work that reasonably suits you. If you can't swim you won't be considered available for work as a lifeguard. If you are not physically strong you won't be considered available for construction work. And, you don't necessarily have to be available to do your previous type of work. For example, if your previous job required that you stand for long periods of time, and your feet continually hurt, you can still be available for a sit-down job.

If you are disabled and cannot do any substantial work, you may be ineligible to collect unemployment benefits. Some states reduce your benefits, some let you collect for a limited time, while others disallow benefits altogether.

If you are disabled because of an accident or injury suffered while on the job, you may be eligible for worker's compensation. If this is the case, file a claim at the local unemployment office as soon as possible. Even if your disability is not job related you can still collect other government benefits. If you've worked long enough, you may be eligible for social security disability payments. Even if you have little or no work history, you may still be eligible to collect Supplemental Security Income benefits. However, to collect under these programs you must be unable to engage in any substantial, gainful employment for at least 12 months or more. For more information, refer to the disability section of Chapter 1 on Social Security.

Available To Accept Work

You must be available to accept suitable work in order to collect unemployment benefits. This means that you must be willing to devote a reasonable number of hours to a job. If you're a full time student you're probably not "available for work". If you have to stay home and watch the kids most of the time, you're probably not "available or work".

You must also be willing to accept reasonable pay. If you want a waitress job but are unwilling to work for less than $25 an hour, you will probably be considered "not available for work". Get the picture?

Most states require that you register for work at the local unemployment office. Further, they require that you accept suitable work that they refer you to. For example, let's say the unemployment office sends you out on a job interview for suitable work. You impress the employer. He wants to hire you at reasonable wages. But you refuse to take the job. In this case you could be denied unemployment benefits. The unemployment office would reason that a suitable job was available. But you refused it. Therefore, you're really not available for work.

How to Collect Unemployment Compensation $$$

Actively Seeking Work

Most states require that you be actively seeking a job in order to start collecting unemployment benefits. The reason for this is to assure that you really want to be part of the "workforce". To meet this requirement you simply have to apply at various businesses potentially offering suitable work. And, it's alright to reapply at businesses that have previously turned you down.

Some states require that you report to them the firms that you contacted to find work. However, few unemployment offices ever check up to make sure you really sought work at a firm. The main reasons for this are staff shortages at most unemployment offices and the difficulty of contacting firms and requesting such confidential information.

Accepting A Job

You cannot be required to take any old job just because it is an available job. The job offered to you must be reasonably suitable based on your age, training, experience and physical condition. Only you can decide whether or not a job is suitable for you. You are the one who must get up in the morning and go to the job. The unemployment compensation people don't have to do any dirty work. They already have comfortable government jobs. Make sure the job is right for you before you accept it.

The definition of "suitable work", of course, varies from state to state. However, the unemployment office will generally consider a job not suitable for the following reasons:

—The job is too far from your home. Such things as availability of transportation, the cost of travel, and travel time are considered.

—Wages are a lot less than other similar jobs in the community.

—The job requires that you join a union or other organization that goes against your beliefs.

If you refuse work that the unemployment office considers suitable for you, benefits may be stopped. Some states may stop benefit payments up to 4 months or more, while others deny benefits entirely. Be sure to find out what the requirements are in your state.

Here's What You Can Collect

The amount of unemployment compensation benefits you can collect depends on a number of factors, such as the amount of your earnings during your base period, when you earned the money and the state's method of computing benefits.

Most states figure your benefits on your highest earnings during any quarter in your base period. For example, if your earnings during your base period were:

January		July	
February	— $800	August	— $1,000
March		September	
April		October	
May	— $750	November	— $1,800
June		December	

Your benefit check would be based on the $1,800—your earnings for the highest quarter. Some states pay additional benefits if you have dependents.

Weekly benefits generally average about 50 percent of your gross weekly wages up to a maximum amount set by the state. Studies have shown that overall unemployment compensation replaces about 64 percent of a person's *net* earnings while working.

The first week after filing your claim is normally a "waiting period" and no benefits can be paid for that week. But do not wait to file because of a waiting period. The waiting period does not start until the claim is filed. The first payment on a new claim is usually about three weeks after the claim is filed.

In most states you can collect benefits for a period of 26 weeks. Some states limit benefits to 20 weeks while others pay up to 36 weeks. In periods of high unemployment states can give an extension of benefits for a period of time up to 65 weeks.

How to Collect Unemployment Compensation $$$

Working Part-Time

Often a person collecting unemployment benefits is unable to find a full-time job, but is offered a job working only part-time. The question of how this will affect unemployment payments arises. Most states allow you to work part-time while still collecting benefits.

Some states encourage claimants to work part-time by offering various incentives. For example, California allows persons to keep up to $25 without having benefit checks reduced. Other states allow persons to earn a certain percentage of their benefit payments before reducing benefits. Michigan pays full benefits if part-time earnings are less than half of the benefit amount.

Collecting While In Job Training

In many states you can collect unemployment benefits while attending an approved training program. Some states even pay additional training benefits. The type of eligible training varies from state to state, but generally it must develop some kind of job skill. The hours of training generally can't be too time consuming because you must technically be available for work.

Some states set up special training programs in conjunction with local colleges. All programs are designed to develop job skills. Check with your local unemployment office to see what they can offer you. Collecting while at the same time furthering your education sounds like a good idea!

You Can Collect in Any State

The unemployment compensation program is a federally-funded program. As such, it operates under general uniform federal rules and regulations. Therefore, you can move to any of the 50 states and collect unemployment benefits. Many people are unaware of this fact. They stay in an uncomfortable climate when they could just as well be collecting benefits in the state and city of their choice.

Filing a claim for unemployment benefits in another state is called an "interstate claim". An interstate claim is no more difficult to collect on than a regular claim. The state you move to simply acts as payment agent for your home state. It may take a little longer to get your first check because of the extra paper shuffling involved. The unemployment compensation office will have to contact your previous state office to have your claim verified. But, the unemployment offices are familiar with out-of-state claims; and they know how to process your claim so you will get your check as soon as possible.

Generally, an interstate claim will involve one of the following situations:

— You get laid off and move to another state to look for suitable work.
— You get transferred to another state, then lose your job.
— You leave a job in one state for a different job in another state, then lose that job.
— You start collecting unemployment compensation benefits in one state and then move to another state.

You can collect benefits in each of the above-mentioned situations. In each case you simply go down to the local unemployment office in the new state and say you want to file an interstate claim.

If you move to another state, continue to work, and then get laid off, make sure your earnings in both states are combined in figuring your benefits. This will probably result in a higher check.

Applying For Benefits

Applying for unemployment benefits is generally a two-step procedure. (1) You must fill out a written application, and (2) you must be "interveiwed" by an unemployment office employee.

When you first visit the unemployment office you will be given application forms and told to return for an interview at a later time. Remember that the written application and face-to-face interview are designed to establish your eligibility for benefits. So at this point, let's briefly review what the

eligibility requirements are. You must:
— have worked long enough in qualified employment,
— have lost your job through "no fault" of your own,
— be physically able to work,
— be available for work, and
— be actively seeking work.

If any of your written or verbal statements indicate that you do not meet the above requirements, you stand a good chance of being denied unemployment compensation benefits.

The Forms

When completing the application forms, your answers should be brief and to the point. Don't add any extra information that is not specifically asked for. Above all, make sure your answers are consistent and make sense. Some of the questions on the forms are more important than others. Your answer could mean the difference between collecting thousands of dollars in unemployment benefits and collecting nothing.

An example of State Unemployment claim forms are included at the back of this chapter.

The following question is probably one of the most important ones you will be asked to answer: "Why are you no longer working at your last job?" Of course, if you were laid off, write that in the space provided. If you were fired, but not for misconduct on your part, write "discharged without misconduct on my part". In a case where you quit for good cause, write "quit for good cause for a work-related reason".

Don't try to fully explain every little detail. Just answer the question simply and to the point. Further explanation can be made during the interview if required.

The Interview

After you complete the necessary forms you'll be asked to go down to the unemployment office for an interview. The interview can take place over the counter or in an office. The unemployment office employee will review your forms to make sure thay are properly filled out. You will no doubt be asked to provide details on some of the answers on your application. Again, only answer the specific question. Don't offer other information. Be brief and to-the-point.

During the interview you don't have to feel humble. Keep in mind that the taxes you paid while you were working helped pay for the unemployment office worker's salary. So keep your head high.

Your Unemployment Compensation Check

In most cases you will have to visit the unemployment office to pick up your check. You will be given a specific time and day to report. The checks are generally issued every week although some states pay every two weeks. When you pick up your check, you'll probably have to tell someone at the unemployment office where you looked for work. remember, in order to be eligible for benefits you must be actively seeking work. You'll have to provide the names of about three places where you went looking for a job. By the way, if you think you'll feel uneasy about standing in an unemployment line, wear sunglasses. Many people wear dark glasses while waiting to pick up their checks.

What if you are unable to report to the unemployment office to pick up your check? Notify them ahead of time. You can still get that benefit check at a later time if you have a good excuse for missing your appointment. Of course, if you had a job interview that's fine. Just forgetting to show may be good enough in most states.

What if you don't show up because you're sick or disabled? You may be denied your full check for that week. Why? Because if you're sick or disabled you can't meet at least two eligibility requirements: Being able to work, and actively seeking work. Here again, find out what the requirements are in your state.

What if you don't show up because you're out of town looking for work? That's fine. The unemployment office will look favorably on your traveling to another part of the state or a different state to look for work, as long as work actually exists there. If you go to a remote island, that won't do. Your type of work must be available in that area. Many people from eastern states travel to Florida in the winter to look for work. That's okay. Just notify your employment office ahead of time.

Appealing a Denial

You will be notified in writing if you are denied unemployment compensation benefits. The reason for the denial should be clearly spelled out. The denial notice will state how long you have to appeal the decision. You generally have 20 days to file an appeal. If you miss the appeal deadline, you can still appeal if you have a valid reason for missing it. In some states the only valid reason is not receiving the denial notice in the first place.

Of course, you will have to fill out a form to appeal. You will be asked to give your reasons for appealing. A simple reason is sufficient. This could be:

"I don't agree with the decision for legal reasons."

It is usually better to pinpoint the specific reason why you are appealing. For example, if you quit your job for a health reason, your statement could read like this:

"I quit my job because the heavy lifting of boxes caused considerable back pain. Often I could not sleep because of the discomfort. Dr. Connell advised me to look for other work."

Having a note from a medical doctor or chiropractor would help your case.

A while after you file your appeal form, you will receive a notice which will tell you the date and time of the hearing. The hearing is informal and usually held at the local unemployment office. Before the hearing, you have the right to review all records affecting your appeal. Also, you may be represented by a union official or lawyer. If you have an attorney, you'll have to pay the fee.

Preparation

At the hearing you can present witnesses to help prove your case. If a witness is unavailable for some reason you can have that person prepare a sworn sttement. Legally, a sworn statement is called an "affidavit". It is the next best thing to having the witness testify in person.

The affidavit should briefly and clearly address your main defense issue. For example, let's say you were fired because you got into a scuffle with your supervisor. But, a fellow employee saw your supervisor shove you. The statement should clearly address what was observed and heard. It should be as detailed as possible, showing names, dates, location and other pertinent information. Under the statement the witness should write: "I certify that the above is true and correct to the best of my knowledge." His or her name and address should be included. Having the signature notarized makes the affidavit even more powerful.

Before the hearing make a list of the key facts that you want to cover. Make sure each point is covered before the hearing comes to an end.

A Second Appeal

Losing an appeal doesn't always end the matter. In most states you can appeal to the State Unemployment Insurance Board.

Like the first appeal, you'll have to file the necessary forms stating your reason for appealing. If new facts become availble to help your case, be sure to emphasize them. You usually don't have to appear in person. The board merely reviews the facts in the case and decides whether the laws and regulations were properly applied. If you lose the second appeal, yet you still believe your claim is justified, get legal advice. Many lawyers will take a promising case on a contingency fee basis. Their fee can be taken from the back proceeds of your claim only if you win.

Where To Go

Each state operates an unemployment compensation office. The exact name may vary from state to state. It will be called something like "Employment Development Department" or "Employment Security Commission". The address and telephone numbers can be found under the state government section of your phone directory. If you can't find the number refer to the list of Federal Information Centers at the back of this book. Call the number nearest your home.

How to Collect Unemployment Compensation $$$

Ask for the number of the unemployment compensation office nearest you.

How To Save Time And Cut Red Tape

Before visiting your local unemployment office, make sure you are going to the one nearest your home. This will save time when you start picking up your checks each week. Also, before you go to the unemployment office, call first. Ask the unemployment compensation representative the best time to come in to avoid crowded conditions. This is important, because at certain times the line can be very long. While other times the office is almost empty. Calling first can save you a lot of time and aggravation.

You should also find out what specific information you need to file a claim. As a minimum, you'll probably need:
— your social security number,
— the name and address of your last employer,
— the name and address of each employer for the last 19 months, including those in other states.

Of course, before filing a claim you should be familiar with the important aspects of this chapter.

Questions and Answers

Q. What groups of people are not normally covered by unemployment insurance?

A. Minor children employed by their parents, parents employed by their children, husbands and wifes employed by each other, and caddies and jockeys. But, in time of high unemployment, most workers not normally covered can still collect benefits. Don't assume anything. Check with your nearest unemployment office.

Q. Why can't self-employed persons collect unemployment compensation?

A. The unemployment insurance program was intended to help workers who become unemployed through no fault of their own. A self-employed person has some control over his employment. Also, with a self-employed person, it is hard to determine the extent of unemployment. For these reasons, self-employed persons are not generally eligible for unemployment compensations benefits. But, don't count yourself out. Sometimes there is a fine line between being an employee and being self-employed. Apply for benefits. Let the unemployment office turn you down.

Q. Can bill collectors get at my unemployment check?

A. In most cases creditors can't touch your unemployment benefits. However, you must keep the unemployment compensation money separate from other funds. If you combine your money, a creditor might be able to get at any money you have. If you are worried about bill collectors keep your unemployment benefits in a separate bank account.

Q. What affect does other income have on unemployment benefits?

A. Unearned income will not affect your benefits. Examples are income from trust funds, gifts, interest, rental income, and dividends. A person could conceivably be getting $1 million a year in interest from savings bonds and still be eligible to collect unemployment benefits. Some states will reduce your benefits when you receive military or National Guard pay, jury and witness fees, or strike benefits. However, supplemental unemployment benefits such as that paid by the large automobile companies are usually permitted without penalty.

Q. Does the unemployment office know about job opportunities in other parts of the country?

A. Yes. The unemployment offices exchange information on job openings throughout the state and nationwide. They may be able to find you a job in the location of your choice.

Q. Can the unemployment office help a person decide what type of work they are best suited for?

How to Collect Unemployment Compensation $$$

A. Yes. Employment counselors are available to help identify your potential for certain types of work. They can also tell you what opportunities are available in a particular field of interest.

Q. Do states pay additional benefits if the unemployed worker has dependents?

A. Presently, 12 states pay an additional allowance for dependent children, the other 40 states do no. Also, 7 states pay an allowance for a non-working spouse. Check with your local unemployment office to find out the requirements in your state.

Q. Can a person collect unemployment benefits and social security at the same time?

A. No. States are now required to reduce unemployment benefit checks by the amount of a pension or other retirement benefit on a dollar-for-dollar basis during any week an individual was eligible for both types of benefits.

How to Collect Big $$$ from Uncle Sam

THIS IS NOT A WORK APPLICATION – PLEASE ANSWER ITEMS 1 THROUGH 17

1. Social Security No.	2. First Name Last Name	3. How long have you lived in this part of California? ____ Years ____ Months

4. Circle highest school grade completed.
1 2 3 4 5 6 7 8 9 10 11 12

College 1 2 3 4 5+   Last year you attended school _____

5. What kinds of work do you plan to look for?

6. In what localities or areas are you willing to seek and accept work?

7. Transportation to and from work (check one)

☐ Automobile   ☐ Bus   ☐ Other

8. How much time are you willing to spend traveling to a job?

9. How do you usually find work?

10. What is the lowest starting wage you will ACCEPT on your next job?

11. Between what hours or which shifts will you work?

12. Are there any days during the week you will not or cannot work?

☐ Yes   ☐ No   If Yes, list days and give reason:

13. Is there any reason that would prevent you from accepting immediate work?

☐ Yes   ☐ No   If Yes, what is the reason?

14. Describe any health condition that may limit work you can accept.

15. List any job-required tools, license, certificate, credential, registration and/or other work-related material you have:

16. List kinds of work you can do.   Length of experience   Last year in this work   Last rate of pay

17. WORK RECORD: Complete the items below for the longest jobs you had during the past 24 months regardless of where work was done. Include your last employer and any significant periods of self-employment, government or military service.

EMPLOYER NAME (Name of Company)	ADDRESS WHERE YOU WORKED	KIND OF WORK YOU HAD & DURATION	PAY RATE	REASON NO LONGER WORKING
LAST EMPLOYER regardless of State, type of work, or length of job.	Street / City / State	Kind or Title: From ____ (Mo.) ____ (Year) To ____ (Mo.) ____ (Year)		☐ Lack of Work ☐ Voluntary Quit ☐ Discharge ☐ Other
NEXT EMPLOYER	Street / City / State	Kind or Title: From ____ (Mo.) ____ (Year) To ____ (Mo.) ____ (Year)		☐ Lack of Work ☐ Voluntary Quit ☐ Discharge ☐ Other
NEXT EMPLOYER	Street / City / State	Kind or Title: From ____ (Mo.) ____ (Year) To ____ (Mo.) ____ (Year)		☐ Lack of Work ☐ Voluntary Quit ☐ Discharge ☐ Other
NEXT EMPLOYER	Street / City / State	Kind or Title: From ____ (Mo.) ____ (Year) To ____ (Mo.) ____ (Year)		☐ Lack of Work ☐ Voluntary Quit ☐ Discharge ☐ Other

A. This space for Department use ONLY –

DE 3893, Rev. 8 (12-76)
State of California
Employment Development Department

CLAIMANT PROFILE

Chapter 5

How To Collect Farm Loan And Rural Housing $$$

Many people dream of the day when they can get out of the daily rat-race of urban living. A day when they can quit the grueling 8-5 grind and find a place in the world where, on their own, they can make a living for themselves and their families. Farming offers such an opportunity in many cases. And Uncle Sam will gladly help you start your own farm if you have the determination and ability to succeed.

Many families just want to get out of the larger cities because of the growing problems of crime, polution and congestion. They want fresher air, less traffic and more space to enjoy life. They dream of owning a nice home in a small town somewhere in America. Uncle Same will gladly help you buy a home in a rural part of the country. Of, if you prefer, you can rent a place in the country and have Uncle Sam help you make your monthly rent payment.

The Farmers Home Administration (FmHA), an agency within the Department of Agriculture, was created to help Americans get established in farming and ranching and to encourage urban families to live in the countryside. To accomplish this, the Farmers Home Administration provides loan assistance to eligible persons for the purchase of farms, ranches and homesites. The FmHA also provides rent subsidies to eligible families.

Farm and Ranch Loans

The Farmers Home Administration provides loan assistance to eligible persons to buy or construct a farm or ranch, or to enlarge or develop farm land and dwellings. Loan help is also extended to include purchase of livestock, drilling wells and improving water supplies. Farms and ranches must be located in rural areas with a population of less than 20,000 people.

To be eligible for loan assistance to purchase a farm or ranch an individual must meet certain general requirements. To be eligible an applicant must:
— be a citizen of the Unites States and be of legal age,
— be unable to obtain a farm or ranch loan from a bank or other private lending institution,
— possess the character and ability to carry out farm and ranch activities,
— have recent farm experience or training needed to succeed in farming or ranching.
— after the loan is made, be the owner/operator of the farm or ranch, and
— rely on farm income to have a reasonable standard of living.

As for the financial condition of the applicant, FmHA has no rigid standards for determining an applicant's eligibility for a farm or ranch loan. Each application for a loan is judged on an individual basis. Therefore, if you have only limited capital, don't rule yourself out. The FmHA is more concerned with your determination and ability to suceed in farming or ranching. Countless numbers of now-successful farmers and ranchers started   from scratch with the help of FmHA.

How To Apply

The Farmers Home Administration (FmHA) is not in

business to compete with private lending institutions. Therefore, it will not provide financial help for a farm or ranch if private financing is available. So before you can get FmHA loan help, you'll have to be refused financing from a bank or other private lender. Only then can you apply for FmHA loan assistance.

Getting Turned Down

You'll have to apply for your farm or ranch loan at a bank or financial institution that is capable of handling your loan request. For the lender to properly assess your loan request, you'll be required to complete a regular loan application form. You'll have to provide information both on the farm or ranch and on your own financial situation.

The Federal Land Bank

You don't have to confine your search for a farm or ranch loan to banks and other private lenders. You can also apply at the Federal Land Bank. The Federal Land Bank was created by Congress to provide long-term loans to prospective farmers and ranchers. Nationwide, there are about 522 Federal Land Banks. They can make loans for up to 85 percent of the appraised value of the farm or ranch. Repayment of the loan can take up to 40 years.

To find the Federal Land Bank nearest you, refer to the list of Federal Information Centers in the back of this book. Call there and ask for the Federal Land Bank nearest your home. Applying for a land bank loan is similar to applying at a regular bank.

After Refusal

At this point, you'll have to consider whether you want to apply directly to FmHA for a loan or have FmHA guarantee a loan from a private lender. Each type of loan assistance is discussed in more detail under the section "Here's What You Can Collect".

Obviously, it is to your advantage to get a loan directly from FmHA. The interest rate is much lower than that available from a private lender and the terms of the loan are also better. However, if loan funds from FmHA are not available, you may have to be satisfied with FmHA's loan guarantee program. In this case, ask your banker to make you the loan under the loan guarantee plan. Under this plan the FmHA guarantees the lender that if you don't repay the loan the FmHA will pay it back. Most lenders look favorably on this arrangement because it is risk free.

Of course, if the lender who initially turned you down is not interested in a FmHA loan guarantee plan, you'll have to find another willing lender. Look in the telephone book to locate other lenders in your vicinity. Call and ask if they would be willing to consider a FmHA loan guarantee plan for your farm or ranch.

Applying for Farmers Home Administration Loan Help

Once you've found a lender willing to go along with a FmHA loan guarantee plan, you'll then have to convince the FmHA that buying your farm or ranch is a good idea. You'll have to complete the necessary application forms and submit them to FmHA for approval. Your application should include a letter from a lending institution indicating your application for a regular loan was rejected. A copy of a FmHA application for loan assistance is included at the back of this chapter.

Evalutating Your Application

Your application for a loan will be decided by the FmHA county committee in the area where the ranch or farm site is located. The committee consists of three individuals, two of whom are farmers themselves. They know local farming and credit conditions and are aware of what it takes to become successful. Before acting on an application the committee may ask to meet with your wife or family, or they may want to visit the farm or ranch you want to buy.

After careful consideration the committee will determine your eligibility based on the requirements discussed earlier. The committee then decides the amount of loan help to provide. And, once your application is approved, the committee will help you work out a plan for making the best use of the farm or ranch's land, labor, livestock, capital and equipment. In all cases labor must be furnished primarily by the owner and his immediate family except during seasonal peak-load periods.

Here's What You Can Collect

The FmHA provides two types of loan assistance to help you purchase a ranch or farm: direct loans and guaranteed loans. Each is discussed below.

Direct Loans

The FmHA can loan money directly to you without the involvement of a bank or other lending institution. The amount of the loan is limited to $225,000 with a maximum repayment period of 40 years. The rate of interest varies with economic conditions. In certain parts of the country there is a waiting list for direct farm or ranch loans. With the favorable rate of interest and terms of the loan, this can be expected. Each county receives direct loan funds on a quarterly basis. So, if funds are not available in one quarter, more will be coming in every three months. However, not all areas have waiting lists. So money to buy a farm or ranch is waiting to be collected on a first come, first served basis.

Guaranteed Loans

The FmHA guarantees your lender (such as a bank, savings and loan, or insurance company, etc.) that if you don't repay the loan the FmHA will pay it back. The FmHA guarantees 90 percent of the loan up to $300,000.

Under a FmHA loan guarantee plan, the rate of interest and loan maturity are agreed upon by the lender and the loan applicant. The FmHA does not establish maximum rates of interest for loan guarantee purposes. However, it can only guarantee a loan for up to 40 years.

Where To Go

There are over 1,800 local FmHA offices throughout the

country that can help you apply for a loan. To find the telephone number of the local FmHA county office, call the Federal Information Center nearest your home. A complete list of Federal Information Centers is included in the back of this book. Ask the information specialist for the number of the FmHA county office nearest your home.

How To Cut Red Tape

As a first step, read this chapter carefully. Then, as you go along, call the FmHA whenever questions or problems arise. It is a good idea to deal with one specific official. Some FmHA officials are former small town farmers. They can really be helpful.

Rural Home Loans

The FmHA provides loans to eligible families for the purchase of homes in rural areas having a population of less than 20,000 people. Home loans may be used to buy an existing home, or to build a new home. The new or existing home can be part of a tract development, or it can be custom built. For new homes, FmHA makes available a number of building plans. Funds are also available for home modernization. This could be to add bathrooms, central heating, improve kitchens, or other improvements.

To be eligible for home loan assistance an individual must meet certain general requirements. To be eligible an applicant must:

— be in need of decent, safe and sanitary housing,
— be unable to obtain a loan from a private lender at affordable terms,
— have sufficient income to make the monthly payments, and
— possess the character, ability and experience to meet the loan obligation.

In addition to the general requirements, specific income requirements must be met. To be eligible for loan assistance, a family's annual adjusted income cannot exceed $23,500.

How to Collect Farm Loan and Rural Housing $$$

The adjusted income is computed by reducing a family's gross income by $450 for each dependent child in the family. For example, let's say a married couple has an overall gross income of $17,000 with 2 children. Their adjusted income would be $16,100, computed as follows:

```
Gross income ........................ $17,000
         minus $450 x 2 = .............     900
Adjusted income ..................... $16,100
```

When a family's adjusted income is less than $21,800, they may be eligible for subsidized house payments. This is explained later in this chapter.

Under FmHA's home loan assistance program, there is no minimum down payment required. The family is required to make a down payment only if it can afford one.

The FmHA limits the size of the home you can purchase depending on your family size. If you are a single person, the homesite can have up to two bedrooms. Of course, if you have a larger family of 8 or more, the numnber of bedrooms allowed can be up to 6 or more.

How To Apply

The FmHA will not provide loan assistance if private financing is available at affordable terms. So, before you can get FmHA home loan help, you'll have to be refused financing from a bank or other private lender. Only then can you apply for FmHA loan assistance.

Getting Turned Down

You'll have to apply for a home loan at a bank or other private lender. You must file a formal application. Your loan application must be rejected.

At this point, you'll have to consider whether you want to apply directly to FmHA for a loan, or have FmHA guarantee a loan from a private lender. Each type of loan assistance is discussed in more detail under the section ''Here's What You Can Collect''.

How to Collect Big $$$ from Uncle Sam

Obviously, it is to your advantage to get a loan directly from FmHA. The interest rate is much lower than that available from a lender and the terms of the loan are also better. However, if loan funds from FmHA are not available, you may have to be satisfied with FmHA's loan guarantee program. In this case, ask your banker to make you the loan under the loan guarantee plan. Under this plan the FmHA guarantees the lender that if you don't repay the loan the FmHA will pay it back. Most lenders look favorably on this arrangement because it is risk free.

Of course, if the lender who initially turned you down is not interested in a FmHA loan guarantee plan, you'll have to find another willing lender. Look in the telephone book to locate other lenders in your vicinity. Call and ask if they would be willing to consider a FmHA home loan guarantee plan.

Applying For FmHA's Loan Help

Once you find a lender willing to go along with a FmHA home loan guarantee plan, you are then ready to apply for FmHA loan assistance. You'll have to complete the necessary application forms and submit them to FmHA for approval. Your application should include a letter from a private lender indicating that your application for a regular loan was rejected.

Evaluating Your Application

Your application for a loan will be decided by the FmHA county supervisor in the area where your homesite is located. The county supervisor will decide your application based on the eligibility requirements discussed earlier. A good deal of reliance is placed on the recommendation of the private lender. Generally, if the private lender is willing to finance your home, the FmHA is willing to guarantee the loan.

Here's What You Can Collect

The FmHA provides two types of loan assistance to help you purchase a home: direct loans and guaranteed loans.

How to Collect Farm Loan and Rural Housing $$$

Each is discussed below:

Direct Loans

The FmHA can make you a direct loan to purchase a home. To be eligible for a direct loan, the family's adjusted income cannot exceed $25,800. The loan amount is usually limited to $58,000, but with special approval, the loan can be any reasonable amount. The rate of interest varies with economic conditions and the maximum repayment term is 33 years. In certain parts of the country there is a waiting list for direct home loans. With the favorable rate of interest and terms of the loan, this can be expected. Each county receives direct loan funds on a quarterly basis. So, if funds are not available in one quarter, more will be coming in every three months. However, not all rural areas have waiting lists. So money to buy a home is waiting to be collected on a first come, first served basis.

Guaranteed Loans

The FmHA guarantees your lender (such as a bank, savings and loan or insurance company, etc.) that if you don't repay the loan the FmHA will pay it back. The FmHA will guarantee a home loan for up to 100 percent of its appraised value. The only limit on the amount of the home loan is the applicant's ability to make the monthly payments. No minimum down payment is required. The interest rate and loan maturity is agreed on by the lender and the loan applicant. The FmHA does not set a maximum rate of interest on guaranteed loans. However, the loan can only be guaranteed for up to 33 years.

Subsidized House Payments

Families with an adjusted income of less than $21,800 may be eligible for both a direct loan and subsidized house payments. Under this program, the FmHA will reduce your monthly house payment by paying part of the interest on your home loan. Depending on the family's adjusted income, the FmHA could reduce the interest on your loan to only one percent. This could substantially reduce your house payment.

For example, let's say your loan amount was $40,000 at 12 percent interest. Your annual interest payment alone would be about $4,800 or $400 a month. But at one percent, the annual interest is only $480, or $40 a month. Again, the amount of the FmHA subsidy depends on your family's size and adjusted income.

Where To Go

As mentioned before, the FmHA operates about 1,800 local county offices which can provide help in processing a home loan application. To find the telephone number of the local FmHA county office, call the Federal Information Center nearest your home. A complete list of Federal Information Centers is included in the back of this book. Ask the information specialist for the number of the FmHA county office nearest your home.

How To Cut Red Tape

As a first step, read this chapter carefully. Then as you go along call the local FmHA county office whenever questions arise. They will be glad to help you. Above all, be persistent. Don't get discouraged. The difference between persistence and giving up could mean many thousands of dollars to you. It could mean getting out of the crowded city and starting a whole new life in the country.

Subsidized Rent Payments

The FmHA has two programs which provide low-cost apartment accommodations in rural areas having a population of less than 20,000 people. Under these programs moderate and lower income families can live in a small town in the country and have FmHA pay part of their apartment rents. These rent subsidy programs are commonly called Section 515 (1) Rural Rental Housing Program, and (2) Rental Assistance Program. Each of the programs is discussed below.

Section 515—Rural Rental Housing Program

Families with moderate or lower income who want nice, rural apartment accommodations at a low cost may be eligible for this program. Under the program, FmHA makes long term loans available to apartment complex owners at low interest rates. The owners then pass the savings along to the tenants. The rent charged at these apartments will vary depending on the location, size and overall operating costs. However, eligible families can expect rents that are substantially lower than comparable accommodations available elsewhere.

To be eligible for the Rural Rental Housing Program, a family's adjusted income cannot exceed $25,800. To compute your adjusted income for eligibility purposes, first add up the family's total gross income from all sources. Then deduct $450 for each dependent child in the family. For example, let's say that a couple has an overall gross income of $17,000 with 2 children. Their adjusted gross income would be $16,100. ($17,000 minus $900 = $16,100). Under the Rural Rental Housing Program, there is no limit on the amount of assets you can have. So you could conceivably own $100,000 or more in stocks, bonds or gold bullion and still be eligible for subsidized rent assistance.

Section 515—Rental Assistance Program

Families with a lower income who want to rent a nice apartment in a small town may be eligible for the Rental Assistance Program. Under the Rental Assistance Program, FmHA can subsidize up to 75 percent of your rent payment. You pay only 25 percent of your family's adjusted income towards your rent payment. To be eligible for this program a family's adjusted income cannot exceed $21,800 a year.

Under this program, FmHA provides a substantial subsidy to the apartment complex owners in small towns who in turn charge lower rent in accordance with a family's income. For example, let's say that you are a one-person family with an adjusted income of $250 a month. The rent at the FmHA financed apartment project is $175 a month. You would pay only $62.50 a month for rent ($250 x 25% = $62.50) and FmHA would pay the remaining $112.50. Under the Rental Assistance Program, there is no limit on the amount of assets you can have. So you could conceivably own $100,000 or more in stocks, bonds or gold bullion and still be eligible for rental assistance.

Where To Go and How To Cut Red Tape

As a first step in getting FmHA rental assistance, you must obtain a list of all Section 515 apartment complexes in the area you are planning to live. The FmHA office can give you this information over the telephone or it can send you a current list in the mail. As mentioned before, the FmHA operates about 1,800 local county offices. To find the telephone number of the local FmHA county office, call the Federal Information Center nearest your home. A complete list of Federal Information Centers is included in the back of this book. Ask the information specialist for the number of the FmHA county office nearest your home.

The FmHA county office should have two lists of available apartment complexes. One list is for the Section 515 Rural Rental Housing Program. This is for families with moderate adjusted incomes under $25,800 a year. The second list should be for the Section 515 Rental Assistance Program. This is for families with adjusted incomes under $21,800 whereby FmHA can pay up to 75 percent of your rent.

Once you know where the Section 515 units are located, you should call the managers and obtain specific information on vacancies and rent. If there are no vacancies you can ask to be put on a waiting list.

Once you have found a Section 515 apartment you want to rent, you'll have to demonstrate your eligibility to the manager. The manager will know all about FmHA income limitations for each program as discussed above. He or she will ask you to provide certain information to show that you are eligible. Most apartment managers will be courteous and cooperative in dealing with you. They want to have you as a tenant. That's how they make their living.

How to Collect Farm Loan and Rural Housing $$$

FORM APPROVED.
BUDGET BUREAU NO. 40R—1071.9.

United States Department of Agriculture
FARMERS HOME ADMINISTRATION

APPLICATION FOR FHA SERVICES

(Please Print or Write Plainly)

.OR COUNTY OFFICE USE

Race (Ethnic Code) Check One

W ☐ 1 N ☐ 2 O ☐ 3 AI ☐ 4 S ☐ 5

1. NAME (FIRST)	(MIDDLE)	(LAST)	SOCIAL SECURITY NO.	NICKNAME OR KNOWN AS

2. WIFE'S NAME (FIRST)	(MIDDLE)	(MAIDEN)	SOCIAL SECURITY NO.	TELEPHONE NO.

3. COMPLETE ADDRESS (ROUTE, POST OFFICE, STATE, ZIP CODE, COUNTY)

5. HIGHEST GRADE OF SCHOOL COMPLETED BY APPLICANT (CIRCLE APPROPRIATE YEAR)
ELEMENTARY:
1 2 3 4 5 6 7 8
HIGH SCHOOL:
1 2 3 4
COLLEGE:
1 2 3 4 5 6
OR MORE

4. AGES OF PERSONS IN HOUSEHOLD	HUSBAND	WIFE	SONS	DAUGHTERS	OTHERS

6. ARE YOU A CITIZEN OF THE UNITED STATES? ☐ YES ☐ NO   IS YOUR WIFE A CITIZEN OF THE UNITED STATES? ☐ YES ☐ NO

7. ARE YOU A VETERAN? ☐ YES ☐ NO   IF "YES" INDICATE SERVICE FROM _____ TO _____

8. MY FARM OR RESIDENCE IS LOCATED (DIRECTION) _____ MILES
FROM (TOWN) _____ ON ROAD _____

IT ADJOINS THE PROPERTY OF:

9. ARE YOU FARMING OR RANCHING NOW? ☐ YES ☐ NO

IF NOT, WHEN DID YOU LAST OPERATE A FARM? 19___   NUMBER OF YEARS EXPERIENCE OPERATING A FARM _____

10. DO YOU OWN OR RENT FARM YOU PLAN TO OPERATE? ☐ OWN & RENT ☐ RENT ☐ OWN

DO YOU LIVE ON FARM YOU PLAN TO OPERATE? ☐ YES ☐ NO

IF YES, HOW LONG HAVE YOU LIVED ON THIS FARM? _____ YRS.
(LAST YR.) (NEXT YR.)   (LAST YR.) (NEXT YR.)
TOTAL ACRES OWNED _____   TOTAL ACRES RENTED _____
(LAST YR.) (NEXT YR.)   (LAST YR.) (NEXT YR.)
CROP ACRES OWNED _____   CROP ACRES RENTED _____

11. IF AN OWNER, WHEN DID YOU ACQUIRE THE LAND? _____ 19___
HOW? (PURCHASED, INHERITED, ETC.)
FROM WHOM?
IF PURCHASED, GIVE PURCHASE PRICE ... $_____

12. IF YOU RENT OR PLAN TO RENT, GIVE NAME AND ADDRESS OF LANDLORD
TERMS AND LENGTH OF LEASE
ANNUAL CASH RENT PAID LAST YEAR ..... $_____
VALUE OF SHARE OR OTHER NON-CASH RENT LAST YEAR $_____

13. NAME AND ADDRESS OF BANK WITH WHICH YOU LAST HAD A
☐ CHECKING OR SAVING ACCOUNT   ☐ LOAN ACCOUNT

14. AMOUNT BORROWED FOR OPERATING PURPOSES OR BUSINESS LAST YEAR ..... $_____
FROM WHOM?

15. HAVE YOU OR YOUR SPOUSE EVER OBTAINED A LOAN FROM FARMERS HOME ADMINISTRATION? ☐ YES ☐ NO
IF YES, WAS THE LOAN PAID IN FULL? ☐ YES ☐ NO

16. WHAT KIND OF NONFARM WORK DO YOU AND MEMBERS OF YOUR FAMILY DO?
_____ (HUSBAND)
_____ (WIFE)
_____ (OTHER)

17. NAME AND ADDRESS OF EMPLOYER(S)
_____ (HUSBAND)
_____ (WIFE)
NUMBER OF YEARS WITH EMPLOYER(S) _____ YRS. $_____ (HUSBAND)
AND INCOME LAST YR. _____ YRS. $_____ (WIFE)

18. TOTAL CASH INCOME LAST YEAR:
LIVESTOCK AND LIVESTOCK PRODUCTS SOLD ... $_____
CROPS SOLD ..... _____
OTHER FARM INCOME ..... _____
NONFARM INCOME (SALARY, PENSIONS, DIVIDENDS, RENTS, ETC.) ..... _____
TOTAL $_____

19. TOTAL CASH EXPENSES LAST YEAR:
FAMILY LIVING ..... $_____
FARM OPERATING ..... _____
NONFARM OPERATING ..... _____
PERSONAL, REAL ESTATE AND INCOME TAXES PAID ..... $_____
OTHER (CAPITAL GOODS PURCHASED, DEBTS PAID, ETC.) ..... _____
TOTAL EXPENSE $_____

20. CASH VALUE OF FOOD PRODUCED FOR HOME USE LAST YEAR $_____

FHA 410-1 (Rev. 12-7-72)

131

21. FINANCIAL STATEMENT AS OF DATE OF APPLICATION
(Show property owned and debts owed by applicant and spouse)

LIST ALL PROPERTY OWNED			LIST ALL DEBTS OWED					
REAL ESTATE (LOCATION):	ACRE	VALUE	NAME AND ADDRESS OF CREDITOR	FINAL DUE DATE	INTEREST RATE	ANNUAL INSTAL.	AMOUNT DELINQ.	UNPAID BALANCE
FARM		$	**LIENS ON REAL ESTATE:**					
OTHER REAL ESTATE								
TOTAL REAL ESTATE		$						
LIVESTOCK:	NO.	VALUE						
LIVESTOCK HELD FOR SALE		$	TOTAL LIENS ON R. E.			$	$	$
DAIRY COWS			**LIENS ON CHATTELS AND CROPS:**					
BEEF COWS						$	$	$
OTHER CATTLE								
BROOD SOWS AND GILTS								
OTHER HOGS								
EWES								
OTHER SHEEP								
POULTRY								
TOTAL LIVESTOCK		$						
MACHINERY AND EQUIPMENT:								
AUTO $ TRUCK $		$						
TRACTOR(S)								
OTHER FARM MACHINERY								
			TOTAL LIENS CHATTELS & CROPS			$	$	$
			JUDGMENTS:					
TOTAL MACHINERY AND EQUIPMENT		$						
OTHER PERSONAL PROPERTY:	QUAN.	VALUE	TOTAL JUDGMENTS:			$	$	$
CROPS HELD FOR SALE		$	TAXES DUE: REAL ESTATE $ PERSONAL $					
GROWING CROPS			INCOME & SOCIAL SECURITY $ TOTAL TAXES DUE					$
FEED			**ALL OTHER DEBTS (DOCTOR, STORE, ETC., DESCRIBE):**					
								$
SEED AND SUPPLIES								
HOUSEHOLD GOODS								
CASH ON HAND								
BONDS AND INVESTMENTS								
ACCTS. OWED US—COLLECTIBLE								
TOTAL OTHER PERSONAL PROP.		$				TOTAL OTHER DEBTS		$
TOTAL PROPERTY OWNED		$				TOTAL ALL DEBTS		$

22. FOR WHAT PURPOSE DO YOU NEED FARMERS HOME ADMINISTRATION SERVICES?

23. I am unable to provide the above items on my own account, and I am unable to secure the credit necessary for such items from other sources upon terms and conditions which I can reasonably fulfill. I CERTIFY that the statements made by me in this application are true, complete and correct to the best of my knowledge and belief, and are made in good faith to obtain a loan.

DATE _____ , 19 ___

_____
(SIGNATURE OF APPLICANT)

_____
(SIGNATURE OF SPOUSE)

24. TO BE COMPLETED BY COUNTY SUPERVISOR

TYPE OF LOAN APPLIED FOR:	☐ OL ☐ EM ☐ FO ☐ RH ☐ SW ☐ EO ☐ OTHER _____ (SPECIFY)
CONDITION OF HOUSE	☐ 1 ☐ 2 ☐ 3
PLUMBING FACILITIES IN HOUSE	☐ 1 ☐ 2 ☐ 3 SYSTEM OF FARMING LAST YEAR: _____

☆ U.S.GPO:1978-0-665-011/1604

Chapter 6

How To Get Free
Legal Assistance

In 1974 Congress established the Legal Services Corporation to provide free legal assistance for eligible Americans. Through support of local programs, the Legal Services Corporation makes available the services of over 4,000 attorneys who offer professional legal advice and representation at over 1,000 neighborhood offices around the country.

The Legal Services Corporation does not provide legal assistance for criminal cases. (If you are ever charged with a crime, the judge could appoint an attorney to defend you if you are unable to afford one.) Instead, the Legal Services Corporation provides legal assistance only in civil matters (all legal areas except criminal law). For example, the Legal Services Corporation could help you:

—collect government benefits such as social security or other assistance payments,

—obtain child support payments,

—take legal action against your landlord,

— obtain damages for any injuries you have incurred from an auto accident, faulty products, etc.,

— obtain settlements from doctors or dentists for medical malpractice,

— get a settlement from merchants or repair shop operators.

The services offered by the Legal Services Corporation are endless. They include specialized legal areas such as consumer law, immigration, and senior citizen problems. The Legal Services Corporation has helped millions of Americans obtain quality legal assistance that would otherwise not have been available because of the cost involved. (A graph at the end of this chapter shows the different kinds of civil cases handled by the Legal Services Corporation without charge to the client.)

Actually, only about 15 percent of the cases handled by the Legal Services Corporation end in court. The vast majority of cases are handled out of court whereby a negotiated settlement is agreed upon by the parties involved. For example, say the Legal Services Corporation takes legal action on your behalf against the Social Security Administration for back payments of benefits. Instead of having the case settled in Federal Court, a Social Security bureaucrat would negotiate a cash settlement with your attorney.

The Legal Services Corporation provides legal services in two basic ways: your case can be handled by a Legal Services staff lawyer, or it can be referred to a local private lawyer. As a general rule, a LSC staff lawyer will handle cases that do not involve suing for damages. Such cases would generally include matters like landlord grievances, child support, civil rights, juvenile matters and immigration. However, when a legal action involves damages, the LSC will generally refer the case to a private lawyer who will work on a contingency fee basis. This simply means that the lawyer will get a specified percentage—usually about 30 percent—of any settlement that comes about. For example, let's say you sue a large company for product liability—you ate a food product which caused you to become ill. Let's say the company settles for $100,000. Of that amount, your lawyer would take about $30,000 to cover his services. However, if you did not get any settlement at all, you would not be obligated to pay the lawyer for the services provided. Most lawyers will take a case on a contingency fee basis if there is a likelihood for a cash settlement.

Regardless of how your case is handled, the quality of legal service is high. Lawyers are well educated and receive extensive training in specialized legal areas. Further, the LSC maintains a staff of experts who continually review case files to assure that legal services provided are of the highest quality possible.

Here's How You Qualify

To be eligible for LSC legal assistance you must fill out a simple form and meet certain income requirements.

The form will ask you to state the total family income. The information you give will not normally be verified unless the LSC has good reason to doubt its accuracy. Having a lawyer verify your income might cause distrust and interfere with the client/attorney relationship.

The following table will give you an idea of the income requirement needed for eligibility before adjustments and special circumstances.

Size of Family	Approximate Maximum Income
1	$ 7,000
2	$ 9,000
3	$11,000
4	$13,000
5	$15,000
6	$17,000
7	$19,000
8	$21,000

For families larger than 8 members, add $2,000 for each family member. Income limits are substantially higher in Alaska and Hawaii.

Before you count yourself out, the LSC can still provide you free legal assistance even if your income exceeds the above limits under certain circumstances. These special circumstances include the following:

—if you're seeking free legal service to collect government benefits due you,

—if you have extraordinary expenses such as child care, transportation, or medical bills,

—the cost of obtaining private legal assistance would be too expensive for you to obtain.

If you need legal assistance but can't afford it, apply to the Legal Services Corporation and let them decide your eligibility. Chances are you can qualify for free legal assistance.

For your information, the LSC defines income as cash receipts before taxes from all family members living in the household. This includes regular payments from all sources including social security, public assistance, unemployment, workers' compensation, strike benefits, veterans' benefits, alimony, child support, pension payments. It also includes income from investments such as dividends, interest, rents and royalties. If you are self-employed, business income is defined as net income after business expenses are deducted.

Where To Go And How To Cut Red Tape

There are over 1,000 LSC sponsored neighborhood offices where you can go to obtain free legal assistance. The specific name of the office will vary from city to city. It could be called something like the "Legal Aid Society", "Legal Services Center", etc.

As a first step, you should call your local Federal Information Center. A complete list of Federal Information Centers is included in the back of the book. Ask the Information Specialist for the telephone number of the LSC sponsored office nearest your home. Then call the LSC office and ask to make an appointment with a lawyer to discuss your legal problem. One word of caution, the secretary or clerk answering the telephone at the LSC office may ask you to state your income to determine your eligibility. Chances are good that this person is a low-level employee with no real knowledge of eligibility requirements. So be careful what you say. You may be told you are not eligible for free legal assistance when in fact you are eligible. Let the lawyer decide whether or not you meet the eligibility requirements. The LSC staff lawyer will be more familiar with the special circumstances that allow higher income persons to receive free assistance.

Questions and Answers

Q. Do more men than women get free legal help from the LSC?

A. About 68 percent of clients are women and 32 percent men.

Q. What are the typical ages of LSC clients?

A. About 53 percent are from ages 18-34. About 30 percent are ages 35-59, 15 percent are age 60 or older, and 2 percent are under age 18.

Q. Can the LSC help a person get a divorce?

A. Yes. About 17 percent of LSC's caseload involves helping persons get a divorce who otherwise couldn't afford it.

Q. Can the LSC help in collecting social security disability?

A. Yes. The LSC has helped many persons collect disability benefits after being turned down by the Social Security Administration. The LSC can take a case to the Federal courts when benefits are being wrongly denied.

How to Collect Big $$$ from Uncle Sam

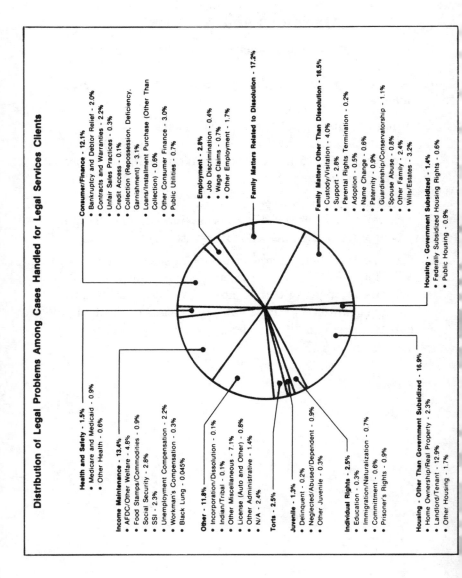

Distribution of Legal Problems Among Cases Handled for Legal Services Clients

Health and Safety - 1.5%
- Medicare and Medicaid - 0.9%
- Other Health - 0.6%

Income Maintenance - 13.4%
- AFDC/Other Welfare - 4.8%
- Food Stamps/Commodities - 0.9%
- Social Security - 2.8%
- SSI - 2.3%
- Unemployment Compensation - 2.2%
- Workman's Compensation - 0.3%
- Black Lung - 0.045%

Other - 11.8%
- Incorporation/Dissolution - 0.1%
- Indian/Tribal - 0.1%
- Other Miscellaneous - 7.1%
- License (Auto and Other) - 0.8%
- Other Administrative - 1.4%
- N/A - 2.4%

Torts - 2.5%

Juvenile - 1.3%
- Delinquent - 0.2%
- Neglected/Abused/Dependent - 0.9%
- Other Juvenile - 0.3%

Individual Rights - 2.5%
- Education - 0.3%
- Immigration/Naturalization - 0.7%
- Commitment - 0.6%
- Prisoner's Rights - 0.9%

Housing - Other Than Government Subsidized - 16.9%
- Home Ownership/Real Property - 2.3%
- Landlord/Tenant - 12.9%
- Other Housing - 1.7%

Consumer/Finance - 12.1%
- Bankruptcy and Debtor Relief - 2.0%
- Contracts and Warranties - 2.2%
- Unfair Sales Practices - 0.3%
- Credit Access - 0.1%
- Collection (Repossession, Deficiency, Garnishment) - 3.1%
- Loans/Installment Purchase (Other Than Collection) - 0.6%
- Other Consumer Finance - 3.0%
- Public Utilities - 0.7%

Employment - 2.8%
- Job Discrimination - 0.4%
- Wage Claims - 0.7%
- Other Employment - 1.7%

Family Matters Related to Dissolution - 17.2%

Family Matters Other Than Dissolution - 16.5%
- Custody/Visitation - 4.0%
- Support - 2.8%
- Parental Rights Termination - 0.2%
- Adoption - 0.5%
- Name Change - 0.6%
- Paternity - 0.9%
- Guardianship/Conservatorship - 1.1%
- Spouse Abuse - 0.8%
- Other Family - 2.4%
- Wills/Estates - 3.2%

Housing - Government Subsidized - 1.4%
- Federally Subsidized Housing Rights - 0.6%
- Public Housing - 0.9%

Chapter 7

How To Collect
Housing $$$

Many Americans dream of owning or renting a decent home in a nice neighborhood. And in order to make that dream come true, the federal government has established a number of programs which are benefiting millions of Americans.

Since few families are able to pay cash for homes, helping them finance the purchase is one of the chief purposes of the Department of Housing and Urban Development (HUD). HUD does not loan money or built homes. It simply provides mortgage insuurance which protects the lender that offers the home buyer a loan. With HUD's assistance, a home buyer makes a small down payment and obtains a mortgage for the rest of the purchase price. The mortgage loan is made by a bank, savings and loan association, mortgage or insurance company, or other HUD-approved lender. Since HUD mortgage insurance protects the lender, he can allow more liberal mortgage terms than the home buyer might otherwise get.

HUD also operates programs to help lower income families pay their rent, or make their monthly house payments.

The key HUD programs are:
—home mortgage insurance;
—mobile home mortgage insurance;
—home improvement loans;
—subsidized house payments, and
—subsidized rent payments.

Home Mortgage Insurance

HUD insurance guarantees the mortgage lender that, in the event of default by the purchaser, HUD will honor the lender's claim. To be eligible for insurance, the follower must have:
—A good credit record;
—the needed cash to close the deal, and
—enough steady income to make the monthly mortgage payments without difficulty.

HUD sets no upper age limit for the borrower; nor does it say he must have a certain income to buy a home at a certain price. However, HUD does consider age and income when judging whether or not the borrower will be able to repay the mortgage.

HUD will consider a wife's income when there is confirmation of employment with a good possibility for its continuation. The confirmation may be based on the length of her employment or on her use of special training or skills in a particular position.

The property must at least meet the objectives of HUD's minimum standards which require that the house be livable, soundly built and suitably located.

Under HUD's home mortgage insurance program, qualified home buyers can obtain up to $101,250 in home mortgage insurance. The amount of insurance which can be obtained and the down payment required depends on the value HUD places on the home.

Where To Go

The home loan application should be made at any HUD-approved lender. In selecting the bank, savings and loan association or mortgage company, be sure to find out whether it is an approved HUD lending institution.

How To Cut Red Tape

In recent years, HUD has been the focal point of considerable criticism because of its mismanagement of housing programs. HUD has had a history of inefficiency and poor public relations; therefore, in dealing with HUD, it is important to have a general knowledge of the procedures you will have to follow to get your loan.

Following is a general outline of the major steps and paper work needed to complete the processing of your loan application:

—The application for the loan is made at any HUD-approved lender.
—The lender will provide the proper forms, help the borrower complete them and then forward the papers to HUD.
—The HUD office reviews the applicant's credit history to judge whether the loan would be reasonable, and the property is appraised.
—HUD tells the lender what it has decided; the lender informs the borrower.
—If HUD has approved the application, the lender arranges with the borrower for the closing of the loan.
—The borrower deals directly with the lender; the lender handles the transaction with HUD.

* * *

HUD charges a small mortgage insurance premium on the average outstanding balance of the mortgage during the year.

Mobile Home Mortgage Insurance

With the soaring cost of permanent housing, in recent years mobile homes have become very popular. As with permanent housing, HUD will provide insurance so that if the mobile home buyer defaults, HUD will pay off the loan. To be eligible for a mobile home loan, a borrower must:

—Have sufficient income to make payments on the loan.

—Intend to use the mobile home as his residence.

—Be buying a mobile home which is at least 10 feet wide and 40 feet long; meets HUD construction standards for mobile homes; and is new or, if not new, formerly financed with a HUD-insured loan.

—Have sufficient funds to make a specified small down payment. Five percent of the total price of the mobile home up to $3,000; 10 percent on amounts more than $3,000. The total price of the mobile home may include furnishings, appliances, tie-downs, set up and initial insurance premium.

—Have an acceptable site on which the mobile home is to be placed. Such site may be rented space in a mobile home park or land owned by the borrower. The site must meet HUD standards and both buyer and seller must certify that there will be no violation of zoning requirements or other regulations applicable to mobile homes.

HUD's mobile home insurance program covers both the mobile home and the lot. The program offers:

—$40,500 for a single unit.

—$54,000 for a double wide unit.

—15 years and 32 days to pay off the loan (longer for double-wide units).

—A maximum annual interest rate that varies with economic conditions.

—Personal loans secured by conditional sales contracts or chattel mortgages on the mobile home.

—Loans repaid in equal monthly installments.

The lender pays HUD for mortgage insurance.

Where To Go

Prospective mobile homeowners may apply at any HUD-approved bank, savings and loan association, credit union or finance company. No application fee is required.

How To Cut Red Tape

The procedures followed in getting a mobile home loan generally are similar to those described under home mortgage insurance.

Several publications offering useful tips on buying a mobile home are available from HUD without cost. Two of these publications are:

Buying and Financing a Mobile Home

Mobile Homes—Alternative Housing for the Handicapped

Order from: U.S. Department of Housing and Urban Development, Public Service Center, Washington, D.C. 20410.

Home Improvement Loans

Many times it is more economical to improve on your existing home than to invest in another one. HUD has a program to insure loans for improvements that increase basic livability or utility of your property. To be eligible for a home improvement loan, you must:

—own your property or have a long-term lease on it;

—have a satisfactory credit rating, and

—have enough income to repay the loan.

The maximum HUD will insure for an individual home is $17,500. For a residence with two or more units, HUD will allow $7,500 a unit, up to a maximum of $43,750.

HUD-insured loans may be used for any improvements that will make your home more livable and useful. They can be used for dishwashers, refrigerators, freezers or ovens which are built-in; but cannot be used for luxury items such as swimming pools or outdoor fireplaces, or to pay for work already done.

Improvements can be handled on a do-it-yourself basis or through a contractor or dealer, with the loan used to pay for labor and materials.

Some of the advantages of a HUD home improvement loan are:

—You do not have to live in any particular area to get one of these loans.

147

- You seldom need any security for loans under $7,500 other than your signature on the note, and you need no co-signer.
- You do not have to disturb any mortgage or deed of trust you may have on your home.
- Your loan can cover architectural and engineering costs and building permit fees, or it can be just enough to pay for materials.

Where To Go

Homeowners may apply at any HUD-approved bank, savings and loan association, credit union or finance company. No application fee is required and a contractor can make the loan application for you.

How To Cut Red Tape

With a home improvement loan you are not hampered by a lot of red tape. Only three simple forms are involved: an application, a note and a completion certificate (if work or materials are furnished by a dealer or contractor). Usually only the lender has to approve your loan, and can give you an answer in a few days.

If you plan to use the services of a dealer or contractor, take care to choose one with a reputation for honesty and good workmanship. There are several ways to check on a contractor:

- Consult your local Chamber of Commerce or the Better Business Bureau.
- Talk with people for whom he has done work.
- Ask your lender about him.
- Check his place of business to see that he is not a fly-by-night opeartor.
- Find out, if you can, how he rates with known building product distributors and wholesale suppliers.
- Ask friends and relatives for names of firms that did good work for them.

Subsidized House Payments

Under the National Housing Act, Congress proclaimed that every American family should have a safe, sanitary and decent home in a suitable living environment. Realizing that many families could not afford to buy and maintain a home, Congress passed Section 235 of the National Housing Act. Under Section 235, HUD can pay part of the low income home buyer's mortgage payment.

Up until the middle 1960s, HUD primarily assisted middle class families in purchasing homes. HUD had strict rules about the type of homes it would help finance; the homes had to be in good condition and be located in a stable neighborhood. In addition, the home buyer had to meet fairly strict personal requirements.

In the late 1960s, Congress mandated that all families, regardless of income, should be able to own their own home. HUD lowered its requirements so that virtually any American —even welfare recipients—could purchase a home. Also, HUD allowed homes to be purchased in declining urban areas never before eligible.

But while HUD arranged for thousands to assume home ownership, it was lax in preparing these families for their new roles. Many families went over their heads in home purchases and couldn't afford the house payment and the utility and maintenance bills. Families by the thousands lost their homes.

Unscrupulous spectators were quickly on the scene to sell homes to unsophisticated home buyers. Speculators made money by following a simple concept—buy low and sell high. Speculators would purchase dilapidated homes for a song, spend a few dollars for paint and cosmetic repairs, and resell the homes with HUD's help to low income families. Thousands of homes were purchased by speculators for a few thousand dollars each then sold under HUD for five times that and more.

Speculators also found that for a few hundred dollars they could often encourage HUD appraisers to place a higher value on the home and overlook needed repairs. Thus, many speculators made millions of dollars by buying and selling homes.

In recent years HUD has corrected many of its problems. HUD homes now have to undergo a thorough inspection to assure all defects are corrected and brought up to city code. Even though most of the appraisers who were taking bribes have been rooted out, it will be a long time before HUD completely sheds the stigma of its housing scandal of the early 1970s.

Americans eligible for the Section 235 housing program under HUD should not hesitate to avail themselves of the program's benefits because of the adverse publicity created by the scandal.

Eligibility under the program will be met if the applicant:

— Is part of a family of two or more persons related by blood, marriage, or operation of law.
— Is a handicapped person.
— Is a single person, 62 years of age or older.
— Has an adjusted family income not exceeding the limit set by HUD. This will vary from city to city. Adjusted family income means income during the past 12 months from all sources, before taxes or withholding, of all adult members of the family living in units, but excluding unusual or temporary income and less $300 for each minor under 21 and earnings of minors. For a family of one person the annual earnings limit is about $14,250. For a family of 8 or more the annual earnings limit is about $25,400.

To be eligible for Section 235 assistance, a family's assets normally cannot exceed $3,500. However, this figure increases $500 for each dependent child in the family. The asset limit goes up to $6,000 if an applicant is over age 62.

Families qualifying for assistance under Section 235 can purchase a home for up to $47,500. This amount goes up to $55,000 if the home has 4 bedrooms and is purchased by a family of 5 or more persons. The family has to make a down payment of only 3 percent of the selling price (5% for anything over $25,000). Up to 30 years is allowed to pay off the mortgage.

Here's the best part. Under Section 235, HUD pays part of

your monthly house payment. HUD can pay the difference between total monthly payment under the mortgage (principal, interest, mortgage insurance premium (MIP), taxes and hazard insurance) and 20 percent of mortgagor's adjusted income.

Mullins Family Collects Housing $$$

Dan Mullins is married and the father of three children. He works in a bar five nights a week as a guitar player and brings home $400 a month. His wife and children have no income. The Mullins family has assets totaling $2,000 which consists primarily of savings bonds, money in a bank account and a few shares of stock.

After renting for several years, the Mullins family is considering buying a home. Recently while home hunting, they found the perfect home—a 3-bedroom ranch in a nice neighborhood for $47,500. However, Dan Mullins is worried that he will not qualify for a mortgage or be able to meet the monthly mortgage payment of $250.

The Mullins family, and others like it, can take advantage of the Section 235 housing program and realize their dream of owning a home. The Mullins family is eligible under 235 because:

—They are a family of two or more persons related by blood or marriage.
—Their adjusted family income does not exceed the limit set by HUD.
—They have only $2,000 in assets. Since Dan has a wife and three children he could have a maximum of $5,000 in assets and still be eligible. This would include $3,500 plus $500 for each dependent in the family.
—They want to buy a $47,500 home and HUD will insure the home mortgage.
—They have the necessary $1,400 down payment.

The Mullins family also is eligible to have HUD pay part of the $250 monthly house payment. The following computation illustrates how much HUD will pay toward the Mullins' house payment:

House payment	$250.00
20 percent of $400 gross income	80.00
Difference	$170.00

HUD will pay $170 of the Mullins' family house payment.

Where To Go

Once you have found the home your family wants to purchase, contact HUD to apply for assistance under Section 235 of the National Housing Act.

To find the telephone number of the local HUD office, call the Federal Information Center nearest you. A complete list of Federal Information Centers is included in the back of this book.

In certain areas there may be HUD approved counseling agencies operating under an agreement with HUD to provide home ownership information, advice and assistance. Contact your local HUD office to find out if there is a counseling agency in your area.

How To Cut Red Tape

The procedure followed in getting a Section 235 home generally are similar to those described under home mortgage insurance.

HUD does not warranty the house being purchased. If the house is new, HUD requires the builder to warranty that it conforms substantially to the plans and specifications on which HUD based its appraisal. But HUD does not approve or disapprove a house or give the design and construction a stamp of approval. Some builders advertise "HUD Approval" to imply that their houses are superior. This is false advertising and could result in a criminal charge.

Subsidized Rent Payments

Many families do not have the financial means to buy a

home while other families do not want the responsibility of home-ownership and choose to rent. Yet, there is a crucial shortage of affordable, decent rental housing in this country. Many families just can't afford the high rent for housing that is suitable for their family.

HUD has estimated that over 18 million families in this country need some form of housing assistance. Six million of these families are living in substandard housing, 10 million are spending far too much of their income for housing, and the remaining 2 million are living in overcrowded housing. HUD, in many cases, can help families obtain suitable rental housing at affordable rates.

HUD operates two major programs designed to help moderate and lower income families with their rent payments. These programs for renters are called Section 8 and Section 236. Each of these programs is discussed below.

Section 8 Housing Program

The Section 8 program was established by Congress in 1974. Section 8 is the government's major program to help lower income families afford decent, safe and sanitary rental housing. Under Section 8, Uncle Sam can pay up to 75 percent of your monthly rent for a house or apartment dwelling.

The Section 8 rental assistance program is administered by local housing authorities, which are generally city or county agencies. HUD allows these local agencies to operate the Section 8 program because they are knowledgeable about the local housing market and the community's housing needs. County or city local housing authorities are funded by the federal government and loperate under federal rules and regulations.

The local housing authority determines eligibility for the Section 8 program. To be eligible for the program, a family's income cannot exceed a specified limit, depending on the number of people in the family. For a "family" of one person the maximum annual income for eligibility cannot exceed $13,450. For a family of 8 or more, the maximum yearly income limit is $24,000.

The amount of money a family has in a savings account or

other investments such as stocks or bonds is also considered in determining annual earnings. Ten percent of the balance over $5,000 on any investment is added to the family's yearly income. For example, let's say that a family of 8, with yearly income of $16,700 has $8,000 in the bank. Ten percent of this savings account balance over $5,000 ($300) would be added on to the family's yearly income of $16,700. So the family's yearly income would be considered to be $17,000 ($16,700 plus $300 = $17,000).

As you can see, eligibility requirements for Section 8 assistance are fairly simple. Therefore, it should not take long to be certified for rent assistance payments.

Once you are certified you are free to find your own rental house or apartment. However, you only have 60 days from the date of certification to find suitable accommodations. Sixty days should be plenty of time to find a house or apartment to rent.

The rental accommodations you find must meet certain standards set by HUD. Generally, these standards require the rental unit to be safe and sanitary for you and your family to live in.

The maximum rent you can pay for a house or apartment is set by HUD. These maximums are based on "fair market rents" established for each county and metropolitan area of the country. In considering the fairness of rents, HUD considers such things as the number of square feet of living space and number of bedrooms in the dwelling. Maximum "fair market rents" may differ depending on the part of the country. Rents would be higher in California than in Iowa. Typically, fair market rent would be about $280 for a one-bedroom and about $471 for a six-bedroom unit. Of course, the maximum rent you are allowed to pay under Section 8 depends on the size and composition of your family and the number of bedrooms required.

Now here's the good news. You pay at least 15 but no more than 25 percent of your monthly income toward your rent payment. Uncle Sam pays the rest up to 75 percent of the total. So, let's say your monthly income is $250 and you are a one-person family. You find a nice, one-bedroom house to rent for $175 which is considered "fair market rent" by HUD. You would pay only $62.50 a month toward the rent payment ($250 x 25% = $62.50) and HUD would pay the remaining $112.50.

Another nice thing about the Section 8 program is that Uncle Sam pays its share of your rent directly to the landlord. Therefore, the landlord is assured of getting regular rent payments. Because of this a landlord may prefer you over other tenants. Further, the local housing authority will enter into a lease agreement with the landlord. The lease will run for a period of 1 to 3 years. This assures the landlord that you will be a tenant for a specified period of time. Many landlords like this arrangement because it cuts down on vacancies. When a rental unit is empty the landlord loses money. The lease arrangement is also good for the tenant because he does not have to worry about an eviction or rent increase during the lease period.

The Congressional Budget Office has estimated that about 40 percent of the nation's households are eligible for Section 8 and other housing assistance programs. Yet, only about 10 percent are now receiving housing assistance.

Section 236 Rental Housing Program

Families who want to rent a quality apartment at a very reasonable cost may be eligible for the Section 236 Rental Housing Program.

Under this program, rent is much lower than other comparable apartment units. This is because HUD pays part of the owner's interest cost on the apartment complex. The owners of the apartment complex then pass the savings on to you.

To be eligible for Section 236 rental housing a family's income cannot exceed a specified limit depending on the size of the family. The following table will give you an idea of the approximate income limits based on family size.

How to Collect Big $$$ from Uncle Sam

Size of Family	Approximate Income Limit
1	$19,350
2	$22,100
3	$24,850
4	$27,600
5	$29,350
6	$31,050
7	$32,800
8 or more	$34,500

In addition to the income requirement, one of the following conditions must be met. The applicant must either:
— be part of a family of two persons related by blood, marriage or operation of law,
— be single and at least 62 years of age, or
— be handicapped.

Under Section 236, there is no limit on the amount of assets you can have. So you could conceivably own $100,000 or more in stocks or other assets and still be eligible for subsidized rent under Section 236.

The amount of rent which is charged for 236 apartments will vary depending on the location, size and operating costs of the apartment project. However, eligible participants can expect rent substantially less than comparable accommodations available elsewhere.

The first step in getting an apartment under 236 is to contact your local HUD office and ask for a listing of 236 housing projects in the area in which you are planning to live. HUD should be able to provide this information over the telephone or send you a listing in the mail. Once you know where the Section 236 apartment projects are located, you should call the managers and obtain specific information on vacancies and rent. If there are no vacancies you can ask to be put on a waiting list.

Once you have found a 236 apartment that you want to rent, you'll have to demonstrate your eligibility to the manager. The manager will know all about the HUD income limitations discussed above. He will ask you to provide certain information to show that you are eligible. This information will include:

—statement of income for the last 12 months;
—proof that you are married;
—proof of your dependents, if any, or
—if you are single, proof of your age.

Most apartment managers will be very courteous and cooperative in establishing your eligibility. They want to have you as a tenant. That's how they make their living.

Where To Go

To obtain rent assistance under Section 8 or Section 236 contact your local HUD office. You can find the number in your telephone directory under United States Government, or you can get the number by calling the Federal Information Center nearest your home. A complete list of all Federal Information Centers is at the back of this book.

Questions and Answers

Q. Specifically, what is a HUD appraisal?

A. HUD appraises a home to determine the maximum amount of a mortgage it would be willing to insure. The appraisal is made to estimate the value of the property solely for mortgage insurance purposes. A HUD appraisal is not an inspection of the construction, nor does it set sales price.

Q. Who paid for the many thousands of homes which were foreclosed because the buyers did not make the house payment?

A. The taxpayers paid through the nose. Everyone else—the banks and the speculators—made piles of money.

Q. Can a person collect social security and get subsidized rent benefits at the same time?

A. Yes. As long as the limit on family income is not exceeded.

Q. With today's housing prices, is Section 235 a viable program in all parts of the country?

A. No. In some states, such as California, it is almost

impossible to buy a home within the price constraints set by Section 235. However, other states such as Florida have plenty of homes in the Section 235 price range.

Q. What are the landlords' responsibilities under the Section 8 Rent Assistance Program?

A. The landlord must continue to provide decent, safe and sanitary housing to the tenant at reasonable cost. If the landlord fails to do this, the local housing authority can terminate the lease.

Q. Does the Section 8 Housing Program suffer from any of the management problems that seem to beset Federal Government Housing Programs?

A. Yes. According to a report by the U.S. General Accounting Office (GAO) several problems were found in a recent audit. Some families were getting as much as $7,000 or more a year in rent subsidies. This exceeds the allowable payment under the program. Also, the GAO found some of the Section 8 apartments were overly luxurious having swimming pools and tennis courts—one had a health club.

Q. What are some examples of families receiving excessive rent subsidies?

A. Acccording to a recent GAO report, a family in the Boston area lived in a 4-bedroom unit with a monthly rent of $604. The family paid only $52 per month toward the rent, and the Federal government paid $552. The annual subsidy for this family was $6,048.

Chapter 8

How To Collect
Veteran Benefit $$$

• After serving two years in the U.S. Army and being honorably discharged in 1970, Tom Miller married his childhood sweetheart and now they have one child and another on the way. Working as a payroll clerk in a department store, Tom has learned that there will be an opening for a much better-paying position in the accounting department within the year. But he needs more education to assume the position.

The company president said he will give Tom the job and a leave-of-absence for a year to finish his accounting education. Although Tom can't afford to stop working for a year because of his family, he knows that this is his only chance for advancement with the company. He isn't quite sure what to do.

• After finishing high school, Walter Stanley served two years of honorable military service. Now, 10 years later, Walter needs a gall bladder operation. His family doctor told him the operation will cost about $4,000. Walter has no medical insurance and simply can't afford the operation. He isn't sure where to turn to get help.

How to Collect Big $$$ from Uncle Sam

Tom and Walter both should turn to the federal government and the Veterans Administration (VA). Tom would be eligible for over $500 per month to finish his schooling, and Walter can get free medical care at any Veterans hospital.

Recognizing the nation's obligation to those who served their country in the interest of national defense, Congress through the years has passed a number of programs designed to assist veterans. This year's outlay for benefits and services to veterans and their families will be about $24 billion. These benefits will allow thousands of veterans to further their education and purchase homes. And, for those veterans who are disabled, pensions and other benefits are available for them and their families.

A recent VA study predicted that veterans will comprise the major portion of the male aged population for the remainder of this century. It stated that:

> "At the present time veterans comprise 45 percent of all American males over the age of 20 years. Because of the large number of veterans of World War II and the Korean War, by 1990 more than half of U.S. males over age 65 years will be veterans, and by 1995 veterans will exceed 60 percent of the total. . . ."

Although many veterans take advantage of benefits available to them, there still is a great number who are eligible for benefits but don't know about them. The VA has made some progress in alerting eligible veterans of assistance available, but much more needs to be done to assure that all eligible veterans get what they rightfully have coming after serving their country.

Many different individuals and organizations have been critical of the VA for not doing more to seek out veterans eligible for benefits. For example, a congressional investigatory agency, in a recent report, found that letters were not being sent to recently discharged veterans explaining benefits available to them. And veterans in need of special assistance, such as educational training, were not being contacted by the VA.

This chapter clearly explains many of the benefits available

to veterans and their families, including:
- GI Bill educational training;
- GI loans for homes, condominiums and mobile homes;
- GI pensions and survivor's death pensions;
- medical and health care;
- payment of burial expenses and free burial; and
- benefits to veterans with service-connected disabilities.

GI Bill Educational Training

The federal government has educational benefits available for veterans of the post-Korean conflict and Vietnam era. To be eligible for benefits under this bill, a veteran:
- Would have had to serve more than 180 days, a part after January 31, 1955 and before January 1, 1977.
- Could not have been discharged dishonorably.
- Could have been discharged for a service-connected disability.
- Could continue on active duty.

Each eligible veteran is entitled to educational assistance for a period of 1½ months for each month of his service on active duty after January 31, 1955, but not to exceed 45 months. This is called his entitlement. Veterans released from active duty after the 1955 date have eligibility for benefits for ten years after release.

Educational and vocational counseling will be provided by the VA upon request. And to qualify for benefits the veteran must be attending an educational institution approved for training by the VA. Those institutions may include:
- Public or private elementary or high school. A veteran who must complete high school or pass the GED examination to quality for higher education may receive educational assistance without a charge against his basic entitlement. VA also permits additional training, such as refresher courses or deficiency courses, needed to qualify for admission to an educational institution.
- Tutorial assistance. Veterans who need tutorial

163

assistance after high school on at least a half-time basis may qualify for payments.

—Vocational or business schools.

—Correspondence school. Veterans will be paid on the basis of 55 percent of the established charge paid by non-veterans.

—Junior and teacher colleges.

—Scientific or technical schools.

—Farm cooperative training. An eligible veteran enrolled in a "farm cooperative" program concurrently must be engaged in agricultural employment related to his courses. When instruction is scheduled for at least 44 weeks in a year, the veteran may receive a full 12-months of benefits.

—Apprenticeship or other on-the-job training. An eligible veteran may pursue on a full-time basis an approved program of apprenticeship or other training on-the-job. Apprenticeship or on-the-job training programs must be okayed by a state-approving agency. The employer's wage rate will be at least one-half of the wages paid for the specific job. Wages are increased on a regular basis until the veteran is receiving 85 percent of the wages for that job by at least the last full month of his training period which cannot exceed two years. These limitations do not apply to apprenticeships.

—Flight training. An eligible veteran may take an approved flight training course if it is necessary for employment in the field of aviation or another vocation. However, he must first possess a valid private pilot's license and meet the medical requirements necessary for a commercial pilot's license. Educational assistance for flight training is computed at the rate of 90 percent of the established charges for tuition and fees for non-veterans. Flight training as a part of an approved college degree program also is available.

—Predischarge Educational Program (PREP). Servicemen with 181 days of active duty may take, without loss of basic entitlement, courses required for a high school diploma or any refresher courses needed to quality for educational training.

The table which follows shows the amount of money per month veterans can receive for education. Payments are increased with the number of dependents the veteran has and the type of program he is pursuing.

Type of Program	Number of Dependents			
	None	One	Two	Each Add'l Dep.
Institutional				
Full time	$376	$448	$510	$32
Three-quarter time	283	336	383	24
Half time	181	224	255	17
Cooperative..................	304	355	404	23
Apprenticeship/OJT				
First 6 months	274	307	336	14
Second 6 months	205	239	267	14
Third 6 months	136	171	198	14
Fourth and any succeeding 6 months	68	101	131	14
Farm Cooperative				
Full time	304	355	404	23
Three-quarter time	228	266	303	18
Half time	152	178	202	12
Active duty or less than half time .	Tuition and fees not to exceed $376 for full time; $283 for three-quarter time; $188 for half time or less-than-half but more than one-quarter time; $94 for quarter-time or less.			

Where To Go

Application forms for GI Bill educational benefits are available at all VA offices, active duty stations and American embassies in other countries. Completed applications should be submitted to the nearest VA office.

To find the number of the local VA office, refer to the list of Federal Information Centers at the back of this book. Call the Center nearest you.

How To Cut Red Tape

If you plan to apply for educational benefits by visiting a VA office, bring along the following proof to expedite the processing of your application:
— discharge papers;
— marriage license, if any, and
— birth certificate of dependent children, if any.

Post-Vietnam Veterans Education Assistance

For persons entering the military service after December 31, 1976, a voluntary education financing plan is available. Under this plan the service person can authorize monthly deductions of $25 to $100 from military pay to be placed in an educational fund. A maximum of up to $2,700 can be deducted and placed in this special fund. The Veterans Administration then matches this contribution at a rate of $2 for every $1 made by the service person.

After discharge from the service, the veteran has 10 years to receive educational benefits from the fund. The veteran can receive payments for the number of months he or she contributed to the fund or 36 months, whichever is less. Veterans choosing to withdraw from the program can get a refund of their contributions.

Questions and Answers

Q. Can a veteran who dropped out of high school get a high school diploma through VA assistance?

A. Yes, without a charge against basic entitlement.

Q. Must the veteran attend an educational institution chosen by the VA?

A. No. Each eligible person may select a program of training at any educational institution which will accept and retain him as a student in any field or branch of knowledge which the institution finds him qualified to undertake.

Q. How much can a veteran expect to receive from his employer while on a full-time job training program?

A. The employer's wages shall be at least one-half of the wages paid for the specific job and shall be increased on a regular schedule until the veteran is receiving 85 percent of the wages for that job by at least the last full month of his training period which cannot exceed two years.

Q. How many months of educational assistance can a veteran expect to receive if he served on active duty for 18 months after January 31, 1955?

A. If he served 18 months or more after that date and has been released under conditions satisfying his active duty obligation, he will be entitled to 36 full months of educational assistance.

Q. Can the expiration date for educational benefits ever be extended?

A. Yes. Veterans who are prevented from starting or completing their educational program because of a physical or mental disability may receive an extention beyond the 10 year limit.

Q. Can a veteran receive benefits while attending school in an institution outside of the U.S.?

A. Yes, as long as the particular institution is approved by the Veterans Administration.

GI Loans for Homes, Condominiums and Mobile Homes

Veterans who served between September 16, 1940, and the present time and spouses of service persons officially listed as missing in action or captured for more than 90 days and service persons who have served at least 181 days may be eligible for loans for homes, condominiums or mobile homes.

The eligibility requirement for:

—World War II veterans includes active duty on or after September 16, 1940 and prior to July 26, 1947; discharge or separation under other than dishonorable conditions, and at least 90 days' total service, unless discharged earlier for a service-connected disability.

—Post World War II veterans includes no other active duty except that which occurred after July 25, 1947, but before June 27, 1950, and at least 181 days total active service, unless discharged with a service-connected disability.

—Korean conflict veterans includes discharge or separation under other than dishonorable conditions; active duty at any time on or after June 27, 1950 and prior to February 1, 1955, and at least 90 days total service, unless discharged earlier for a service-connected disability.

—Post-Korean veterans includes active duty for 181 days or more after January 31, 1955, and before August 5, 1964, unless discharged earlier for a service-connected disability.

—Vietnam veterans includes active duty for 90 or more days after August 5, 1964, and before May 8, 1975, unless discharged earlier for a service-connected disability.

—Post-Vietnam veterans includes active duty for 181 continuous days or more after May 7, 1975, unless released earlier for a service-connected disability.

A surviving spouse may also be eligible for a loan for a home, condominium or mobile home. To be eligible a surviving spouse must have been married to a veteran serving between September 16, 1940, and the present and who died of service-connected disabilities, or be the spouse of a service person officially listed as missing in action or captured for more than 90 days.

The VA makes it possible for the veteran to buy a home:
—at an interest rate usually lower than conventional mortgages;
—with no down payment (unless required by the lender or for other reasons); and
—with a long repayment period.

How to Collect Veteran Benefit $$$

Here's how it works. A lending instituion such as bank, savings and loan association, insurance or mortgage company makes a home loan to the veteran; while VA enters into an agreement with the lender to guarantee or insure the loan, so the lender probably will not suffer any loss in the event the veteran fails to repay the loan. Because of this the private lender is able to provide the home loan at more favorable terms.

The VA will insure loans for an eligible veteran:
—To buy or build a home.
—To buy a condominium unit.
—To repair, alter or improve a home.
—To refinance an existing home loan.
—To buy a mobile home with or without a lot.
—To buy a lot for a mobile home the veteran already owns.
—To install solar heating and/or cooling system or other weatherization improvements.

The maximum entitlement (guarantee or insurance benefits available to an eligible veteran) is:
—$27,500 for a home loan.
—$20,000 for a mobile home and/or lot.

Although the VA insures loans up to the above amounts, there are no established loan maximums. However, the loan amount has to be reasonable in light of the appraised value of the particular property and the veteran's ability to make the payments on the loan.

The repayment period for the loan can be as long as 30 years and 32 days. The VA does not require any down payment. However, the veteran is required to pay all home closing costs, including title search and recording and prepaid taxes. The veteran has the right to pay off the loan in full at any time without penalty.

Veterans who used their entitlement before October 1, 1980 may have additional entitlement available for GI home loan purposes. Veterans' maximum home loan entitlement was raised from $4,000 to $7,500 in 1950 and continues to rise to the present limit of $27,500. The amount of the additional entitlement is the difference between $27,500 and the amount of entitlement used on prior home loans.

A veteran may be eligible to have his or her entitlement restored upon sale of the home to a veteran-buyer who agrees to substitute his or her entitlement for that of the original veteran.

Where To Go
How to Cut Red Tape

One of the main problems in obtaining benefits under federal programs is finding out where to go and what procedures to follow in establishing your eligibility. Below are step-by-step procedures on how to obtain loans for homes, condominiums and mobile homes.

STEP 1: Veteran must establish his eligibility for a VA loan and a Certificate of Eligibility must be obtained from a VA office by:

—"Walk-in" procedure. Veteran brings discharge or separation papers (World War II veterans bring discharge, Korean or Vietnam veterans bring separation papers) to the VA office and completes Form 26-1880, Request for Determination of Eligibility and Available Loan Guaranty Entitlements. VA eligibility clerk reviews application form and discharge or separation papers, then issues VA Form 26-8320, Certificate of Eligibility for Loan Guaranty Benefits.

VA Form 26-8320, Certificate of Eligibility for Loan Guaranty Benefits.

—Mail procedure. Veteran writes or calls the VA office and requests an application for the eligibility certificate. He completes the application form and mails it with discharge for World War II or separation papers for Korean or Vietnam Service to the VA regional office. Eligibility clerk reviews service papers and application and returns the discharge or separation papers with Certificate of Eligibility to veteran by mail.

STEP 2: Veteran selects property and discusses purchase with seller or selling broker and signs a purchase contract with a condition that the agreement is subject to the availability of a VA loan.

170

STEP 3: The Veteran contacts a lender and the lender interviews the veteran and prepares a mortgage application. If it is obvious that the purchaser will not qualify because of unsatisfactory credit or insufficient income, the lender has the responsibility to decline the application.

STEP 4: If the lender determines that the veteran may qualify for the requested mortgage, the lender will order an appraisal of the property. Lenders have been advised that if there is any question as to the veteran's qualifications, to submit the loan application to the VA so as to assure that a qualified veteran will not be denied a loan. While the appraisal is being processed, the lender will expedite processing by ordering the credit report, employment verification, bank deposit verification as well as other documents that will be necessary to complete processing.

STEP 5: The VA assigns an appraiser who inspects the property and submits a report. If the location and condition of the property are acceptable, VA issues a Certificate of Reasonable Value establishing the maximum amount of the loan available. One copy of the certificate is sent to the lender, another copy to the veteran.

STEP 6: When the lender receives the Certificate of Reasonable Value, he normally will have all the necessary items (credit report, employment letter, etc.) and the veteran will be able to return to the lender to review his application and sign the required certifications including one that he is aware of the reasonable value of the property.

STEP 7: In most cases, the lender submits the application to the VA for its approval prior to closing the loan. If the veteran is qualified for the loan, a Certificate of Committment is sent to the lender, who can then close the loan and receive the VA guaranty.

Questions and Answers

Q. Are there any charges made for obtaining a GI loan?

A. The VA makes no charge for guaranteeing or insuring a loan. No commission or brokerage fees may be charged to a veteran for securing a GI loan. However, the lender may charge reasonable closing costs, usually paid by a borrower. In the case of a home loan, such closing costs generally include the VA appraisal, credit report, survey, title evidence and recording fees. The lender, as provided in schedules issued by VA, also may make a reasonable flat charge to cover all other loan origination costs.

Q. Is time spent in the National Guard or Reserve units considered eligible service to meet the requirement of active duty for benefits for post-Korean veterans?

A. No.

Q. Are veterans of World War I eligible for GI loans?

A. No.

Q. May children of deceased veterans obtain a guaranteed or insured loan?

A. No.

Q. May several veterans use their entitlement to acquire property together?

A. Yes. Their total entitlement would be the sum total of each veteran's entitlement.

Q. If both a husband and wife are eligible veterans, may they acquire property jointly and increase the amount which may be guaranteed?

A. Yes.

Q. May a veteran join with a non-veteran in obtaining a GI loan?

A. Yes, but the amount of the loan on which the guaranty is based is in proportion to the veteran's interest in the loan.

Q. Will a veteran be able to get a GI loan indefinitely?

A. Yes, there is no time limit on eligibility.

Q. May a veteran transfer or sell the property purchased with a GI loan to another person?

A. Yes, either to a veteran or a non-veteran. Such transfer does not require VA approve.

Q. Is it required that the existing GI loan be paid in full in order for the veteran to transfer or sell the property?

A. No. The buyer may purchase the property subject to or by assumption of the existing GI mortgage debt.

GI Pensions

Pension benefits are awarded to eligible veterans who took up arms in defense of their country during time of war. The Congress has proclaimed that the nation owes a special obligation to these veterans.

Accordingly, needy veterans of World War I, World War II, the Korean conflict and the Vietnam era who are 65 or older or any age with a non-service connected disability may be eligible for pensions. Benefits are available for war-time veterans discharged under other than dishonorable conditions after 90 or more days of service.

A veteran is considered disabled if he or she is generally permanently incapable of earning a living because of a physical or mental impairment. Needy veterans age 65 or older are considered eligible for pensions even though they do not suffer from a disability.

To be eligible, a veteran must have served:

—In World War I from April 6, 1917 to November 11, 1918; extended to April 1, 1920 for those veterans who served in Russia; also extended through July 1, 1921 for those veterans who had at least one day of service before November 12, 1918, and who served after November 11, 1918 and before July 2, 1921.

—In World War II from December 7, 1941 to December 31, 1946.

—In the Korean conflict from June 27, 1950 to January 31, 1955.

—In the Vietnam era from August 5, 1964 to May 7, 1975.

The yearly disability pensions range up to $5963 for a single veteran and up to $10,500 or more for veterans with dependents. The following annual rates are available to the qualified veteran:

Veteran without dependent spouse or child ... $5,963
Veteran with one dependent 7,811
Veteran in need of regular aid and attendance . 9,539
Two veterans married to one another 7,811
Increase for each dependent child 1,012

Other Income

It is important to note that the pension benefits may be reduced by countable income less specific exclusions over a certain limit. The reduction in the pension is on a dollar for dollar basis. Income of the veteran's spouse may also be counted under certain circumstances. The adjusted income limitations are $6,273 for a veteran with no dependents and $8,435 for a veteran with dependents.

Other Assets

VA can deny or discontinue pension benefits if the veteran's net worth is "substantial". In such cases the VA may determine that the support should come from the veteran's estate rather than the VA. In evaluating a veteran's net worth, the VA considers factors such as the veteran's life style, living standards of the community, housing costs, family obligations and state of health. VA also considers the nature of the veteran's assets, their marketability and convertibility into cash. All these factors are considered before the VA arrives at a decision affecting payment of a pension.

As you can see, there are no clear cut rules relating to the value of a veteran's assets and the possible impact on pension payments. The VA makes these decisions on a case-by-case basis.

The VA requires that veterans receiving pensions complete a questionnaire at the beginning of each year. Veterans are asked to report income and resource data for themselves, their spouse and dependent children.

Residence Outside Country

Veterans receiving pension benefits can reside in a foreign country indefinitely and still receive pension checks. It is estimated that over 50,000 veterans and survivors of veterans live outside of the U.S. and receive monthly pension benefit checks.

Survivor's Death Pensions

Surviving spouses and unmarried children up to age 18 (or

23 if attending school) may be eligible to collect pension payments for a veteran who has *died of causes not related to military service.*

Generally, to be eligible the widow or widower:

—must have been married to the veteran at least one year prior to the veteran's death. This requirement does not have to be met if a child resulted from the marriage relationship.

—must have lived with the veteran continuously from the time of marriage until the veteran's death.

Remarriage following the death of the veteran makes the spouse ineligible for pension payments. Also, openly living with a person as man and wife makes the spouse ineligible for payments. Should the remarriage end in divorce or the live-in relationship terminate, the surviving spouse is then re-eligible for pension payments.

Also, eligible children who become permanently incapable of self-support because of mental or physical disability before age 18 may receive a pension as long as the condition exists (or until they marry).

The yearly pension payments range from up to $3,996 for a surviving spouse with no dependent children to $6,347 or more for a surviving spouse with one dependent in need of regular aid and attendance. The following annual rates are available to eligible surviving spouses and dependents:

Surviving spouse without dependent children . $3,996
Surviving spouse with one dependent child ... 5,235
Surviving spouse in need of regular aid and
   attendance without dependent child 6,392
Increase for each additional child 1,012

It is important to note that income of the surviving spouse and dependent children may reduce the pension payments. Despite this, the program can be of great benefit to those having little or no other source of income.

Where to Go and
How to Cut Red Tape

To find the telephone number of your local VA office, call the Federal Information Center nearest your home. A complete list of Federal Information Centers is included in the back of this book. Ask the information specialist for the number of the VA office nearest your home.

Before calling the VA to begin filing a claim, be sure you are familiar with the information in this book.VA officials answering questions over the telephone very often provide erroneous information to callers. So, if you get an answer to a question that doesn't seem right, call back and talk to another official—or call another VA office.

In applying for a veteran's pension, you will need the following information to establish your eligibility:
—discharge papers;
—proof of dependents, if any, and
—proof of income.

Questions and Answers

Q. Are veterans in prison and parolees still eligible for benefits?

A. Yes, in most cases.

Q. How do the various classes of discharges from the military service affect benefits?

A. *Honorable* and *general* discharges qualify the veteran for benefits. Dishonorable discharges bar a person from VA benefits. Undesirable and bad conduct dischargees may or may not qualify for benefits depending on the circumstances. The VA decides each of these discharges on a case-by-case basis.

Q. Will the pension of a veteran with a nonservice-connected disability be reduced if he is a patient in a VA hospital?

A. Yes. For example, the pension of a single veteran will be reduced up to $60 a month after two full months of care. Full pension resumes after release from the hospital.

Q. Did a veteran have to be in combat to be eligible for a nonservice-connected disability pension?

A. The veteran only has to serve during specified war-time periods.

Medical and Health Care

The VA maintains a massive network of medical and health care services for veterans who have honorably served their country. It operates 172 medical centers, 220 clinics, 92 nursing homes, and 16 domiciliaries throughout the country. In addition, the VA helps pay for about 45 state-operated hospitals, nursing homes and domiciliaries which also provide care for eligible veterans.

Medical and health care for veterans is expected to expand significantly in coming years. As previously mentioned, veterans comprise about 45 percent of all American males over age 20. By 1990 more than 50 percent of all U.S. men over 65 will be veterans.

The large number of aging veterans will put a particular strain on VA's nursing home facilities. The number of veterans requiring nursing home care is expected to increase steadily over the next 20 years. And, by the year 2,000, over 270,000 veterans will be in need of nursing home care. The VA is currently planning the construction of a large number of nursing homes to meet the expected demand.

Eligibility

Generally, any needy veteran can receive medical or health care from the VA if she or he has been discharged under conditions other than dishonorable. The eligible veteran merely has to sign a statement of inability to pay for comparable care in a private facility. The statement of inability to pay is not required for veterans age 65 or older. Veterans with a service-connected disability are generally eligible by virtue of their disability alone. The VA has not established specific income or asset requirements for eligibility, and no investigation is normally made to determine a veteran's financial condition.

Types of Care Available

The VA provides three types of health care to eligible veterans—hospitals, nursing home, and domiciliary care. Each is discussed below.

How to Collect Big $$$ from Uncle Sam

Hospital Care

Hospital care is provided to eligible veterans who need inpatient treatment and diagnosis for medical, surgical or psychiatric conditions. Generally, these veterans require the services of a physician on a daily basis with attendant diagnostic, therapeutic and rehabilitative services.

Nursing Home Care

Nursing home care is provided to veterans who are *not* acutely ill or in need of hospital care, but still require skilled nursing care and related medical services.

Domiciliary Care

VA domiciliaries provide shelter, food and necessary medical care on a "self-care" basis to veterans who are disabled by age or disease, but not in need of hospitalization or skilled nursing care facilities.

As a general rule, veterans placed in a domiciliary must be self-sufficent and be able to handle daily living activities without assistance. This would include performing without assistance such things as brushing teeth, bathing, combing hair, and body elimination.

Veterans needing substantial assistance in performing normal daily activities would likely be eligible for nursing home care rather than domiciliary care.

Nursing home care and domiciliary care provided by the VA has been called excellent by independent observers. The facilities are well-maintained and the services provided are exemplary. VA nursing home and domiciliary facilities are clean and comfortable while presenting a pleasant atmosphere. The residents are well-cared for and provided various social and recreational activities.

With the wide spread reported inadequacies and high cost of private nursing homes care, VA nursing homes and domicilaries offer a welcome alternative for qualified veterans. Yet, few veterans or veteran family members know of these excellent facilities.

Impact of Veteran Pension Payments

Most veterans provided care in a VA hospital, nursing home or domiciliary also receive a veteran's pension. As discussed on page 173, the benefits received under veteran's pensions are based on the eligible veteran's income, marital status, and number of dependents.

When a veteran is provided care by a VA hospital, nursing home or domiciliary the veteran's pension is reduced. However, the pension amount is not reduced until after 2 full calendar months of domiciliary care or 3 months of hospital or nursing home care. And, in some cases, the veteran's pension will not be reduced at all. This may occur in cases where a veteran is a resident of a VA-supported, state-operated facility. Each of the VA-supported, state-operated facilities has its own rules governing whether veterans must give up part of their pension money when receiving care.

Payment of Burial Expenses and Free Burial

The VA will pay a $300 burial allowance for any eligible deceased veteran. Also, a $150 burial plot allowance will be paid for a veteran not buried in a national cemetery. The claim must be filed within 2 years of permanent burial or cremation.

NOTE: A deceased veteran's family may also be eligible for a lump sum payment of $255 under Social Security. See page 36.

Burial in a national cemetery is also available to eligible deceased veterans. The burial can be in any national cemetery having space, except Arlington. The free burial includes opening and closing of the grave, the grave marker, and if available, an honor guard. Burials are also available to an eligible veteran's spouse and minor children. Under certain conditions an unmarried adult child can be buried in the same site.

Where To Go and How To Cut Red Tape

You can apply for reimbursement of burial expenses at any VA office. To find the number of your local VA office, call the Federal Information Center nearest your home. A complete list of Federal Information Centers is included in the back of this book.

As for free burials in a national cemetery, requests can only be made at the time of death by contacting the director of the National Cemetery desired. Several publications are available to help you:

Interments in National Cemeteries — Describes services available to veterans and dependents.

List of National Cemeteries — Name and status of each federally-owned national cemetery.

Application for Headstone or Marker — DOD Form 1330.

These informative publications and other information on free burial services for veterans can be obtained by writing: Office of Chief of Support Services, Memorial Division, Department of the Army, Washington, DC 20315.

Benefits to Veterans with Service-Connected Disabilities

There are many benefits available to veterans who have been disabled while serving in the military service. If you are a veteran with a service-connected disability, contact the VA to see if you are eligible for benefits. Listed below are some of the benefits available to disabled veterans:

—automobiles or other conveyances;
—compensation;
—annual clothing allowance;
—hospitalization;
—nursing home care;
—domiciliary;
—outpatient medical treatment;
—outpatient dental treatment, and
—vocational rehabilitation.

* * *

How to Collect Veteran Benefit $$$

In addition the VA administers some benefits for certain widows, children and parents of veterans. If a member of your family lost his life while in military service, contact the VA to see if you are eligible for specific benefits. Some of the benefits available to the veteran's family are:

—Compensation. If the veteran's death was service connected, the widow and minor children may be eligible for dependency and indemnity compensation.

—Pension. A service-connected death may entitle the widow and veteran's minor children to pension payments.

—Parents' compensation. In certain cases, parents may be eligible for dependency and indemnity compensation.

—Children's education. Children of veterans who die or become permanently and totalled disabled because of service-connected disabilities or of servicemen who are missing in action or prisoners of war may be eligible for orphans' education assistance.

—Widow's education. Widows of veterans who died as the result of service-connected disabilities are eligible for education assistance.

—Wives' education. Wives of veterans who are permanently and totally disabled because of a service-connected disability or of servicemen who are missing in action or prisoners of war are eligible for educational assistance.

—Death gratuity. Paid by the armed services to widows, children, and, if designated by the deceased, to parents, brothers or sisters.

Wherever possible, veterans should acquaint their families with the location of their military records, their file number and their insurance numbers to save delay.

Chapter 9

How To Collect Education $$$

With the ever soaring cost of education many people who want to go to school and are qualified can't afford it. And things seem to be getting worse. Many families who in past years were able to send their children to school now find it impossible to do so without outside financial help.

Uncle Sam has various programs that can help pay for the high cost of going to school. This help falls into three categories: grants, loans, or employment. Grants are outright gifts of money—they do not have to be paid back. Loans are borrowed money which you must repay with interest. Employment allows you to work and earn the money you need for school.

The federal government's Department of Education administers several student financial aid programs. These programs are:
—Pell Grants,
—Supplemental Educational Opportunity Grants,
—Perkins Loans (formerly National Direct Student Loans),
—Guaranteed Student Loans, (Stafford Loan)
—Plus Loans, and
—College Work-Study.

Here's How You Qualify

Generally, you may be eligible for financial aid under one of the programs if you meet these requirements:

—You are enrolled as a regular student in an eligible program at one of over 7,000 colleges, universities, vocational schools, technical schools or hospital schools of nursing that take part in the Department of Education's Aid program;

—You are a U.S. citizen or eligible non-citizen;

—Make satisfactory progress in the school work;

—You are not in default on another government loan program;

—You sign a statement that you have registered for the selective service;

—You sign a statement that money received will be used solely for educational purposes; and

—Show you need the money.

Most Federal student aid is awarded on the basis of need. Financial need is defined as the difference between your educational costs—tuition, fees, room, board, books, supplies, and miscellaneous expenses—and the amount you and your family can be expected to pay for your education. There are several different systems used to establish need. Other eligibility requirements, such as satisfactory progress in completing your studies, must also be met to obtain assistance.

Your need is determined by a standard formula which evaluates the information you put on your application for aid. Use of this standard evaluation formula assures all students receive equal treatment in awarding money. This formula evaluates important factors like sources of income and ownership of assets such as savings accounts, stocks, bonds, real estate, home and business values.

Validation

The Department of Eduation or your school selects certain applications for a process called "validation". Under this validation process, you may be asked to demonstrate that the information on your application is correct. If you're "lucky" enough to be selected you may be asked to produce important documents like Federal tax returns and other information showing your income and assets owned. Failure to provide requested proof may result in cancellation of financial aid.

Here's What You Can Collect

The amount of assitance available to further your education under each program is discussed below.

PELL Grants

Pell Grants provide money to help undergraduates pay for educational expenses. The Pell Grant program is the largest of the Federal student aid programs. Thousands of students are able to stay in school because of these grants. Grant awards range up to $2,200 depending on your need. Remember, you are not required to pay back any portion of the grant money you receive.

Supplemental Educational Opportunity Grants

Supplemental Educational Opportunity Grants provide money to help undergraduates pay for educational expenses. You can collect up to $4,000 a year depending on your need. Keep in mind you are not required to pay back any portion of the money you receive.

Guaranteed Student Loans (Stafford Loan)

Under the Guaranteed Student Loan program, you may borrow up to $2,625 a year as an undergraduate and up to $7,500 a year as a graduate or professional student.

The total amount you can borrow for undergraduate or vocational study is $17,250. The total for graduate or professional study is $54,750, including loans made at the undergraduate level. The interest rate varies with economic conditions.

A guaranteed student loan is made to you by a private lender such as a bank, credit union, or savings and loan. These loans are then insured by the Federal Government.

Under this arrangement the lender is able to offer the loan at a lower interest rate because it is risk-free. It's risk-free because if you don't pay back the lender, the Federal Government will.

Depending on your family income, you may have to show financial need. And the amount of your loan will depend on the amount of your family income.

From the date of your graduation, you have up to 10 years to repay the loan.

Perkins Loans (formerly National Direct Student Loans)

A Perkins Loan is a low-interest loan to help you pay for educational expenses. These loans are for both undergraduate and graduate students. Depending on your need, you may borrow up to:
—$4,500 if you're an undergraduate and have finished less than two years toward a Bachelor degree program, or enrolled in a vocational program;
—$9,000 if you're an undergraduate student and have finished more than 2 years toward a Bachelor degree program;
—$18,000 for graduate or professional study.

The maximum loan amounts include total amount borrowed under the Perkins program. For example, if you borrowed $4,000 as an undergraduate, you can borrow a maximum of only $14,000 as a graduate or professional student.

Generally, you begin repaying the loan 6 months after you graduate. You may be allowed up to 10 years to repay the loan.

Part of your loan may be cancelled for each year you teach handicapped children, or each year you teach in a designated elementary or secondary school that serves low-income students. Your entire loan will be cancelled after the fifth full year of teaching. What's more, part of your loan will be cancelled for each year you work in specified Head Start programs. Your entire loan will be cancelled after the seventh full year.

Plus Loans

Plus Loans provide supplemental money for educational expenses beyond what the other programs offer. These loans are made by a private lender such as a bank, credit union or savings and loan. The interest rates on Plus Loans are higher than the other basic educational loan programs.

Those eligible for Plus Loans and the maximum amounts available are as follows:

—Parents may borrow up to $4,000 per year for each dependent undergraduate student. The total maximum loan amount is $20,000.

—Undergraduate students may borrow up to $4,000 a year.

—Graduate students may borrow up to $4,000 a year, to a total maximum loan amount of $20,000.

Unlike the other loan programs, borrowers do not have to demonstrate need.

College Work-Study

The College Work Study program provides jobs for students who need financial aid and who must earn part of their educational expenses.

Under this program the educational institution arranges jobs on campus or off campus. You can work as many as 40 hours a week. In general, the wages you receive are based on the current minimum wage plus the skills required for the job.

Undergraduates are paid by the hour. Graudate students may be paid by the hour or receive a salary. You get paid at least once a month.

Where To Go and
How To Cut Through Red Tape

As a first step in finding out more comprehensive information on these programs you can write the U.S. Department of Education, Office of Public Affairs, Washington D.C. 20202 or call the Federal Student Aid Information Center at 1-800-333-4636.

The Information Center provides the following services:

—Explaining general eligibility requirements,

—Explaining process for determining cash award,

—Checking the status of your application,

—Solving payment problems, and

—Mailing you helpful publications.

You can call between 9:00 a.m. and 5:30 p.m. EST, Monday through Friday.

If you write the Department of Education ask for the free booklet *The Student Guide*. Also ask for other publications that may be helpful.

For those who recently enrolled in an educational institution, you can find out more about these programs from the school's financial aid officer.

Before applying for any of these financial aid programs, it is advisable to obtain as much information about them as possible. With this first-hand knowledge you'll be better able to understand the specific eligibility requirements that you must satisfy before you start collecting.

Questions and Answers

Q. Does aid from federal financial assitance programs continue from year to year without reapplication?

A. No, You must reapply annually.

Q. For what purpose can money obtained under federal financial aid programs be used?

A. Aid received from these programs must be used for educational purposes only. These include expenditures for such things as tuition, fees, room and board, books, and supplies.

Q. If a student transfers from one school to another, does the financial aid automatically follow?

A. No. The student must take the action necessary to continue receiving it at the new school.

Q. What other sources of financial aid are available to students?

A. There are many other financial aid sources to help students complete their studies. To find out about them, contact the financial aid office at your school. It is probably your best and most direct source of information.

Q. What happens if I don't pay back a Department of Education loan?

A. The school or the Federal Government may notify credit bureaus of your loan default. This may affect your future credit rating.

Q. What is meant by "satisfactory progress" in my school work?

A. Satisfactory progress varies from school to school. Each school that takes part in Federal student aid programs must have a written standard of satisfactory academic process. To receive Federal aid, you must meet that standard.

Q. What kinds of jobs are available under the College Work-Study Program?

A. Jobs are available both on and off campus. Jobs must be for either a public or private, non-profit organiation. For example, jobs working for a Federal, State or local public agency or commission are common.

Chapter 10

How To Collect
Job Training $$$

• Joyce Adams is employed as a files clerk, but she can't earn enough money to make ends meet. Joyce wants to get training to do some other kind of work that pays more, but she doesn't know where to turn.

• Henry Rossi is employed as a floor sweeper in a dress factory and, for the fourth time in seven years, he has been laid off. Henry has an eighth-grade education with no specific job skills and he realizes that his low educational level has had something to do with his continual layoffs. Whenever the economy gets bad he seems to be the first one to be out on the street. Recently, Henry's unemployment benefits and family savings were depleted causing him to go on public assistance. He wants to get off public assistance as soon as possible, finish high school and get training in the tool and dye trade.

The federal government's Department of Labor has a number of programs to help people like Joyce Adams and Henry Rossi. These programs are designed to develop the employment potential of unemployed, or underemployed persons so they can become self-sufficient and contribute more to the economy. The programs are operated by state and local units of government under guidelines established by the Department of Labor. The major job training programs are the Work Incentive Program (WIN) and various other programs under the Job Training Partnership Act.

Job Training Partnership Act

Joyce Adams may qualify for job training under the Job Training Partnership Act (JTPA). Under the JTPA the Federal Government's Department of Labor gives money to State governments to provide job training and related assistance to eligible persons. States then oversee programs in local areas where the training and other services are carried out. The local training programs are set up through the joint efforts of business and industry representatives and local governments. The type of training offered will depend on the need for certain types of jobs within each state. That's the reason for having business and industry representatives involved in the training. They know what training and skills are needed to fill specific jobs in business. The goal of JTPA training is to move eligible persons into a permanent job that provides enough income to be self-sufficient.

Training Services for the Disadvantaged

This program provides a wide range of training and related services for economically disadvantaged persons. The assistance available includes counseling, testing, classroom instruction, vocational training, on-the-job training and help in finding a job. This program can also help persons who encounter special problems finding a job. This includes displaced homemakers, teenage parents, older workers, school dropouts, the handicapped, veterans and others.

Employment and Training Assistance for Dislocated Workers

This program provides job training and other related assistance to:

—workers who have been laid off because of a permanent plant shut-down;

—workers who have received notice of impending layoff or permanent plant shut-down;

—workers who are laid off with little hope for finding work in their previous occupation.

The long-term unemployed worker with little hope for finding a job locally is also eligible under this program.

The program can provide retraining, job search assistance, relocation, and support services.

Employment and Training Program for Native Americans, Migrant Workers and Seasonal Farmworkers

This program offers a wide variety of training, employment and supportive services. This program is administered by the Federal government.

Veterans Employment Program

This program provides training and employment services for disabled veterans, veterans of the Vietnam era, and veterans who recently separated from military service.

Job Corps Program

The Job Corps Program is designed to assist youths age 16 to 21 who are both out of work and out of school. The program helps youths develop talents, self-confidence and motivation. Enrollees spend a maximum of 2 years in the Job Corps. The average enrollment is about 6 months. This is normally enough time to provide training and improve employability.

Eligible youths actually live at a Job Corps center during their training period. At the center, the youth is provided with all food, medical and dental care. A monthly allowance is given to cover incidental expenses. In addition, for each month the youth stays in the Job Corps program, money is set aside to be paid upon completion of training.

To be eligible for the program, youths cannot have any serious physical or mental handicaps and normally must be from a lower-income family. Youths 18 or over can enroll in Job Corps on their own, while youths under 18 must be enrolled by a parent or guardian.

Specific Eligibility Criteria

The specific requirements for Job Corps Eligibility are:
—Be age 16 through 21 (male or female).
—Need job training.
—Have a low family income.
—Be out of school, either a drop-out or graduate.
—Be in school but recommended by a counselor.
—Be able to benefit from the Job Corps.
—Be willing to work hard and obey the rules.
—Be without a history of serious criminal or anti-social behavior problems.

The Job Corps is not designed to be a program for juvenile delinquents or criminals. Moreover, it is not a rehabilitation program. It's a program for job training, academic upgrading, and social skills development followed by job placement.

Training Approach

The Job Corps is a multi-pronged approach designed to develop the young person's overall abilities. Some of the important aspects of the program include:

Academic Training — Intensive, individualized reading, writing, math skills, high school equivalency GED preparation.

Vocational Training — Intensive skills training for entry level positions in a variety of vocations. Some of these vocations include auto mechanics, bricklaying, carpentry, electronics, welding, nursing, and office skills.

Resident Living — Job Corps is primarily a live-in program with a disciplined and well-regulated setting.

Counseling — Personal counseling is provided on a one-on-one and group basis. Potential skills are evaluated and vocational opportunities are explained.

Placement — About 70 percent of Job Corps graduates are

placed in jobs. About 20 percent go on to advanced schooling. Generally, about 10 percent enter the military service.

Other Advantages

In addition to academic and job training the Job Corps offers the following benefits:
—A nice place to live.
—Meals.
—Clothing allowance.
—Drivers education.
—Medical and dental care.
—Recreation, sports, movies.
—$40 a month spending money.
—$75 a month for each month of program participation, paid at completion of training.
—A chance to make new friends.

Work Incentive Program

Under the Work Incentive Program (WIN), Henry Rossi may finish high school and at the same time get valuable on-the-job training in tool and dye. WIN is a national effort created by Congress in 1967 to help people on AFDC become productive workers. This program offers job-finding aid to recipients who are ready to work and it provides services such as job training, counseling, medical aid and child care to those who need such help in order to get ready for work.

This year about 300,000 WIN participants will find jobs after training; and 65 percent will still be working after 90 days. Presently, the program costs about $400 million.

Mothers receiving AFDC may take advantage of WIN provided that adequate child care arrangements can be made. Unemployed fathers on AFDC automatically are eligible for WIN. The program refers participants to jobs after they have been appraised and it is determined that they have the aptitude, skills and other qualifications needed to work.

While an individual is in a training program he will continue to receive assistance checks plus $30 a month. The duration of training may vary from four weeks to 18 months depending on the type of training received. The individual also gets $4 for car fare and lunch money for each day of training. If needed, WIN will provide:

1. Basic educational skills, such as training in reading, arithmetic, etc.
2. High School equivalency training leading to the General Education Development (GED) Test, equal to a high school diploma.
3. Vocational training.
4. Medical services.
5. Child care services.
6. Homemaker services.
7. Guidance, counseling, and other supportive services.
8. Eye glasses, hearing aids, braces, dentures, and other such devices necessary to obtaining and keeping employment.

Any job a WIN participant gets will pay about the same wages other people earn for doing similar work, and after the WIN training period, the employer generally must keep the individual on for at least one year.

When considering the type of training you want to participate in under WIN, you should give serious consideration to the following factors:

—Look to the future. What are your chances for advancement? Where will the job lead you in five or 10 years?

—Look for work that uses your abilities and interests.

—Look at the general working conditions, the environment of the job, not solely at the salary.

When you are seeking a job, remember that the employer wants satisfied and efficient workers. Any mistakes in hiring may be costly to him and you.

As you can see Uncle Sam has a training or job program for just about everyone who wants to improve themselves.

Where To Go and How To Cut Red Tape

Job Training Partnership Act (JTPA)

As a first step, call the Federal Information Center nearest you. The numbers are listed at the back of this book. When you call, ask for the telephone number of the local JTPA office. The information specialist may ask you if you are interested in a job, job training or both. For job and job training information, you will most likely be referred to a local employment office. For job training only, you'll be referred to a county or city agency which administers the JTPA program. The name of the specific local agency handling the JTPA program may vary from state to state.

Once you have obtained the proper telephone number of the local governmental agency which operates JTPA, call to obtain some general information. Try to find out as much as possible over the phone. Depending on your particular interests, find out about specific eligibility requirements. Ask hypothetical questions. Ask probing questions. Get a general insight on what's available and how to qualify. Remember, specific programs and eligibility requirements differ from state to state. For example, in some states, to be eligible for JTPA job training, you may have to be unemployed at least 12 weeks. Other states may have completely different requirements. That's why it is important to find out the specific requirements in your own state.

Above all, be persistant. Demand clear, complete answers to your questions. Learn all you can before you go down and apply in person. Then when you finally file a written application, your chances of success will be very good.

Work Incentive Program (WIN)

To find the number of your local WIN office, call the Federal Information Center nearest your home. A complete list of Federal Information Centers is included at the back of this book. Ask the information specialist for the number of the WIN office in your area.

Questions And Answers

Q. Under WIN, does the participant receive wages from the employer?

How to Collect Big $$$ from Uncle Sam

A. Yes. Wages must equal the prevailing wage rate for the occupation in the area.

Q. Where do WIN participants train and work?

A. On-the-job trainees usually are placed in private industry. They work and learn in factories, shops and other business establishments which are operated for profit.

Q. How many youths are participating in the Job Corps Program?

A. The Job Corps Program now provides training opportunities for about 45,000 youths.

Q. When did Congress enact the Job Training Partnership Act?

A. JTPA became effective October 1, 1983. Before then the Federal government's principle Job Training effort was under the Comprehensive Employment and Training Act (CETA).

Q. Why is JTPA called a "Partnership"?

A. Because the job training activities are supposed to be a joint effort between local governments and representatives from the business and the private sector. This "partnership" encourages more permenent jobs in business. Past Federally funded training often placed trainees in temporary government jobs.

Chapter 11

How To Collect
Family Support $$$

• George Adams was a factory worker in a large automobile firm for 10 years. Because of the slump in auto sales, he was indefinitely laid off. His company benefits and unemployment compensation have been exhausted completely. George is the sole supporter of a wife and two children.

• Mary Travers had worked as a sales clerk in a large department store for several years. Being caught in a massive layoff last year, she has no source of income. Mary is divorced with two children.

George and Mary are bitter and have every right to be. After all, they have worked hard their whole lives, been good citizens and have paid their fair share in taxes. They feel as thousands of others do, that their current unfortunate situation is no fault of their own and they are victims of the present economic slump.

With a family to maintain and children to feed they feel deserted and have no one to turn to. But George and Mary can get financial help.

How to Collect Big $$$ from Uncle Sam

Congress recognized that in peoples' lives there would be periods of economic hardship where financial assistance would be needed and established Aid to Families with Dependent Children (AFDC).

AFDC is designed to assist children who are deprived of necessities because of their parents' reduction or loss of income. Accordingly, it is available to families who are in need of assistance due to temporary periods of economic recession. AFDC sometimes is called welfare.

Probably no other federal program has caused so much alarm as AFDC and the concern is justified because welfare costs to the taxpayer continue to swell. For example, federal costs for AFDC have increased from $625 million in 1970 to a present cost of about $10 billion. Since the states also are required to contribute to AFDC, the total cost to the taxpayer is billions of dollars a year.

As you would expect, the AFDC rolls also have increased to a present total of about 11 million recipients. One reason why AFDC rolls are growing is that more and more people are finding out about the program and taking advantage of it.

Unlike most federal assistance programs, AFDC is widely known and understood by most people. The main reason is that the federal government has, in the past, granted money to large urban cities for the purpose of seeking out those eligible for AFDC and encouraging them to get on the rolls.

Under this approach, many people were making welfare a way of life; therefore, in recent years, the emphasis has been on getting people off welfare and making them self sufficient through job upgrading and training.

In this chapter, we are addressing those families who are experiencing extreme financial distress due to the nation's slumping economic conditions and are in need of temporary assistance. This includes families who are victims of mass layoffs and soaring inflation.

Since AFDC is designed to provide the essentials of life for dependent children, parents should not feel ashamed or embarrassed about receiving benefits from the program. Most parents are willing to work hard and support their families but because of economic conditions they temporarily are unable to find a job. While they were working the government was not hesitant to take taxes out of their paychecks, so they should hold their heads high and take advantage of AFDC—they paid for it.

Here's How to Qualify for Support

To be considered for AFDC you must be a parent of a needy child who is under 18; or 21, if attending school; or related to the child, living with him and responsible for his care and support. Pregnant women are eligible for benefits in some states.

All states allow benefits for dependent children without a father in the home. About half of the states allow benefits for families with an unemployed father in the home; however, the states allowing families with unemployed fathers to participate in AFDC are expected to increase with worsening economic conditions.

Here's What You Can Collect

The benefits available under AFDC vary significantly from state to state. This is because each state is allowed to decide the needs to be covered under the AFDC program and the amount of benefits to be paid. State control over need standards and payment levels has resulted in a situation where AFDC family benefits are determined more by the state they live in than by family needs. The diversity of coverage between states creates inequities because families with similar needs and circumstances are treated differently.

The political, economic and social climate of a state largely dictates the amount of AFDC benefits to be paid. Some states believe in welfare and provide substantial benefits, while other states frown on it and pay a meager amount even to desperately needy families.

For example, a family of four in Milwaukee, Wisconsin, could get a maximum grant of over $500 a month while the same family could receive just over $120 a month in Jackson, Mississippi.

Supplemental Benefits

There are three major supplemental benefits that some states pay for. These benefits are for:
— pregnant women,
— emergency assistance, and
— unemployed fathers.
Each of these benefits is discussed below.

Pregnant Women

In about 18 states a pregnant woman with no other children is eligible for AFDC benefits. In some states, benefits are granted to the woman as soon as the pregnancy is verified. In other states, AFDC pays only for the last 6 months of the pregnancy.

Providing benefits for pregnant women may help protect the unborn child. It provides money to the expectant mother for such things as adequate food, medical attention and shelter.

Emergency Assistance

Emergency assistance can take several different forms, depending on the state. Generally, it covers such emergencies as civil disorders, avoidance of potential evictions and prevention of utility shutoffs. Emergency assistance has prevented many families from being thrown out onto the streets with no place to go. It has also helped needy families keep the heat on during cold winters, thus preventing possible physical harm to children.

Unemployed Fathers

Over half of the states allow benefits for families with an unemployed father in the house. Years ago, AFDC was not allowed if the father lived in the home. This requirement created a situation where the father was often "forced" to leave the home so the family could start collecting AFDC. The result was many families were needlessly broken up with great psychological damage to the children and the family unit. More and more states are realizing it is often better to provide temporary assistance to the entire family unit.

Other Benefits Available to AFDC Recipients

Families eligible for AFDC are automatically eligible for Medicaid (see page 229 for further information on Medicaid). All states provide Medicaid benefits. Depending on the state, families may be able to receive dental services, eyeglasses, chiropractic services, prescriptions and private duty nursing service.

Of course, AFDC recipients may be eligible for other Federal programs such as food stamps and subsidized housing.

Figuring the Grant Amount

After you have filled out the forms, an AFDC representative will consider all the information about your family's income, property and other resources. The amount of money your family needs for housing, utilities, food and personal needs will be figured according to standards set by your state.

When you have met the requirements you will receive a monthly grant for the following necessities:
— housing allowance (rent or house payment);
— personal needs (food, clothing and transportation), and
— utilities (heat, light, telephone).

In addition, allowances for the purchase or repair of needed appliances will be granted. This includes appliances considered essential for the family's health and safety. For example, if your oven breaks down you would be unable to cook for your family and in turn the health of your family would be jeopardized. And, if your furnace is not working, this may present a safety hazard. In each instance, funds may be provided to correct the problems.

The following example shows a typical monthly grant for a family of three with no income: housing allowance—$200; personal needs—$248 and utilities—$55 or a total of $503.

If a parent is working, the first $30 per month of income is not counted in reducing the grant. In addition, one-third of the remainder of the income is not counted in reducing the grant. Also, all taxes are subtracted as well as $40 for other expenses related to work such as transportation, lunches, extra clothing, etc. For example, in the above illustration the family was receiving a grant of $503 per month. Suppose a parent gets a job making $330 per month after taxes. The grant would be computed as follows:

Monthly earnings	$330.00
Exclusions: first $30	30.00
	$300.00
1/3 of remainder	100.00
	$200.00
$40 for transportation	40.00
	$160.00
Monthly earnings	$330.00
Minus exclusions	160.00
Reduction in grant	$170.00

After exclusions the grant would be reduced by $170. This means the family would receive $333 ($503 – $170). But the total family income including the grant is $663 a month ($330 income plus $333 grant).

You can expect to receive your first check about one month after you qualify for AFDC. Checks normally are mailed twice a month. While you are receiving assistance your family's circumstances will be reviewed periodically to determine whether the amount of your grant is adequate.

General Relief

The AFDC program helps needy families who have dependent children. But how about single people and couples without children? Is there a federal welfare program comparable to AFDC to help them? The answer is no. However, most counties in the U.S. operate programs designed to help needy people who are not eligible to collect AFDC. These county programs are normally called "General Relief" or "General Assistance". They are paid for by county taxes and operated by county employees. The federal government does not help pay for these relief programs.

A single person, or a family with no children can get help from General Relief programs. Eligibility requirements vary considerably from county to county. Generally, a person has to be in dire need of help, and have no other place to turn. An applicant generally cannot have cash on hand over a specified amount, usually about $50 to $100. If a car is owned, it cannot be over a certain value, usually about $500 to $1,000. Most counties require that an applicant be a resident of the county for a certain period of time, usually about 30 days. Some states will not allow benefits if the applicant quit a job or was fired within about 90 days before applying for assistance.

The assistance available under General Relief, of course, varies from county to county. However, cash benefits are much less than that available under AFDC. The maximum monthly benefit is usually under $300.

Social Services

In addition to cash assistance, state social service agencies may provide a number of other services. Among the services which may be available are:

- Information and Referral—to help you find someone in a private or public agency who can help you with a problem.
- Child Health Disability Prevention Program—to arrange for free health checkups for persons in your family under 21 years old.
- Family Planning—to help you decide whether and when you or other members of your family (including minors) want to have children.
- Child Day Care Services—to arrange for your child's care during part of the day when you are at work or in training.
- Protective Services for Children—to help in cases of neglect and abuse of children.
- Protective Services for Adults—to help in cases of neglect and abuse of adults who cannot protect themselves.
- In-Home Supportive Services—to pay for necessary care so that aged, blind or disabled persons can stay in their own homes.
- Out-of-Home Care Services for Children—to help

decide whether a child should be placed in a foster home or treatment facility; to work with the child and others in a place suitable to meet the child's needs.

- Out-of-Home Services for Adults—to help decide whether an adult should be placed in a treatment facility; to work with the adult and others in a place suitable to meet the adult's needs.

Food Program for Women, Infants and Children

This special supplemental food program for women, infants and children—called WIC—provides extra food for pregnant women, new mothers and young children who cannot afford an adequate diet. WIC supplements the regular diet with iron, protein-rich foods and infant formula.

The WIC program is administered by the Department of Agriculture which provides funds to local social service organizations. The social service organizations, in turn, provide food supplements to WIC recipients. About 2 million persons are now receiving benefits, but nutritional experts estimate that over 6 million more women, infants, and children are presently eligible for WIC benefits.

Child Support From Absent Parents

Right now about 4 million women are due child support payments but only about 2 million get the full amount owed them. Fathers are abandoning families and refusing to pay child support at alarming rates. For some fathers, the problem is the economic times that make it hard to make a dollar. Other fathers make enough to pay support but give support obligations the lowest priority. First comes other women, entertainment and the pleasures of life. Then, if any money is left, the kids might get their fair share. But all too often nothing is left over for the kids. Meanwhile, mothers struggle to keep the family intact, shouldering the full burden of the children.

How to Collect Family Support $$$

To combat this continuing problem Congress passed the Child Support Enforcement Program. Under this program, the Federal government oversees State and local government efforts to collect overdue child support payments. The efforts to collect are powerful and get results. They include:
— withholding of child support from the father's paycheck;
— placing liens on property owned by the father; and
— intercepting income tax refund checks.
This program can help if you have a child who needs the financial support of an absent father.

Establishing Paternity

The Child Support Enforcement Program can also help you establish the legal father of a child. This is extremely important because many benefits are available to a child through the legal father. These benefits include monthly social security checks upon the death, injury or retirement of the father and a large number of veterans benefits. Other benefits include inheritance from the father's estate and private pension plans.

Where To Go

Each state operates a social service agency which is funded principally by the federal government. This agency normally is called the Department of Social Services. To find the number of the local Social Services office, call the Federal Information Center nearest you. A complete list of Federal Information Centers is included at the back of this book. When calling the Social Services office, be sure to state the specific services you are interested in—AFDC, General Relief, Etc. Each service may have a different telephone number.

How To Cut Red Tape

When you visit the Social Services office to apply for AFDC, bring along certain documents which will speed up the processing of your application. As a minimum you will need proof:

—that you are living at your present address and the amount of your rent or house payment;

—that you are the parent or legal guardian of children who depend on you for support;

—of your income and resources.

Federal law requires that your application be handled promptly and that information provided to the AFDC representative be kept strictly confidential.

If you believe there has been a problem in processing your application (your application has been unfairly denied, your grant has been canceled or reduced without good cause, or your grant has been figured incorrectly) you should discuss your grievance with the AFDC representative. If your problem still is not solved to your satisfaction you are entitled to a hearing with AFDC officials and can be represented by an attorney, friend or family member.

Since most of the AFDC program is funded by the federal government, it must obey the provisions of the Civil Rights Act. If you think you are being discriminated against because of race, color, religion or national origin you can file a complaint with the Civil Rights Commission.

Questions and Answers

Q. Are most welfare children illegitimate?

A. No, but a sizable majority are. About 31 percent of the more than seven million children in welfare families are illegitimate, according to data compiled by the Social and Rehabilitation Service.

Q. Are most AFDC families black?

A. No. The largest racial group among AFDC families—48.3 percent—is white. Blacks represent 43.3 percent. Most of the remaining 8.4 percent are American Indians, Orientals and other racial minorities. Statistics show blacks comprise about 11 percent of the U.S. population, but 34 percent of the black population has incomes below the established poverty level, compared to 13 percent of the white population with income below the poverty level.

How to Collect Family Support $$$

Q. Is it true that once a family is on welfare, it always will be on welfare?

A. No, half the families on welfare have been receiving assistance for 20 months or less. Two-thirds of families have been on the rolls less than three years. About one in five families (17.7 percent) have been on welfare for five years or more, and about one in 16 families (6.1 percent) have been on the rolls 10 years or more. Current figures show that about 65 percent of cases are on welfare for the first time; about one-third of cases have been on the rolls before.

Q. Should a welfare recipient get a Social Services photo I.D. card?

A. It's free, and it's to the recipient's advantage to get one, especially when you cash your public assistance checks. Many supermarket chains and banks have instructed their employees not to cash public assistance checks without an accompaning I.D. card. It can be obtained at your district office.

Q. If a recipient does not get along with her social worker can she be assigned a new worker?

A. Yes, if the problem cannot be resolved by the worker's supervisor or the district office supervisor.

Q. Where can needy persons get immediate emergency assistance during times when a government agency is not open (weekends, holidays, etc.)?

A. Most people can get emergency help from the Salvation Army, United Way or the Catholic Church.

Q. Are mothers caring for young children forced to get jobs while collecting AFDC?

A. No. Mothers with children younger than 6 years are permitted to stay home to care for the children.

Q. What percent of the welfare mothers have children under 6?

A. About 60 percent.

Q. What percent of the U.S. population receives "needs based" assitance such as AFDC?

How to Collect Big $$$ from Uncle Sam

A. Based on a study by the Bureau of Census, about 1 in 5 Americans.

Q. Can the information on my application for AFDC be verified by the AFDC office?

A. Yes. States now have access to earnings information reported to the federal government for purposes of verifying AFDC (and food stamp) eligibility.

Chapter 12

How To Collect
Food $$$

- Howard Stone works in a tool shop five days a week and often puts in overtime. Although his job seems secure he finds it difficult to feed his family on the income he makes.
- Dave Lick recently was laid off because of a steel mill shutdown. His unemployment benefits do not provide an adequate standard of living for him, his wife and three children. In order to pay the bills, his wife has cut the food budget drastically.

Marilyn Stone and Judy Lick have been trimming the grocery bill by buying lower quality foods for their families and some days cutting meat out of the family diet completely. Howard and Dave feel confused by the economic slump our nation is facing and they don't know where to turn for help. Moreover, they do not realize that the food budget trimming their wives are doing may retard the growth of their children, destroy resistance to disease in the whole family and cause infection.

How to Collect Big $$$ from Uncle Sam

Although they do not know it, the Stones and Licks probably are eligible for federal assistance to increase their food purchasing power and maintain an adequate diet.

In 1964 Congress mandated that every American family should have an adequate nutritional diet. To carry out this goal, the Department of Agriculture was given the responsibility to administer the Food Stamp Program. Under the program eligible families get stamps that can be exchanged for food at authorized retail outlets.

Today, 22 million people are getting food stamps, costing taxpayers about $9 billion yearly. But several studies show that 27 to 39 million people may be eligible under the program. This means that millions of Americans may not be getting what Congress intended—an adequate diet.

The consequence of an inadequate diet is not immediately noticeable, but the long term effect can be disastrous. Improper diets can affect a child's educational advancement, social development and ultimately his success in life. Adults also may suffer from an inadequate diet by reduced productivity, susceptibility to disease, and even premature death.

You may ask: How could this possibly happen in America?

With mass communication one would think that every eligibile family would know about food stamps. But the Food Stamp Program suffers from the same old bureaucratic problem plaguing other federal programs. The bureaucratic administrators are not reaching out to the people to inform those who are eligible for benefits and explaining what those benefits are. Even though Congress appropriates billions of dollars to the bureaucrats to run the program, very little is spent to inform the public.

While the bureaucrats do produce food stamp pamphlets, they do little good because the pamphlets are not reaching the people. In order to reach more people who may be eligible for food stamp benefits, we have included the most important information on the Food Stamp Program in this chapter.

In brief, the program involves the issuing of stamps to eligible persons for the purchase of food for human consumption. You may qualify for food stamps if you:

—work for low wages;

—are unemployed or work part-time;

—are elderly or disabled and live on a small income, or
—receive public assistance.

Food stamps can be used to buy most foods except for certain ineligible items such as alcoholic beverages, tobacco or cigarettes and hot food that is ready to eat.

Here's How to Qualify for Food $$$

If you are single or a family household meeting certain income and resource requirements you may be eligible to receive food stamps.

Each household is allowed up to $2,000 in resources, and households of two or more with a member age 60 or over, are allowed up to $3,000 in resources.

Resources include:
—cash on hand;
—cash in bank or savings institution;
—U.S. Savings Bonds;
—stocks and bonds;
—buildings, except your home;
—land; and
—certain real or personal property.

Your family home or automobile are generally not considered a resource.

Each household's net income must be within certain limits. Income refers to any money received by members of the household, except students under 18 years old, including:
—wages;
—public assistance;
—old age benefits;
—survivors benefits;
—strike benefits;
—support payments;
—alimony;
—scholarships;
—educational grants;
—fellowships and veterans educational benefits;
—dividends;
—interest.

The following current income limits will give you an idea of whether or not you qualify for food stamps.

How to Collect Big $$$ from Uncle Sam

Income Limits for Food Stamp Eligibility

Household Size	Monthly Income Limit
1	$ 581
2	785
3	988
4	1192
5	1396
6	1599
7	1805
8	2007

For each additional person add $203
Alaska and Hawaii have higher income levels

Before you count yourself out, there are a number of deductions that reduce your monthly income for food stamp eligibility purposes. These deductions are:
—a standard deduction of $106,
—a deduction of 20 percent from gross earned income to cover work-related expenses.
—a deduction of up to $170 for "excess shelter costs". This is the total rent (or house payment) plus utilities in excess of 50 percent of the household's income after all deductions.
—a dependent care deduction up to $160 per month per dependent.

Individuals age 60 or older (or disabled) may also deduct all medical costs over $35 and any excess shelter costs beyond the regular $170 maximum.

Once these deductions are applied to income, a surprising number of so-called middle class families become eligible for food stamps. As mentioned earlier, as many as 20 million Americans are right now eligible for food stamps but are not taking advantage of them. Also, remember that income limits are adjusted periodically to keep pace with the rising cost of living. As living costs continue to soar, more and more families will become eligible for food stamp assistance.

To help you understand how food stamp eligibility and benefits are computed, we have prepared the hypothetical case of the Varga family. Don Varga has earned income of $800 monthly, with resources of $1500. Don has a wife and 5 children. Don's wife is not employed and spends full-time caring for the family. Don pays $350 monthly for rent.

The first step is to compute Don's income for food stamp eligibility purposes. In arriving at this figure, Don is allowed several deductions from his monthly income of $800. Each of the following deductions corresponds to the allowable deduction discussed above.

A. A standard deduction of $106.
B. A 20 percent deduction from monthly income, so Don's deduction is $160 (20 percent of $800).
C. A deduction of $83 for excess shelter costs ($800 minus $266 = $534; $534 ÷ 2 = $267; $350 (rent) minus $267 = $83. Since Don's wife cares for the 5 children, there is no child care expense to consider.

Don's total deductions from income are $349 ($106 + $160 + $83) so his net food stamp income is only $451 ($800 - $311.50).

To compute Don's food stamp allotment, refer to the benefit schedule below.

Food Stamp Allotment

Household Size	Amount
1	$ 90
2	165
3	236
4	300
5	356
6	427
7	472
8	540

Add $68 for each additional person

A household with no net income would receive the entire allotment. A household with some net income would receive the allotment minus 30 percent of their net income.

Don's net income is $451, and since there are 7 members of the household, Don's monthly food stamp allotment is $336.70 ($472 - $135.30 = $336.70).

Applying For Food Stamps

The Food Stamp office is required to provide an application the same day you request one. You can request an application by telephone, mail or in person. You can even have someone else get you an application.

Once you turn in your application a food stamp representative will hold a confidential interview with you (or another member of the household). If you cannot get to the Food Stamp office you may qualify to be interviewed by telephone or at home.

After your interview, the Food Stamp office will send you a written notice stating whether or not you qualify for benefits. If you qualify the notice will explain the amount of your monthly food stamp benefits. You'll get your food stamps within 30 days of your application. If your household has little or no money, you may be able to get your stamps in only a few days.

If for some reason the Food Stamp office believes you don't qualify the notice will explain why.

Benefits Wrongly Denied

If you believe your application for food stamps has been wrongly denied (or you've been shorted for food stamps) you can request a fair hearing. You can request a hearing by telephone, mail or in person. At the hearing you'll be able to explain why you disagree with the Food Stamp office.

To prepare for the hearing the Food Stamp office must give you a copy of the program regulations. You can also examine your case file to find information that will help your case. You can bring a friend or relative to the hearing with you.

Where To Go

The federal government pays for the food stamp program but it is administered by local State Social Service offices. To find the local office where food stamps are distributed, contact the Federal Information Center nearest your home. A complete list of Federal Information Centers is included at the back of this book. Ask the information specialist for the number of the Food Stamp Office nearest your home.

How To Cut Red Tape

When you apply for food stamps bring along the following information which will speed up the processing of your application. You will need:
- —social security card;
- —rent receipts, house payment book, utility bills;
- —proof of income of all in your household (latest pay slips);
- —bank books or other papers to show any savings;
- —proof of medical bills,
- —proof of tuition for education, and
- —dependent care costs such as a babysitter, day care center or attendant for a disabled adult.

Services under the Food Stamp Program are provided without discrimination on the basis of race, religion, color, national origin or political beliefs. Any person who believes he has not been treated fairly should file a complaint or request a hearing. The complaint or hearing request should be filed with the U.S. Deartment of Agriculture, Washington, D.C. An investigation will be made and corrective action will be taken if discrimination is found.

Quesions and Answers

Q. Can the recipient sell, give away, or pay old food bills with food stamps?

A. No.

Q. Can a friend or relative shop for the food stamp recipient?

A. Yes, Any member of the family or a friend may shop for the recipient if he has the recipient's I.D. card.

Q. Will owning a "luxury" car disqualify a person from eligibility for food stamps?

A. Owning an automobile worth over about $5,000 may disqualify a person from getting food stamps.

How to Collect Big $$$ from Uncle Sam

Q. How many Amercians are presently getting food stamps?

A. Accoridng to the Department of Agriculture, over 22 million Americans are receiving food stamps. This represents 1 in every 10 Americans.

Q. Can persons on strike collect Food Stamps?

A. No. Households with persons on strike are not eligible unless they were eligible the day before the strike.

Q. Specifically, what does dependent care mean?

A. Dependent care includes care for children and disabled adults if this care is needed so a household member can work, look for a job, or get training or education leading to a job.

Q. Specifically, what items can food stamps not be used to buy?

A. Alcholic beverages, tobacco products, household supplies, soaps and paper products, medicine or vitamins, hot foods such as barbeque chicken and pet foods.

Q. If a person believes he or she has been wrongly denied food stamps what further action can be taken?

A. After exhausting all efforts to get help through the food stamp office, the applicant can go to the Legal Services Corporation for help. For further information, refer to the Chapter How To Get Free Legal Services.

Chapter 13

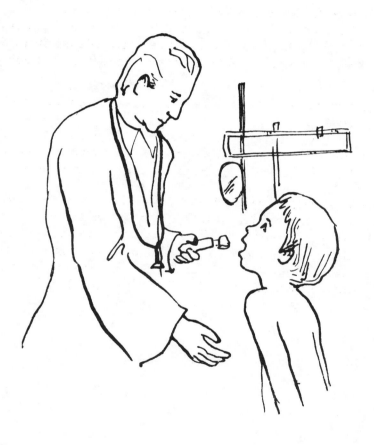

How To Collect
Medical Assistance $$$

• The Jeff Randles family really has hit on hard times. After being layed off from his job as a machine tool operator, Jeff received unemployment compensation until it expired. The day after his unemployment benefits ran out, his wife became ill and will be laid up for several weeks.

Jeff has no health insurance and his wife's medical bills are high. To keep his family together, Jeff took a temporary, part-time job as a dishwasher in a school cafeteria. But, this income was not sufficient to meet normal household costs and he had to sell many of the family's assets to put food on the table. Jeff believes he can make ends meet if he only could get help with his wife's medical bills.

The Randles family can get medical assistance through Medicaid. Medicaid is a joint federal and state-financed program designed to cover costs of medical care for persons having trouble paying their medical bills. All states are now participating in Medicaid.

Congress passed the Medicaid program in 1965 as part of the Social Security Act. The federal government pays for about 55 percent of the Medicaid program with state governments paying the rest. The Medicaid program is supported by general tax revenues.

The Medicaid program helps about 22 million Americans each year. Many of these people could not otherwise afford medical treatment and may have suffered without help. With the high cost of health care, Medicaid helps break the vicious cycle that keeps the "poor sick" and the "sick poor". Overall, the Medicaid program saves money through early detection and treatment of disease, especially in children.

Here's How To Qualify for Assistance

The eligibility requirements for Medicaid vary from state to state. In all states, persons receiving (or eligible for) AFDC can get Medicaid benefits. In most states persons collecting Supplemental Security Income (SSI) are eligible for Medicaid. Other states provide Medicaid benefits to any "medically needy" person whether or not they're receiving AFDC or SSI. The political, economic and social climate of a state to a great extent dictates the eligibility requirements for Medicaid benefits. This diversity of coverage between states creates inequities because families with similar medical needs and circumstances are treated differently.

To get an idea of whether you may be qualified for Medicaid benefits, refer to the eligibility requirements for AFDC and SSI. In addition to income requirements you normally can't have assets over $2,000 for a single person and $3,000 for a couple. A home and car of reasonable value are normally not considered in determining eligibility.

Here's What You Can Collect

While Medicaid benefits vary from state to state the following health care services are generally offered in all states.

How to Collect Medical Assistance $$$

Inpatient Hospital Services: Room and board, operating room expenses, delivery room, X-ray, lab tests, medication provided during hospital stay.

Outpatient Hospital Services: Treatment, X-rays, tests and related services.

Skilled Nursing Facility Services: Includes home and health services for persons over 21.

Physician Services: Charges for office visits, care given in hospitals and hospital outpatient departments.

Family Planning Services: Counseling and latest approved methods of birth control.

Children's Screening Examinations: To check a child's general health and early detection of disease. Helps to find and correct problems before they result in permanent disability. Also covers eye glasses, hearing aids and dental care if needed.

Children's Immunization Program: To protect children against disease such as measles, polio, whooping cough, diphtheria, smallpox and other ailments.

The above medical services are generally provided by all states under the Medicaid program. The following medical services are provided only in some states:

—prescription drugs,
—dental services,
—eye glasses,
—prosthetic devices such as pacemakers and artificial limbs,
—ambulance services,
—physical therapy,
—podiatrists, and
—mental hospitals and intermediate care facilities, clinics and private duty nursing.

Where To Go

Each state operates a social services agency which is funded principally by the federal government. This agency normally is called the Department of Social Services. To find the telephone number of the local Social Services office, call the

Federal Information Center nearest your home. A complete list of Federal Information Centers is included at the back of this book. Ask the information specialist for the telephone number of the Social Services office in your area.

How to Cut Red Tape

Applicants may request medical assistance in person, by telephone or by writing the social services department in the county where he lives.

When you go to apply for Medicaid bring along the following information which will speed up the processing of your application:
  —proof of income for all of those in the household (latest pay slips);
  —bank books or other papers to show all savings;
  —rent receipts, house payment book, utility bills, and
  —social security number.

People receiving public assistance do not have to make a separate application for Medicaid.

An individual or family found eligible will be issued an authorization card which shows the names of persons for whom the card may be used to obtain medical services. This card is issued monthly.

An applicant may request a hearing if he is dissatisfied with the action taken on his request for assistance. He should first discuss the matter with a Medicaid representative in the county. If a satisfactory agreement cannot be reached, he has the right to a hearing before a representative of the director of the state Department of Social Services. If a hearing is desired, arrangements may be made by contacting the county department or the state office.

Medicaid services are to be provided without discrimination on the basis of race, religion, color, sex, national origin or political opinions. Any person who believes that he has been subjected to such discrimination may file a complaint or request a hearing. The complaint or hearing request may be filed with the county or State Department of Social Services, or the Federal Department of Health and Human Services, Washington, D.C. A prompt investigation will be made and corrective action taken.

Questions and Answers

Q. How many children in the United States are eligible for medicaid services?

A. An estimated 10 million children, however a much smaller number are actually receiving benefits under the program.

Q. Can people over age 65 qualify for both Medicare and Medicaid?

A. Yes. In such cases, Medicaid may supplement Medicare by paying all or part of the deductible and co-insurance costs of Medicare's hospital and medical insurance. Medicare benefits must be utilized before any payments can be made under Medicaid.

Q. How is Medicaid financed?

A. The federal government pays from 50 to 81 percent of the costs incurred by the states in providing medical services under the programs.

Q. Are persons living in public institutions, such as prisons, eligible for Medicaid?

A. No. However, patients in public medical institutions may be eligible. Patients in an approved institution for tuberculosis or mental illness (public or private) may be eligible for Medicaid only if they are 65 years of age or older.

Q. In determining eligibility for Medicaid, will a home be counted in the property limitation?

A. No, a home is exempt in determining the value of a family's property.

Q. How long does it generally take for the state to process a Medicaid application?

A. The state must decide whether you're eligible within 45 days; 60 days if you're disabled.

Chapter 14

How To Help Others Through American Volunteer Programs

If you're the kind of person who wants to help people less fortunate than yourself, this chapter is for you. The U.S. government operates a number of volunteer programs designed to help needy people here in America and in foreign nations.

You don't get a lot of money for being a volunteer, but the work can be satisfying and rewarding. The compensation is mainly the personal satisfaction of knowing you are helping others. Beyond that, these programs can offer ample opportunity for foreign travel, personal growth, and a wealth of experience.

Unlike other benefit programs discussed in this book, volunteer programs demand a good deal of effort and hard work by participants. Yet, most volunteers believe they gain much more than they give.

The principal U.S. volunteer programs are:
—The Peace Corps,
—Volunteers in Service to America (VISTA),
—Retired Senior Volunteer Program,
—Foster Grandparents Program, and
—Senior Companion Program.
Each of these volunteer programs is discussed below.

237

The Peace Corps

The Peace Corps sends volunteers overseas to help countries solve social and economic problems hampering their development. Host countries specifically request Peace Corps assistance. Peace Corps volunteers offer their knowledge and skills in finding solutions to problems.

Peace Corps volunteers work and live with people of developing nations around the world. Volunteers work to solve some of the following problems.

Education. Developing nations want knowledge and skills. Volunteers meet this need with classroom instruction and by teaching vocational skills. Subjects include family planning and programs for the handicapped.

Economic development. Volunteers help develop community services and advise small businesses. Engineering-minded volunteers help in road design and construction and sanitation systems development.

Food and Water. Developing nations need food and water. Peace Corps volunteers help develop water supplies, fishery and livestock production.

Health. Volunteers work on disease control, immunization and nutrition projects. They help remote villages create community health services of their own.

Qualifications

Peace Corps volunteers must be at least 18. There is no upper age limit. Volunteers must be willing to devote two years of service to others who need help. Married couples can serve if both work and they can be placed together. Handicapped persons are eligible. Some of the most successful volunteers have been handicapped.

There is no education or degree requirement for many assignments. However, professional experience or specialized training is helpful. If you lack a specific skill the Peace Corps will teach you a skill. As part of your training, you'll learn about the culture of the host country, and how to speak the local language.

How to Help Others Through
American Volunteer Programs

What Volunteers Get

The Peace Corps pays for your travel and medical needs. While on assignment, you'll receive an allowance to cover housing, food and the essentials. You'll also get about $300 a month spending money. And, when you come home, you get $125 for every month you served, including the training period. This will help you get started again.

The real compensation you get is valuable professional and personal experience. A chance to travel and broaden yourself and as much responsibility as you can handle. You'll get plenty of independence and more challenge than most people face in a lifetime.

VISTA

Volunteers work here in the U.S. with urban and rural poor persons to find innovative solutions to community problems. Volunteers actually live in the communities they serve.

VISTA volunteers serve in the 50 states, Puerto Rico, the Virgin Islands, Guam and American Samoa. Volunteers organize community action groups or work with established organizations. Some major areas volunteers work to improve are:

Health/Nutrition. Malnutrition is a widespread problem among poor, especially the elderly. Volunteers help persons get food stamps, or assist in providing food for elderly persons. Volunteers also work with local organizations to promote better health services to the poor.

Knowledge/Skills. Volunteers work with tribes to improve education for Indian children. They also work with migrant workers to help start programs for handicapped children. Volunteers serve in Appalachia areas starting community service programs.

Economic Development. Volunteers work with low-income groups to help them become more self-sufficient. Some activities include counseling small business in management and financial matters.

How to Collect Big $$$ from Uncle Sam

Qualifications

Volunteers must be 18 or older and willing to live and work in an assigned community for at least one year.

Specific college degrees are not required. However, the capacity for hard work, imagination and patience is required.

What Volunteers Get

VISTA pays for transportation, training, and medical care. A spending-money allowance is also provided. The amount varies from region to region. When you finish, you get $50 for every month of VISTA service including periods of training. This will help you get started again.

Another important benefit is that repayment of many federally-insured student loans can be deferred during VISTA service.

Retired Senior Volunteer Program

These older volunteers serve in various community activities to improve the daily lives of the needy. They work in hospitals, nursing homes, schools, and other community services.

About 250,000 volunteers serve in all 50 states, Puerto Rico, the Virgin Islands, and Guam serving in a wide variety of community service projects. General areas of service include health-care, nutrition, and fixed income counseling. Specific assignments could include:
— distribution of donated books to hospital patients and prison inmates;
— visiting patients in local hospitals;
— assisting elderly persons in preparing income tax returns.

Qualifications and What Volunteers Get

Volunteers must be 60 or older and retired. There is no income or education requirement. Volunteers select assignments from a broad list of available service activities.

Volunteers are provided with pre-service orientation and training before assignments. They are paid a transportation allowance to and from assignment sites.

Foster Grandparents Program

Foster grandparents offer guidance and companionship to handicapped children. They visit children in hospitals, institutions, day-care centers and private homes. Volunteers normally are assigned to work with 2 children. Visiting sessions usually last about 4 hours a day. Foster grandparents generally work 5 days a week.

Foster grandparents can offer the children wealth of experience and knowledge. Foster grandparents work with the children keeping track of their progress and reporting to professional staff members.

Qualifications and What Volunteers Get

Foster grandparent volunteers must be 60 or older (men or women) and be able to devote 20 hours a week to helping children. Volunteers are given an initial 40-hour training period followed by monthly on-the-job training sessions. Foster grandparents are provided with spending money, meals, accident insurance, and an annual physical examination.

The most important payment is the satisfaction of helping handicapped children and seeing the progress resulting from your efforts. Foster grandparents are considered part of the team of professionals.

Senior Companion Program

Volunteers help homebound elderly persons having physical or mental handicaps continue independent living. They also help elderly persons obtain available community services. Other volunteers serve in institutions, working with persons who are about to return home. Companion volunteers help needy elderly persons in many ways including shopping, home budgeting and providing transportation for doctors' appointments.

Qualifications and What Volunteers Get

The Senior Companion Program is open to men and women 60 years or older who can devote about 20 hours a week assisting needy elderly persons in their community. Volunteers receive tax-free expense money, transportation allowances, hot meals and an annual physical examination. They also receive 40 hours of orientation, and monthly on-the-job training.

Where To Go

The Peace Corps and VISTA maintain a toll-free number where you can call to get further information. This number is 1-800-424-8580. A staff member will be standing by to take your call and answer any questions you have.

As for the Retired Senior Volunteer Program, the Foster Grandparent Program, and the Senior Companion Program, call the Federal Information Center nearest your home. A completed list of numbers is included at the back of this book. An information specialist will give you the number to call for further information on these volunteer programs.

Chapter 15

How To Collect a Loan to Start a Business in a Foreign Country

The Overseas Private Investment Corporation (OPIC) is an independent U.S. Government corporation which helps Americans finance businesses in friendly foreign countries around the world. Formed in 1971, OPIC has helped countless small (and large) businesses get started in over 90 developing countries. Some of these countries include Brazil, Greece, Granada, Costa Rica, Jamaica, Taiwan, Trinidad and Venezuela.

Why does Uncle Sam want to help American businesses get started in a foreign country? The answer may surprise you: Your business can help the friendly foreign nation develop economically—and this could also benefit the U.S. as a whole. As the developing country becomes more prosperous, it will be able to afford U.S. products. When a foreign nation buys U.S. goods it helps the United States economy by creating jobs and improving our balance of payments.

U.S. exports to developing nations have grown substantially over the years to a present annual figure of over $50 million. Developing countries are now America's fastest growing market. Hence, acceleration of the economic growth of these developing nations is very much in the interest of the U.S. That's why Uncle Sam will bend over backwards to get your busines started in a foreign land.

In addition to helping America, developing nations also benefit from having American business on its soil. For example, new businesses provide opportunities for more jobs and increasing prosperity. New businesses help accelerate the economic and social development of the host country. That's why many developing nations are crying for the establishment of American small businesses on their soil.

Many different kinds of OPIC financed businesses are right now operating in friendly foreign countries around the globe. Some examples of these American-owned businesses include:

—a shrimping fleet business in Nigeria,
—cattle breeding ranch in Argentina,
—a helicopter transportation service in Indonesia,
—a popsicle business in Nigeria,
—a fertilizer plant in India, and
—a cattle ranch in Morocco.

OPIC loans are available to start a business in over 90 approved foreign countries. These nations are not presently as economically advanced as the United States; however, they have the potential to grow and become important trading partners.

In addition to helping you start a business in a foreign nation, OPIC can also insure your business against financial loss resulting from war, revolution, or expropriation. This is an everpresent risk when doing business in a foreign country. OPIC has already paid U.S. companies millions of dollars due to losses from economic or social upheavals in a host country.

How To Qualify

To qualify for OPIC financial assistance to start (or expand) a business in a friendly foreign country, several requirements must be met. First, the business venture must be in the mutual interest of both the foreiogn country and the

How to Collect a Loan to Start a
Business in a Foreign Country

U.S. The business must be approved by the host country and promote its social and economic development.

OPIC considers various factors in deciding whether a business is in the best interest of a friendly foreign country. Some of these factors include whether the proposed American business will:

—increase the availability of goods and services at a lower price or better quality,

—create employment or training opportunities,

—promote managerial and technological skills,

—increase savings or increase tax revenues,

—stimulate local business in the host country.

Hence, a wide variety of business ventures qualify for OPIC loan assistance. Some of the business areas qualifying include agricultural, manufacturing, fishing, forestry, mining, energy development, processing, storage, even hotels, motels and tourist facilities.

OPIC-financed business ventures must be in the economic and political interest of the U.S. For example, applications for OPIC loan help will be turned down if the proposed business could result in loss of U.S. jobs, or have an adverse impact on our balance of payments. However, if you plan on starting a small business, you probably don't have to worry about its impact on the U.S. economy. This is a concern only of larger business ventures.

OPIC has certain ownership and finance requirements for business ventures it finances. To qualify for loan assistance a business firm must be either owned solely by U.S. investors, or owned jointly with local citizens of the host nation.

Business ventures must be soundly financed to assure the ongoing success of the enterprise. The ratio of debt to equity is an important financial consideration. Ratios of 60 percent borrowed funds to 40 percent equity are generally considered financially stable.

Feasibility Surveys

OPIC may help pay for studies that help determine whether a particular business venture is feasible and likely to succeed. Qualified businesses are eligible for OPIC feasibility study assistance for amounts up to $50,000.

Business Ventures Excluded From
OPIC Financial Assistance

OPIC may deny loan assistance to certain business ventures. These exclusions may vary from time to time depending on political considerations. Presently, OPIC will not provide loan assistance for any business producing certain military equipment or alcoholic beverages. In addition, OPIC does not generally finance housing, apartment or condominium projects.

Here's What You Can Collect

OPIC loan assistance generally ranges from about $50,000 up to $50 million. OPIC has two programs for providing business loans: (1) direct loans, and (2) guaranteed loans.

Under the direct program, OPIC uses its own funds to provide the business loan. Direct loans are generally used to finance smaller business ventures. The loan amounts generally range between $50,000 up to about $4 million. The interest rate for direct loans is generally about two percentage points above the yield of U.S. Treasury securities. The repayment schedule will vary depending on the type of business involved and the cash flow generated. Generally, loans are made for periods of between 5 and 12 years.

OPIC uses its guaranteed loan program to finance larger business ventures ranging up to $50 million. Under the guaranteed loan program, OPIC assures a bank or other financial institution that it will repay the loan in case the business cannot do so. This guarantee of payment is backed by the full faith and credit of the U.S. Because the U.S. government takes all the risk, many banks and financial institutions are more than happy to finance your business.

The interest rate on business loans varies depending on market conditions and the risks involved with the loan. In addition, OPIC charges the borrower a small loan fee figured on the unpaid loan balance. The loan repayment period is generally between 5 and 21 years.

How to Collect a Loan to Start a
Business in a Foreign Country

Where To Go and How To Cut Red Tape

As a first step in obtaining a loan call OPIC's small business information office. The toll-free number is 1-800-424-OPIC. An OPIC information officer will be available to answer your questions.

After discussing your loan needs you may be asked to submit some preliminary information on the proposed business venture. OPIC officials will review the information and decide whether it qualifies for loan help.

The preliminary information you should submit to OPIC should include:

—name, location and type of project;

—background and financial status of principal investors;

—information on the product or service you plan to sell, including source of supply, expected sales or output, distribution channels, and projected market share;

—summary of costs and sources of capital goods;

—proposed financing plan, including the OPIC financial assistance required;

—a brief statement of the expected contribution your business will make to the economic and social development of the host country.

If the proposed business venture qualifies, you will be asked to fill out a formal application giving more detailed information. The time required for review and approval of your application can vary between one month to six months. A major factor affecting approval time is the completeness of the information on your application.

OPIC officials claim they are more than willing to work with investors to get a business venture started as soon as possible. Persons wanting further information can write: Information Officer, Overseas Private Investment Corporation, 1129 Twentieth Street NW, Washington, D.C. 20521.

Chapter 16

How To Get
Good-Paying Federal Jobs

During economic slumps when business firms are laying people off, the federal government often increases its work force. This paradox occurs because as economic conditions worsen more people are needed in the federal ranks to administer programs to help those who are out of work.

Congress also may appropriate more money for federal positions during recessionary periods to absorb those who were laid off by the private (business) sector.

Types of Jobs Available

Many interesting and good paying jobs are available in the federal government. For example, federal employees inspect foods and drugs; they maintain national parks; they take care of disabled veterans, and they explore the ocean depths and reaches of space. In fact almost all types of occupations found in private industry also are found in federal civil service.

Although a variety of federal jobs are vacant at almost any point in time, few people know they exist. Most people when seeking employment turn to local newspapers for information about available positions because business firms regularly place newspaper ads in an effort to attract qualified applicants. This, however, is not the case with the federal government.

The federal government, as a matter of policy, seldom publicizes job vacancies. Instead it waits for qualified applicants to come to it; and the problem is that most people don't know where to go or how to apply for a federal job.

This chapter explains how to find out what federal jobs are available and how to apply and qualify for them.

Office of Personnel Management

The Office of Personnel Management acts as an "employment agency" for the federal government. The personnel office administers a merit staffing system whereby appointments to jobs are made on the basis of demonstrated ability in competition with other applicants. This system assures that federal jobs are filled on the basis of qualifications and fitness rather than personal preference or political considerations.

Out of more than 3 million federal employees, only about 12 percent are stationed in Washington, D.C., where most federal agencies are headquartered. Most federal employees work at field offices which are scattered throughout the United States, its territories and some foreign countries.

Finding Job Openings

The Office of Personnel Management operates a network of federal job information centers which maintain complete listings of federal job vacancies. Openings for specific types of positions are announced at these centers. The announcement tells about the jobs—what experience or education you must have before your application will be accepted, whether a written test is required, where the jobs are located and what the pay is.

The Federal Job Information Center will send you a Job Opportunity Listing which highlights the important aspects of federal jobs available in your area. For example, the listing shows the job titles, job locations and pay grade. You can scan this listing and pick the jobs you may be interested in. You can then request the specific announcement to get full details on the job opening.

You can apply for some jobs by directly contacting the federal agency you want to work for. Most temporary jobs are filled this way. What's more federal agencies may consider you for some jobs without competition from the general public. To be hired directly through the federal agency you must be a former federal employee, Vietnam era veteran or 30 percent or more disabled veteran, returning Peace Corps Volunteer or disabled person.

Here's How to Qualify for Jobs

Before you apply, read the announcement carefully. Many disappointed applicants would have been saved time and trouble if they had read the announcement carefully. If the announcement says that only persons with two years of experience along certain lines will qualify and you don't have that experience, don't apply.

Experience credit may be granted an applicant for unpaid volunteer work such as in community, cultural, social service and professional association activities on the same basis as for paid experience, if it is of the type and level acceptable under the announcement. To receive credit, you must show the actual time, such as number of hours a week, spent in such activities.

If you're a veteran of the military service, you may be eligible for a Veterans' preference. Simply stated, you are given preference over non-veterans in consideration for a federal job.

If you are sure that you meet the requirements listed in the announcement, the next step is to fill out the application forms. At first you will only have to fill out a small card, but eventually you will be asked to fill out a 2- or a 4-page personal qualifications statement. It is very important that you do this carefully. Make sure you answer every question. If you don't, the Personnel Office will have to write to you asking for the information, thus delaying your chances to get a job.

How to Collect Big $$$ from Uncle Sam

For many positions, written tests are not required and applicants are rated only on their training and experience.

Be sure to follow the instructions in the announcement as to when and where to send your personal qualifications statement. Be sure to send it to the right office before the closing date.

If the announcement says that a written test will be given, you will get a notice in the mail telling you when and where to go for the test. The written test will be practical. It will test your ability to do the job that you applied for or it will test your ability to learn how to do it.

If you fail a written test, you usually can take it again as long as applications are being accepted for it.

You will be notified whether or not you qualified in the examination by the office that announced it. Be sure to notify that office of changes in essential information, such as address, name or availability. When writing, use your full name, the title of the announcement, the rating you received and your date of birth.

People who are found to meet the requirements in the announcement are called eligibles. Their names are put on a list of other eligibles and their chances of getting a job depend on how well he or she meets the requirements of a specific position and how fast agencies are filling jobs from the list.

An appointing officer makes a choice from among the top three available people on the list. If the selected person accepts the appointment, the names of the others are put back on the list to be considered for future openings.

If you are offered a job, a letter or telegram will show what kind of appointment is involved. Most appointments are either career, term, career-conditional or temporary. You should know what each of these mean.

A temporary appointment does not ordinarily last more than one year. A temporary worker can't be promoted and can't transfer to another job. And temporary employees are not under the retirement system.

A term appointment is made for work on a specific project that will last more than one year, but less than four years. A term employee can be promoted or reassigned to other positions within the project for which that employee was hired. He also is not under the retirement system.

If you accept a temporary or term appointment, your name will stay on the list of eligibles from which you were appointed. This means that you will remain eligible for permanent jobs that normally are filled by career-conditional or career appointments.

A career-conditional appointment after three years' continuous service leads to a career appointment. For the first year, the employee serves a probationary period. During this time, it must be demonstrated that the employee can do a satisfactory job or he or she may be dismissed for failure to do so. Career-conditional employees have promotion and transfer privileges. After career-conditional employees complete their probation, they cannot be removed except for cause. However, in reduction-in-force (layoff) actions, career-conditional employees are dismissed ahead of career employees.

A career employee serves a probationary period, as described above, and has promotion and transfer privileges. After completion of the probation, this type of employee is in the last group to be affected in layoffs.

Layoffs may occur if there is a cut in appropriations, a decrease in work or some similar factor. Four things determine whether an employee goes or stays. They are:
1. Type of appointment.
2. Whether the employee is a veteran.
3. Seniority.
4. Job performance.

Here's What Pay You Can Expect

Once you get a federal job appointment, you may wonder what pay you can expect. Government policy is that salaries of federal employees should be comparable to those paid by private employers for work at the same level of difficulty and responsibility.

The federal government has several pay plans. For most trade positions, wages are set from time to time to bring them into line with prevailing wages paid in the same locality by private industry. A few agencies (The Tennessee Valley Authority, U.S. Postal Service, and Department of State) and a few classes of employees (doctors, dentists and nurses in the Department of Medicine and Surgery of the Veterans Administration) have other pay plans.

About 45 percent of all federal employees are paid under the General Schedule (GS), which applies to most white-collar employees and to protective employees, such as guards. Positions are graded by number according to the type of position, starting with GS-1 and going up to GS-18.

Each grade has a set salary range; thus the grade of a position sets the pay. Employees usually are hired at the first level of a grade. If they do their work at an acceptable level, they receive within-grade increases at intervals. Employees may be awarded additional within-grade increases for exceptionally meritorious work.

Aside from pay, federal employees enjoy other benefits. Most federal employees earn annual leave for vacation and other purposes according to the number of years they have been in the federal service. They are:

—13 days a year for the first three years;

—20 days a year for the next 12 years; and

—26 days a year after 15 years.

Sick leave is earned at the rate of 13 days a year. You can use this leave for illnesses serious enough to keep you away from your work and for appointments with a doctor, dentist or optician. Sick leave that is not used can be saved for future use.

Federal employees also enjoy holidays off such as New Year's Day, Washington's birthday, Memorial Day, the Fourth of July, Labor Day, Veterans Day, Columbus Day, Thanksgiving and Christmas.

How to Cut Red Tape

As a first step in finding a federal job, call your local Federal Job Information Center. To find the telephone number of the local office call the Federal Information Center nearest your home. A complete list of Federal Information Centers is included in the back of this book.

How to Get Good-Paying Federal Jobs

Some Federal Job Information Centers provide a recorded message of new job openings. This will give you a quick overview of what's available in your area. You can request the job center to send you appropriate job announcements, application forms and pamphlets. Using the telephone can save you a lot of time and trouble.

Federal job information centers are open Monday through Friday, except holidays, and the best time to call is from 9 to 11 a.m. or 2 to 4 p.m.

The federal job information center can provide information on:

—federal employment opportunities outlook;
—vacancies in shortage categories and occupations in high demand;
—job requirements and qualications;
—application and examination procedures, and
—special employment counseling services.

Questions and Answers

Q. To be considered for a federal job, what age range must an individual fall in?

A. The usual minimum age is 18, but for most jobs high school graduates may apply at 16. If you are 16 or 17 and are out of school, but not a high school graduate, you may be hired only (1) if you have successfully completed a formal training program preparing you for work, and (2) if you have been out of school for at least three months. Remember, job opportunities are best for those who graduate.

Q. May handicapped individuals apply and be tested for federal jobs?

A. Yes. Whenever it is appropriate, special examinations for the handicapped are arranged to assure their abilities are properly assesed and they are not discriminated against because of their handicaps.

Q. Are any groups of individuals given preference for federal employment?

A. Yes. If you are a veteran, you may be eligible for additional benefits in getting and keeping a government job. For example, veteran preference will add extra points to an individual's passing score on examinations. The pamphlet "Opportunities in the Federal Service for Veterans," gives more information about who is entitled to veterans preference and what its benefits are. It is available at Federal Job Information Centers.

Q. Can more than one member of a family work for the federal government?

A. No, unless you are entitled to veteran preference, you generally may not be appointed (except temporarily) if two or more members of your family who live under the same roof have career-conditional federal appointments.

Q. Can a federal worker get involved in political activities?

A. The law protects federal employees from improper political pressures by placing certain restrictions on their political activity. As a federal worker you may, of course, vote as you please and express your opinions as a private citizen.

Q. Can federal employees engage in other work while in government employment?

A. Yes. As a federal employee, you are permitted to take another job or to engage in any other work activity which does not interfere with your government employment. Officials at your agency will help you decide if a particular bit of "moonlighting" will or will not be compatible with your regular job.

Q. Can a federal employee transfer between government agencies?

A. One advantage of working for the federal government is the possibility of moving to a better job by transferring from one agency to another. Agencies consider the qualifications of an employee for promotion as higher grade positions become vacant.

Chapter 17

How To Use The Privacy Act
To Get Documents The Government
Has On You

The federal government maintains a vast storehouse of information on private citizens. Chances are the federal government has at least one file on you. For example, the government has a file on you if:

—you ever applied for or collected from social security, supplemental security income, medicare or any other federal government assistance program,
—you worked for or were a member of any branch of the federal government,
—you were ever arrested by local, state, or federal authorities and your fingerprints were taken.

What's more, if you have ever engaged in any activity that could be of interest to the government such as picketing, protesting or marching for some cause, you are probably on file.

Until 1974 citizens did not have access to any information the government held on them. But now, thanks to the Privacy Act of 1974, you can easily obtain any document, record, or file the federal government has on you.

How to Collect Big $$$ from Uncle Sam

Background on The Privacy Act

The Privacy Act of 1974 was passed by the Congress after many years of public debate over the threat posed by the federal government's accumulation of vast amounts of information on American citizens. During the 1960s the Congress held hearings and conducted investigations on the government's information gathering methods. The Congress found that the federal bureaucrats had developed streamlined ways to pry into a citizen's private life. These information gathering techniques included telephone tapping, use of lie detectors on federal employees, maintenance of federal data banks and military spying on private citizens.

The purpose of the privacy act is to give private citizens control over and easy access to the information collected on them by the federal government. The rights available to you under the Privacy Act could be powerful. The Privacy Act could be helpful in obtaining federal benefits that are rightfully yours but are being denied by the federal bureauracy. For example, let's say you have applied for disability benefits under social security or supplemental security income but have been turned down. The bureaucrats have not clearly explained why you are being denied benefits. You may have been examined by a government doctor. But you are not sure what the examination showed. Now, because of the Privacy Act, you can get any record—including medical records—that the government is keeping on you. You can examine the records, or have someone else, such as your family doctor, look at them. Then you can determine for yourself what is really going on.

Government benefits are sometimes denied because the government is keeping inaccurate information on an applicant. For example, let's say you are denied social security survivor's benefits because the government has your age improperly recorded. They think you are 50 instead of 60, your true age. You can request the Social Security Administration to provide you with documents being used to determine your age. Under the Privacy Act they must give you the specific information you request.

How to Use the Privacy Act to Get Documents the Government Has on You

Making A Request

You can make a request for documents in writing, by telephone, or in person. One advantage to writing is that it enables you to document the dates and content of the request, and the agency's reply. This could be helpful in the event of future disputes. Be sure to keep copies of all correspondence concerning the request.

Your request should be addressed to the head of the agency which maintains the records you want. Be sure to write "Privacy Act Request" on the bottom, left-hand corner of the envelope. Include your name and permanent address. Your request should always give as much information as possible about the record you are seeking. The more specific the inquiry, the faster you can expect a response. If you want access to a record concerning your application for a government loan, for example, you should give the date of the application, the place where the application was filed, the specific use to which the loan was to be put, and any relevant identifying numbers.

Most agencies require some proof of identity before they will release records. Therefore, when making your request, it would be a good idea to provide some identifying data such as a copy of an official document containing your complete name and address. Remember to sign your request since a signature provides a form of identification. You might also want to consider having your signature notarized. If you are seeking access to a record which has something to do with a government benefit, it could be helpful to give your social security number. Some agencies may request additional information from you, such as a document containing your signature and/or photograph depending upon the nature and sensitivity of the material to be released.

Anyone who "knowingly and willfully" requests or receives access to a record about an individual "under false pretenses" is subject to criminal penalties. This means that a person can be prosecuted for deliberately attempting to obtain someone else's record.

Fees

Under the Privacy Act, agencies are permitted to charge fees to cover the actual costs of copying records. However, they are not allowed to charge for the time spent in locating records or in preparing them for your inspection. Copying fees are about 10 cents a page for standard copies of 8½ x 11 inches and 8½ x 14 inches.

The Privacy Act clearly intended that access to records not be obstructed by costs. So, if you feel that an agency's fees are beyond your means, you should ask for a reduction or waiver of the charges.

Sample Request Letter

Agency Head or Privacy Act Officer
Title
Agency
Agency Address
City, State, Zip

Re: Privacy Act Request

Dear _____:

Under the provisions of the Privacy Act of 1974, 5 U.S.C. 522a, I hereby request a copy of (or: access to) _____ (describe as accurately and specifically as possible the record or records you want, and provide all the relevant information you have concerning them).

If there are any fees for copying the records I am requesting, please inform me before you fill the request. (Or, . . . please supply the records without informing me if the fees do not exceed $_____.)

If all or any part of this request is denied, please cite the specific exemption(s) which you think justifies your refusal to release the information. Also, please inform me of your agency's appeal procedure.

In order to expedite consideration of my request, I am enclosing a copy of _____ (some document of identification).

Thank you for your prompt attention to this matter.

Sincerely,

Signature
Name
Address
City, State, Zip

How to Use the Privacy Act to Get Documents the Government Has on You

Requirements for Agency Responses

The Privacy Act imposes no time limits for agency responses. However, the guidelines for implementing the Act's provisions state that a request for records should be acknowledged within 10 working days of its receipt. Further, the acknowledgment should indicate whether or not access will be granted and, if so, when and where. The records themselves should be produced within 30 working days. And, if this is not possible the agency should tell you the reason and advise you when it is anticipated that access will be granted.

Most agencies will do their best to comply with these time requirements. Therefore, it is probably advisable to tolerate some reasonable delay before taking further action.

Disclosure of Records

Agencies are required to release records to you in a form that is "comprehensible". This means that all computer codes and unintelligible notes must be translated into understandable language.

You can examine your records in person or have copies mailed to you, whichever you prefer. If you decide that you want to see your records at the agency but the agency does not allow this, you cannot later be charged copying fees. If you look at your records in person, you are entitled to take someone along with you. If you do this, you will probably be asked to sign a statement authorizing the agency to disclose and discuss the records in the other person's presence.

Special rules apply to the release of medical records. In most cases, when you request your medical records, you will be permitted to see them directly. However, if it appears that the information contained in the medical records could have an "adverse effect" on you, the agency may give them to someone of your choice, such as your family doctor, who would be willing to discuss them with you.

Exemptions

The Congress made certain types of records exempt from availability under the Privacy Act. These exemptions include:

— Files maintained by the Central Intelligence Agency (CIA),

— Files maintained by federal criminal law enforcement agencies,

— Classified documents on national defense,

— Secret Service intelligence files, and

— Files used solely for statistical purposes.

Keep in mind that federal agencies are not required to invoke all the exemptions allowed them. Therefore, if you really want to see a particular record, go ahead and make your Privacy Act request.

Appeal Procedure for Denial of Access

The Privacy Act provides no standard procedure for appealing denials to release information. However, many agencies have their own regulations governing this. If your request is denied, the agency should advise you of its appeal procedure and tell you to whom to address your appeal. If this information is not provided, you should address your appeal to the head of the agency. Include a copy of the rejection letter along with a copy of your original request and state your reason for wanting access, if you think it will help. If an agency withholds all or any part of your record, it must tell you which Privacy Act exemption it is claiming as justification.

Sample Letter for Appealing Denial of Access

Agency Head or Appeal Officer
Title
Agency
Agency Address
City, State, Zip

Re: Privacy Act Appeal

Dear _____:

On _____ (date), I received a letter from _____ (individual's name) of your agency denying my request for access to _____ (description of the information sought). Enclosed is a copy of this denial along with a copy of my original request. By this letter, I am appealing the denial.

Since Congress intended that information sought under the Privacy Act of 1974, 5 U.S.C. 552a, be released unless it could be withheld under an exemption, I hereby request that you consider this appeal.

(Optional) I am seeking access to these records (state the reasons for your request if you think it will assist you in obtaining the information and give any arguments you might have to justify its release).

Thank you for your prompt attention to this matter.

> Sincerely,
>
> Signature
> Name
> Address
> City, State, Zip

Amending Your Records

The Privacy Act requires agencies to keep all personal records on individuals accurate, complete, up-to-date and relevant. Therefore, if after seeing your record, you wish to correct, delete or add information to it, you should write to the agency official who released the information to you, giving the reasons you might have to justify the changes. Some agencies may allow you to request these corrections in person or by telephone.

While you should have no trouble in determining whether the information contained in your file is accurate, complete, and up-to-date, it might be somewhat more difficult to ascertain whether it is "relevant" to the agency's purpose. However, if you have doubts about anything you find in your records, you should challenge the information and force the agency to justify its retention. There is one thing in particular you might look for: The Privacy Act prohibits the maintenance of information concerning how an individual exercises his first amendment rights unless (1) the maintenance is authorized by statute or the individual to whom it pertains, or (2) unless it is pertinent to and within the scope of an authorized law enforcement activity. In most instances, you would be on solid ground in challenging any information in your file describing your religious and political beliefs, activities, and associations, unless you have voluntarily given this information to the agency.

The act requires agencies to acknowledge in writing all requests for amending records within 10 working days of receipt. In addition, individuals must be notified what action will be taken regarding the requested amendments. Moreover, agencies are directed to complete action on all such requests within 30 working days of receipt.

If the agency agrees to amend your record, it must notify all past and future recipients of the changes made. However, unless the agency has kept some record of disclosures prior to September 27, 1975—the date the act went into effect—it might not be possible for it to notify all prior recipients.

Sample Letter for Request to Amend Records

Agency Head or Privacy Officer
Title
Agency
Agency Address
City, State, Zip

Re: Privacy Act Rquest to Amend Records

Dear _____:

By letter dated _____, I requested access to (use same description as in request letter).

In viewing the information forwarded to me, I found that it was (inaccurate) (incomplete) (outdated) (not relevant to the purpose of your agency).

Therefore, pursuant to the Privacy Act of 1974, 5 U.S.C. 552a, I hereby request that you amend my record in the following manner: (Describe errors, new information, irrelevance, etc.)

In accordance with the Act, I look forward to an acknowledgment of this request within 10 working days of its receipt.

Thank you for your assistance in this matter.

Sincerely,

Signature
Name
Address
City, State, Zip

Appeal Procedure for
Agency Refusal to Amend Records

If an agency refuses to amend your records, it must advise you of the reasons for the refusal as well as the appeal procedures available to you within the agency. It must also tell you to whom to address your appeal. Amendment appeals are usually handled by agency heads or a senior official appointed by the agency head.

Your appeal letter should include a copy of your original request along with a copy of the agency's denial. You should also include any additional information you might have to substantiate your claims regarding the disputed material.

A decision on your appeal must be rendered within 30 working days from the date of receipt. In unusual circumstances, such as the need to obtain information from retired records or another agency, an additional 30 days may be granted.

If the agency denies your appeal and still refuses to make the changes you request, you have the right to file a brief statement giving your reasons for disputing the record. This statement of disagreement then becomes part of the record and must be forwarded to all past and future recipients of your file. However, as previously noted, unless the agency has kept some record of disclosures prior to September 27, 1975, it might not be possible to notify all past recipients. The agency is also permitted to place in your file a short explanation of its refusal to change the record. This, too, becomes a part of your permanent file and is forwarded along with your statement of disagreement

If your appeal is denied or if the agency fails to act upon it within the specified time, you can take your case to court.

Sample Letter for Appealing
Agency's Refusal to Amend Records

Agency Head or Designated Official
Title
Agency
Agency Address
City, State, Zip

Re: Privacy Act Appeal

Dear _____,

By letter dated _____ to Mr. _____
(official to whom you addressed your amendment request),
I requested that information held by your agency concerning me be amended. This request was denied, and I am
hereby appealing that denial. For your information, I am
enclosing a copy of my request letter along with a copy of
Mr. _____'s reply. (If you have any additional
relevant information, send it too.)

I trust that upon consideration of my reasons for seeking
the desired changes, you will grant my request to amend
the disputed material. However, in the event you refuse this
request, please advise me of the agency procedures for filing a statement of disagreement.

(Optional) I plan to initiate legal action if my appeal is
denied.

Thank you for your prompt attention to this matter.

Sincerely,

Signature
Name
Address
City, State, Zip

Taking Your Case To Court

Under the Privacy Act, you can sue an agency for refusing
to release your records, for denial of your appeal to amend a
record, and for failure to act upon your appeal within the
designated time. You can also sue if you are adversely
affected by the agency's failure to comply with any of the
provisions of the Act. For example, if you are denied a job
promotion due to inaccurate, incomplete, outdated or irrele-
vant information in your file, you can contest this action in
court.

How to Use the Privacy Act to Get Documents
the Government Has on You

Judicial rulings favorable to you could result in the release or amendment of the records in question. In addition, you can obtain money damages if it is proven that you have been adversely affected as a result of the agency's intentional and willful disregard of the Act's provisions. You might also be awarded court costs and attorney fees.

If and when you do decide to go to court, you can file suit in the federal district court where you reside or do business or where the agency records are situated. Or you can take the case to the U.S. District Court in the District of Columbia. Under the Privacy Act, you are required to bring suit within 2 years from the date of the violation you are challenging. However, in cases where the agency has materially or willfully misrepresented information, the statute of limitations runs 2 years from the date you discover the misrepresentation.

Chapter 18

$ $

$ $

$ $

$

$

$

How To Collect Free
Information, Services
and Items

The federal government's activities have reached into almost every realm of human endeavor, from underwater research to space exploration. These vast operations have been ongoing for about 200 years both here and across the globe. Arising from these federal government activities through the years has been an enormous accumulation of (1) information on almost every imaginable subject; (2) services that are little-known to the general public; and (3) useful items you can obtain free, just by asking.

This chapter tells you how to collect thousands of dollars worth of useful information, services and items from Uncle Sam. It tells you the specific government source to contact to get exactly what you want. And in some cases, you are given a toll-free telephone number which puts you in contact with the people in government who can give you fast, personal attention.

Free Financial and Economic Newsletters — Every Month

You can get free monthly newsletters on latest business conditions affecting you and your family.

The 12 Federal Reserve Banks, making up the Federal Reserve System, publish monthly newsletters which discuss various business, economic and financial matters. This information can be a valuable tool for forecasting possible periods of coming severe inflation or economic depression. Many investors use this free information in making decisions on the stock market and other investments.

You could easily pay several hundreds of dollars a year to get comparable data from private sources.

To get monthly copies of these valuable newsletters simply write one or more of the Federal Reserve Banks listed below and ask to get their newsletter on a regular basis. The most popular newsletter (and probably the best) is the one published by the Federal Reserve Bank in St. Louis, MO. Another good newsletter, which is concise and extremely easy to read and understand, is the one published by the Federal Reserve Bank of Cleveland.

To be sure that you get the newsletter you like best, you could request one copy from each of the 12 banks. Then decide which one is best for you and request to be put on the regular monthly mailing list.

Each of the 12 Federal Reserve Banks is listed below:

Federal Reserve Bank
30 Pearl Street
Boston, MA 02106

Federal Reserve Bank
925 Chestnut Street
Philadelphia, PA 19101

Federal Reserve Bank
100 North 9th Street
Richmond, VA 23261

Federal Reserve Bank
104 Marietta St. N.W.
Atlanta, GA 30303

Federal Reserve Bank
411 Locust Street
P. O. Box 442
St. Louis, MO 63166

Federal Reserve Bank
73 South 5th Street
Minneapolis, MN 55480

How to Collect Free Information, Services and Items

Federal Reserve Bank
230 South LaSalle St.
Chicago, IL 60690

Federal Reserve Bank
33 Liberty Street
New York, NY 10045

Federal Reserve Bank
1455 East 6th Street
P. O. Box 6387
Cleveland, OH 44101

Federal Reserve Bank
400 South Akard St.
Station K
Dallas, TX 75222

Federal Reserve Bank
925 Grand Avenue
Kansas City, MO 64198

Federal Reserve Bank
400 Sansome Street
San Francisco, CA 94120

Free Retirement Advice for Senior Citizens

In 1975 the President of the U.S. established the Adminisration on Aging. This vital organization provides information on services and other opportunities available to the elderly. A considerable amount of free or nominal cost information is available to senior citizens. This information can be of material assistance for older people and could cost hundreds if not thousands of dollars if obtained from private sources. Some of the available publications are:

Every Tenth American — Describes the programs administered or supported by the Administration on Aging.

Are You Planning on Living the Rest of Your Life? — A do-it-yourself planner for persons working for small companies without in-plant, pre-retirement counseling.

You, the Law and Retirement — Tells why, how and when to see a lawyer.

Consumer Guide for Older People — A convenient wallet-size folder outlining ways an individual can protect himself against frauds and swindles.

The Fitness Challenge...in Later Years — Outlines an exercise program for maintaining youthful health and energy and suggests ways of enhancing the enjoyment of leisure.

These and other informative publications can be obtained by writing: U.S. Department of Health and Human Services, Commissioner on Aging, 200 Independence Avenue SW, Washington, D.C. 20201.

Vacation Home
Architectural Plans

This is one of the nicest services offered by Uncle Sam. You can get complete architectural designs to build your own vacation home for you and your family.

Here are a few of the available plans you might be interested in:

	ORDER NO.
Vacation House, Plan No. 5997	1052
2-bedroom House for Retired Couple, Plan No. 7195	M1272
2-bedroom Duplex, Plan No. 7200	M1289
3-bedroom House, Plan No. 7185	M1153
2-bedroom Farm Dwelling, Plan No. 7176	M1042
4-bedroom House with 2 baths, Plan No. 7193	M1286

This is only a partial list. Many other plans are available.

Order from: Publications Division, Office of Communications, U.S. Department of Agriculture, Washington, D.C. 20250. Be sure to give title and order number as shown above. You might also want to ask for their complete list of free plans.

How to Enjoy the Over
2,000 Islands in the Pacific
and Caribbean
Owned or Controlled by Uncle Sam

Almost everyone has dreamed about living happily and carefreely on the beach of a tropical island. Believe it or not,

How to Collect Free Information, Services and Items

Uncle Sam owns or controls over 2,000 islands comprising millions of square miles in the Pacific and Caribbean. These islands are not for sale. But you can live on them or invest in them. Not only is living good, but there are many excellent opportunities for doing your own thing. The islands in the Pacific are Micronesia (also called the Trust Territory of the Pacific Islands), and American Samoa. The climate of these islands is tropical and pleasant. Temperatures range between 70 and 90 degrees, with trade winds providing cooling breezes. For prospective investors, the economic future of American Samoa and the Trust Territory of the Pacific Islands is well worth looking into. They have something special to offer Americans and it would be worthwhile to visit these islands and see for yourself.

For those adventurous souls wanting to visit or to invest in these Pacific tropical islands, several publications are available to assist you:

Investing in the Future of American Samoa
American Samoa
Guidelines for Doing Business in the Trust Territory of the Pacific Islands

For these and other publications concerning "American Samoa", write: Government of American Samoa, Pago Pago, American Samoa 96799. For the above publication and other information on "The Trust Territory of the Pacific Islands," write: Trust Territory of the Pacific Islands, Office of the High Commissioner, Siapan, Marianna Islands 96950.

The U.S. Virgin Islands are a tropical paradise lying approximately 1,100 miles from Miami, Florida in the Caribbean Sea. The U.S. Virgin Islands lie directly in the path of easterly trade winds. This position enables the Islands to enjoy a near perfect climate condition. The temperature ranges from 70-90 degrees year round, with a mean average of 70 degrees. The continuous trade winds keep the humidity at a comfortable level. Permanent residents of these beautiful islands are U.S. citizens and share the same language, currency, and tax structure as the native Islanders. Whether you want to establish a new business or merely live in the Caribbean, the U.S. Virgin Islands are the ideal location. Several publications are available which explain tourist and investment opportunities in the Virgin Islands. These publications are:

> *Business Guide—U.S. Virgin Islands*
> *The Settlers Handbook—Everything You Need to Know About the U.S. Virgin Islands*

These and other informative publications can be obtained by writing: Government of the Virgin Islands of the U.S., Department of Commerce, Charlotte Emily, St. Thomas, Virgin Islands, USA 00801.

Boating Guides and Maps

The U.S. Army Corps of Engineers makes available to the public a variety of maps and information covering inland waterways and harbors throughout the United States. This information can be of real value to boating and fishing enthusiasts.

To get the telephone number of the U.S. Army Corps of Engineers Office nearest your home, call your local Federal Information Center. A complete list of Federal Information Centers appears at the back of this book. When calling the Corps of Engineers office, ask for the Waterways and Harbors section. You can also get information by writing: Public Affairs Office, Office of Chief of Engineers, Washington, D.C. 20310.

Free Guide on How to Incorporate a Small Business

If you have ever thought of forming a corporation, Uncle Sam's publication "Incorporating a Small Business" can help you. This guide shows you the basic steps involved once you have decided to incorporate. Important aspects are discussed such as articles of incorporation, bylaws, tax obligations, and compliance with state, local, and federal laws.

This valuable guide can be obtained by contacting the Small Business Administration field office listed in your local telephone directory or by writing: The Small Business Administration, Office of Public Information, Washington, D.C. 20416.

Food and Nutrition Library

Uncle Sam can help you in the kitchen and in the super-market with information on planning, buying, and preparing foods that are vital to your family's health. Here are some free publications that will save you money and help you pre-pare more nutritional food for the family:

A Guide to Budgeting for the Family

Family Food Budgeting...For Good Meals and Good Nutrition

Vegetables in Family Meals...A Guide for Consumers

Poultry in Family Meals...A Guide for Consumers

Consumers' Guide to Meat

USDA Yield Grades for Beef

Consumers' Guide to Seafood

How To Buy Cheese

Ten Ways to Save on Food

For these and many, many other valuable publications free or at a nominal cost write: Office of Information, Depart-ment of Agriculture, Washington, D.C. 20250.

Collect a Grant to Advance Your Career in the Arts

The National Endowment for the Arts is an independent government agency created in 1965 to encourage and assist in the Nation's progress in the arts. In establishing the Endow-ment the Congress declared:

"It is necessary and appropriate for the federal government to help create and sustain not only a climate encouraging freedom of thought, imagination and inquiry; but also the material conditions facil-itating the release of this creative talent."

To accomplish this goal the Endowment awards a limited number of fellowships to artists of "exceptional" talent to enable them to set aside time to work and advance their careers.

Presently, endowments are available for: architects, art critics, artists, choreographers, composers, craftsmen, designers, filmmakers, museum professionals, opera singers, photographers and creative writers.

For more information write: Program Information Office, National Endowment for the Arts, Washington, D.C. 20506.

How to Prospect for Gold in the U.S.

Prospecting for gold is something that probably everyone dreams of trying at least once. To the person who is mainly concerned with this activity as a vacation diversion, prospecting offers a special excitement. There is a constant hope that the next pan of sediment may be "paydirt" and no other thrill can compare with that experience when one sees even a few tiny plates of gold glittering in the black sand at the bottom of the pan. Uncle Sam publishes information that tells you what parts of the country are principal gold-producing districts plus helpful hints on goldmining activities in general. These publications are:

> *Prospecting for Gold in the U.S.*
> *Principal Gold Producing Districts, Professional*
> *Paper Six-Ten*

These publications are available free or at nominal cost from: U.S. Geological Survey, Public Affairs, 12201 Sunrise Valley Drive, Reston, VA 22092.

When you write ask them for their total list of publications concerning prospecting for gold.

How to Buy Government
Surplus Property

Each year the federal government purchases millions of dollars in real and personal property to keep the wheels of government rolling. Also each year, Uncle Sam finds that he has more items left over than what he needs. This is called government surplus. This surplus is available to interested parties for purchase. Surplus property such as office machines, furniture, hardware, textiles and motor vehicles can be purchased by interested parties. Some publications made available free or at nominal cost on how to purchase government surplus are as follows:

How to Collect Free Information, Services and Items

Disposal of Surplus Real Property
Sale of Government Personal Property
Facts About the General Service Administration
Doing Business with the Federal Government

These and other informative publications are available by writing: Director of Publications, General Services Administration, Washington, D.C. 20405.

Library of Publications for Parents

Uncle Sam provides a number of guides helpful in bringing up children. These publications are available free or at nominal cost. Some of these publications are:

Infant Care
Accidents and Children
Breast Feeding Your Baby
A Creative Life for Your Children
Child With a Speech Problem
Day Care for Your Child in a Family Home
Food for Your Baby's First Year
Moving Into Adolescence
When You Adopt a Child
Your Child From Age 1-6
Your Child From Age 3-4

Are these publications useful? You bet they are. For example, the publication "Infant Care" has been one of the most read publications ever in the history of America. It has outdone the Bible. Almost 9 million copies have been distributed. It has been revised at least 10 times since its introduction in 1914. It provides essential information on caring for a baby based on experiences of many doctors and other experts concerned with infant care. Important topics such as feeding, clothing, growth and development are discussed. The same informative quality can be expected in all of these publications.

These and other valuable publications can be obtained by writing to: U.S. Department of Health and Human Services, Office of Community Services, 1200 Nineteenth Street NW, Washington, D.C. 20506.

Free Business Management Assistance Publications

Valuable management assistance publications on how to start and operate a small business are available free from Uncle Sam. You could easily pay hundreds of dollars for comparable information obtained from private sources. A few of these informative publications are:

The ABC's of Borrowing
Checklist of Going into Business
Keeping Records in Small Business
Advertising Guidelines for Small Retail Firms
Insurance Checklist for Small Businesses

These great publications can be obtained free by contacting the Small Business Administration field office listed in your telephone directory or by writing: The Small Business Administration, Office of Public Information, Washington, D.C. 20416. The SBA also makes other small business publications available. Ask for their list of publications—there are hundreds of them.

Free Camping in National Forests and Grasslands

You can enjoy a super vacation in a setting of scenic charm and beauty in one of the 154 national forests which comprise over 187 million acres.

At the national forests you can camp, go hiking, swimming, boating, or horseback riding. You can pick berries, collect rocks, or watch birds. You can spend time socializing and singing around an evening campfire. This and much more is offered when you visit one of the national forests which stretch from coast to coast and border to border. No reservations are required. Campsites are filled on a first come, first served basis. Find out more about these exciting vacation opportunities.

The Forest Service makes several publications available on each of the national forests. These publications are:

How to Collect Free Information, Services and Items

National Forest Vacations
Backpacking in National Forest Wilderness
National Forest Wilderness Camping

For copies of these publications and other information, write: The National Forest Service, U.S. Department of Agriculture, Washington, D.C. 20250.

Free X-Ray and Vaccination Card

A wallet-size personal record of X-rays and vaccinations is available free of charge from Uncle Sam. The card is helpful in avoiding excessive exposure to radiation and duplication of recent X-rays. The card also provides easy reference to dates and types of vaccinations received.

You may obtain a card for each member of your family by writing to: Bureau of Radiology Health (HFX-70), Food and Drug Administration, 5600 Fisher Lane, Rockville, MD 20857.

Do You Need Flood Insurance?

If you live in one of the many areas of the country that is flood prone, you should check your eligibility for low-cost disaster protection under the National Insurance Program.

Congress created the flood insurance program in 1968 because such insurance from private sources was often unavailable or the cost was too high for most people to afford. There are presently more than 1 million homeowners receiving protection under this program.

A booklet explaining the program called "Questions and Answers—National Flood Insurance Program" is available and may be obtained by writing: Federal Insurance Administration, Housing and Urban Development, Washington, D.C. 20410, or call this federal agency's toll free number—1-800-638-6620.

How to Get Free Meals Delivered to Your Home

"Meals on Wheels" is the name given to a government program whereby meals are actually delivered to a person's home. Persons eligible must be age 60 or over and physically handicapped or not able to prepare their own meals. To qualify for this program you must also be eligible for food stamps.

If you know someone who may qualify for this beneficial program, find out more by writing: U.S. Department of Agriculture, Food and Nutrition Service, Washington, D.C. 20250.

Crime/Riot Insurance

Businessmen and property owners can get low-cost insurance to cover such things as fire, vandalism, burglary and robbery. The rates are lower than that available from commercial sources because the Federal Government helps underwrite the risk. Millions of these policies have already been issued.

For more information write: Crime/Riot Insurance, Department of Housing and Urban Development, 451 Seventh Street SW, Washington, D.C. 20410; or call toll-free, 1-800-638-8780.

How to Raise Rabbits or Hamsters for Profit

Uncle Sam shows you how to raise these little fellows. They make nice pets or you can even breed them at a profit. Topics such as care and feeding are covered.

Two informative publications are available at nominal costs:

Raising Rabbits   *Hamster Raising*

Write: Government Printing Office, Washington, D.C. 20401.

Travel Information on Foreign Countries

Most foreign embassies make available a wide variety of

free publications on their countries. These publications contain information on such things as travel, food, lodging, investment and employment opportunities. Most embassies are located in Washington, D.C. They will be happy to send you any information you request. For example, if you wanted information about travelling in Mexico, you would write the Mexican Embassy in Washington, D.C. and include a short note stating that you wanted information on vacationing in Mexico.

How to Sell Things to Uncle Sam

Got something to sell? Well, Uncle Sam could become your very best customer. Uncle Sam wants small businessmen to get their fair share of the billions of dollars of federal contracts awarded each year. What does Uncle Sam need? Everything from nails to airplanes.

And Uncle Sam makes available a publication that will help you sell products to him. This publication called "Doing Business with the Federal Government," tells you most everything you'll need to know. It covers each government department and what their product needs are. If you find you can provide a needed product, you're all set.

To get the publication "Doing Business with the Federal Government" write: General Services Administration, Washington, D.C. 20405.

Free Weekly International
Monetary Market Report
(Non-Government)

You can receive free each week a report on prices of gold, currencies, futures and U.S. Treasury Bills. Needless to say, this information can be a valuable tool in keeping abreast of the various potential investments around the world. There is no charge for your subscription. Write: International Monetary Market, 444 W. Jackson Blvd., Chicago, IL 60606.

How to Get Space, Travel, and Historical Pictures, Posters, Charts, and Decals at Nominal Cost

How would you like to have a color picture of Mars taken July 21, 1976, the day following the Viking I's successful landing on the planet? Or, how would you like to have pictures showing highlights of man's return to the moon actually pinpointing the landing? How would you like to have a set of pictures of Mars taken by the federal government's Mariner 9 spacecraft? You can have all these photographs plus many, many more. Uncle Sam makes them available at a very nominal cost way below what you would expect to pay from private sources. Some of the posters, charts, picture sets and decals are:

—Posters of America in 20 x 40 inch sizes. A separate one is available for each state.

—Armed Forces posters covering various periods from 1781-1965. Each 9 x 10½ inch reproduction dramatizes a story of the U.S. Army.

—Space Shuttle wall chart includes 9 illustrations of spacecraft configurations, the space shuttle mission profile and the many uses of the space shuttle.

To obtain these beautiful reproductions write: Superintendent of Documents, U.S. Government Printing Office, Washington, D.C. 20402. Be sure to ask for their complete catalog of posters, charts, picture sets, and decals. You'll be absolutely amazed at the beauty of these items and the low, low cost for which you can obtain them.

How to Lease Campsites in National Parks

Would you like to enjoy snow-capped peaks, mountain meadows, swift flowing streams, trout fishing amid scenic grandeur, a variety of wildlife and a profusion of colorful flowers and shrubs, countless birds and small animals in a forest setting? You can enjoy all this and more at one of Uncle Sam's beautiful campgrounds. Uncle Sam, through the

How to Collect Free Information, Services and Items

National Parks Service, maintains a network of more than 280 historic and recreational areas for public use. Visitor services at the nearly 29,000 campsites include lectures and tours by professional guides, boating and swimming facilities and much more. Some of the available publications covering the wide range of activities in these natural parks are as follows:

Camping in the National Park System — Lists all National Park camping sites and includes fees, facilities, and seasons.

Fishing in the National Park System — A park-by-park review of fishing opportunities including map.

National Parks & Landmarks — A complete listing of all areas administered by the National Parks Service.

Maps, National Parks of the U.S. — A packet of 8 maps covering more than 260 acres of the National Park System.

The National Register of Historic Places — Listing of over 1,100 historic properties owned, preserved, and managed by city, county, state, federal, and private agencies and individuals throughout the U.S. and territories.

You can obtain these publications and other valuable information by writing to: Office of Public Affairs, National Park Service, U.S. Department of Interior, Washington, D.C. 20240.

How to Join the Smithsonian Institute

You can have an opportunity to participate in the activities of the highly prestigous Smithsonian Institute. Members are accepted at all age levels and for various interests.

Members of the Smithsonian Institute may participate in a wide variety of travel programs and enjoy discounts on books and other purchases. The Smithsonian makes available a wide variety of publications including reports of scientific research and books of popular interest on a variety of topics.

For more information on national memberships write to: Smithsonian Associates, Reception Center, Great Hall, Smithsonian Institution Building, Washington, D.C. 20560.

Library of Publications on Earthquakes

In certain parts of the U.S. the threat of an earthquake looms constantly; yet few people know how to protect themselves, their families and homes during and after an earthquake. Uncle Sam provides free publications on this subject. These publications are as follows:

The San Andreas Fault — Explains the fracture that cuts through rocks of the coastal region of California with maps and photos.

Active Faults in California — Locates the most earthquake-prone areas, gives Richter scale readings of past California quakes.

These and other valuable publications can be obtained by writing: U.S. Geological Survey, 12201 Sunrise Valley Drive, Reston, VA 22092.

Free Guide — How to Save a Person's Life

Keep this handy, wallet-size card with you at all times. It may help save a life.

It describes the correct procedure for administering mouth-to-mouth resuscitation. One side of the card illustrates the procedure for infants and small children; the other side adults and children 5 years and older.

You never know when you'll need this vital, life-saving information. So be prepared. This valuable guide is called "First Aid Rescue-Breathing Card." You can obtain it by writing: Superintendent of Documents, Government Printing Office, Washington, D.C. 20402.

Library on Clothing and Laundry Care

Here's all you need to know to take some of the drudgery out of wash day—and how to keep your family's wardrobe free of stains, mildew, and moths. Clothing costs a lot of money these days. Learn the proper way to care for your clothes from government experts. Several publications are available free. They are:

Sanitation in Home Laundering
Removing Stains From Fabrics
How to Prevent and Remove Mildew
Home Laundering: The Equipment and the Job
Clothing Repair
Washing Machines—Selection and Use
Protecting Woolens Against Moths and Carpet Beetles

These and other informative publications can be obtained from: Agricultural Research Service, Department of Agriculture, Washington, D.C. 20250.

Is Your Microwave Oven Safe?

Cooking with a microwave oven can reduce the time you spend in the kitchen. However, cooking with a microwave oven can be dangerous to your health if it is leaking radiation. Your microwave can leak without you knowing it. So every time you cook, you could be taking a risk.

But how can you have your microwave checked for radiation leaks? The Food and Drug Administration (FDA) will do it for you—free of charge. Simply call the local FDA office in your area. Tell them you're concerned about radiation leaks from your microwave oven. They will dispatch an FDA inspector to your home. The inspector will check for leaks using a radiation detection device. If there is a problem you can contact the manufacturer to make repairs. If there is no problem, you can set your mind at ease.

To find the telephone number of your local FDA office, refer to the list of Federal Information Centers at the back of this book. Call the Center nearest your home. Ask for the telephone number of the local FDA office. They'll be happy to give it to you.

Birth and Death Records

For every birth and death taking place in the United States, an official certificate should be on file where the event occurred. These certificates are prepared by doctors, funeral directors or hospital authorities and are filed permanently by state and local government units.

The Federal Government makes available a publication which tells where to write to get birth and death records. It explains what information is needed to get a duplicate record and any cost involved. This publication called *Where to Write for Birth and Death Records* (stock No. 017-022-00618-9) is available from the Superintendent of Documents, U.S. Government Printing Office, Washington, D.C. 20401, or you can telephone order by dialing 1-202-783-3238.

Epilogue —

Where To Get Help

Dear Reader:

Today is the biggest era ever for government benefits. American citizens can get more benefits now than in the days of the deep depression. And, government benefits are getting bigger and broader everyday.

Politicians are constantly dreaming up ways to improve the lot of mankind. These ideas are often transformed into laws passed by Congress, creating new give-away programs. Millions of dollars are made available to eligible citizens; and countless people have a chance for a better existence.

Although more government benefits are available today than ever before, the number of citizens actually collecting these benefits has not kept pace with the growth of federal programs. The reason for this is that many Americans do not know what benefits are available because the federal government does not advertise them. There are many reasons why the government does not advertise. First of all, it would have to obtain competitive bidding from the various advertisers. Then the government bureaucracy would have to sift through the various proposals to determine which one was the lowest possible bid. This would be a monumental task because the quality of the advertising would have to be weighed against the cost. It is likely that the cost of selecting an advertising medium might be more than the cost of the actual advertisement or commercial.

How to Collect Big $$$ from Uncle Sam

Aside from the government "red tape", there are other problems involved in advertising government benefits. If all government departments, agencies and offices decided to advertise the benefits and services available to the American public; our newspapers, magazines, radio and T.V. would be flooded with government paid advertisements. Then there would probably be charges that the federal government was subsidizing the media.

On the other hand, some Americans know of the available benefits but get discouraged and frustrated in dealing with the federal bureaucracy. They actually "give up" and benefits that are rightfully theirs go uncollected.

Almost every American has experienced or heard of cases where government employees have been rude, apathetic and abrupt. When I worked for the federal government I observed many cases where the public was not treated properly. For example, I can recall a particular agency I will not mention here. Citizens calling into the agency had to wait for long periods of time before the phone would be answered. The federal employees were not busy; they simply ignored the ringing of the phones. On other occasions the bureaucrat would be abrupt and act as though the caller was interfering with his work day. I'm sure that we've all, on occasion, called a government agency only to be put on hold for long periods of time, or even cut off. Then, of course, your call can be referred to 3, 4, or 5 individuals before you find someone who can help you.

The problem seems to be the attitude of the bureaucrats working in these federal agencies. They don't believe or cannot understand that they actually work for the public. They seem to forget that public taxes pay their salaries. Some bureaucrats are under the mistaken impression that they are working in government merely to enhance their own comfort.

Fortunately, President Carter recognized the long-standing problem of bureaucratic non-responsiveness to the public. When taking office he listened to story after story of bureaucratic apathy, rudeness, and irresponsibility. He heard case after case where American citizens got the run-around from public employees.

President Carter was the first President in history to do

something about this problem. He got legislation through the Congress that will have a sobering effect on many bureaucrats. Under this legislation, a bureaucrat can be fired if there are a certain number of reports from citizens charging him with being rude. This rule governing bureaucratic behavior with the public is very encouraging and long overdue.

When you deal with a government bureaucrat you no longer have to be intimidated. You no longer have to stand for their rudeness or apathy. If you are not satisfied in your dealings with them, you can tell them you plan to file a formal complaint charging them with rudeness. Then watch their attitude change from a lion to a helpful lamb.

This long-overdue legislation is going to turn the tables on the relationships between the government employees and the American taxpayers. The true relationship between them is now exposed and they will have to become more responsive to the needs and desires of the public for whom they work.

* * *

In this book, I have tried hard to cover the major government benefits available to Americans. With each printing, the book is improved and updated. I hope the book has helped you and I wish you the very best.

R. Emil Neuman

P.S. To better help you obtain every possible benefit available to you as an American, I have compiled a list of federal government services by subject matter. This guide will help you answer questions such as: What kind of benefits and services are offered and which federal department or agency can help me? To be of further service to you, I have also compiled a list of federal information centers where you can call to get help. The list is arranged by state and then city. A specific telephone number is listed for each major city. If you have any questions about any federal program or agency, call the number nearest your home. A staff member will be available to help answer any question you may have.

List of Federal Government Services by Subject

ADVERTISING
Director, Bureau of Consumer Protection, Federal Trade Commission, Washington, DC 20580; phone 202-326-2222.

AIR TRAVEL/ROUTES AND SERVICE
Director, Office of Consumer Protection, Civil Aeronautics Board, Washington, DC 20423; phone 202-366-4000.

AIR TRAVEL/SAFETY
For general information contact the Community and Consumer Liaison Division, Federal Aviation Administration, APA-430, Washington, DC 20591; phone 202-366-4000.

ALCOHOL
Chief, Trade and Consumer Affairs Division, Bureau of Alcohol, Tobacco, and Firearms, Department of the Treasury, Washington, DC 20226; phone 202-566-7581.

ALCOHOLISM, DRUG ABUSE AND MENTAL ILLNESS
Office of Public Affairs, Alcohol, Drug Abuse and Mental Health Service, 5600 Fishers Lane, Rockville, MD 20857; phone 301-443-3783.

ANTITRUST
Bureau of Competition, Federal Trade Commission, Washington, DC 20580; phone 202-326-2222.

Consumer Affairs Section, Antitrust Division, Justice Department, Washington, DC 20530; phone 202-326-2222.

AUTO SAFETY AND HIGHWAYS
National Highway Traffic Safety Administration; toll-free hotline **800-424-9393**. In Washington, DC call 426-0123.

Receives reports on auto safety problems. Provides information on automobile recalls and various complaints received about specific makes and models.

BANKS

Federal Credit Unions

National Credit Union Administration, Washington, DC 20456; phone 202-254-8760.

Federally Insured Savings and Loans

Consumer Division, Office of Community Investment, Federal Home Loan Bank Board, Washington, DC 20552; phone 202-377-6237.

Federal Reserve Banks

Office of Saver and Consumer Affairs, Federal Reserve System, Washington, DC 20551; phone 202-452-3000.

National Banks

Consumer Affairs, Office of the Comptroller of the Currency, Washington, DC 20219; phone 202-447-1600.

State Chartered Banks

Office of Bank Customer Affairs, Federal Deposit Insurance Corporation, Washington, DC 20429; phone 202-389-4427.

BOATING

Chief, Information and Administrative Staff, U.S. Coast Guard, Washington, DC 20590; phone 202-426-1080.

BUS TRAVEL

Consumer Affairs Office, Interstate Commerce Commission, Washington, DC 20423; phone 202-275-7849.

BUSINESS

Office of the Ombudsman, Department of Commerce, Washington, DC 20230; phone 202-377-3176.

Director, Women-in-Business and Consumer Affairs,

Small Business Administration, 1441 L St., NW, Washington, DC 20416; phone 202-653-6074.

CANCER INFORMATION
Operated by the National Cancer Institute, Department of Health and Welfare. Provides information about all aspects of cancer to the general public, cancer patients and their families. All calls are confidential. Call toll-free, **1-800-638-6694.** In Maryland, call **1-800-492-6600.**

CHILD ABUSE
National Center on Child Abuse and Neglect, P.O. Box 1182, Washington, DC 20013; phone 202-245-2856.

CHILDHOOD IMMUNIZATION
Office of the Assistant Secretary for Health, Office of Public Affairs, Washington, DC 20201; phone 703-235-2600.

CHILDREN AND YOUTH
Commissioner, Administration for Children, Youth and Families, Washington, D.C. 20201; phone 202-755-0590.

CONSUMER INFORMATION
For a copy of the free *Consumer Information Catalog,* a listing of more than 200 selected Federal consumer publications on such topics as child care, automobiles, health, employment, housing, energy, etc., send a post-card to the Consumer Information Center, Pueblo, CO 81009.

COPYRIGHTS
Copyright Office, Crystal Mall, 1921 Jefferson Davis Highway, Arlington, VA 20559; phone 202-479-0700.

CREDIT
Director, Bureau of Consumer Protection, Federal Trade Commission, Washington, DC 20850; phone 202-326-2222

CRIME INSURANCE
Federal Crime Insurance, Department of Housing and Urban Development, P.O. Box 41033, Washington, DC

20014; toll-free hotline **800-638-8780.** In Washington, DC call 652-2637.

Provides information and applications for benefits for Federal low-cost crime insurance for both residential and commercial property.

CUSTOMS

Public Information Division, U.S. Customs, Washington, DC 20229; phone 202-566-8195.

DISCRIMINATION

U.S. Commission on Civil Rights, 1121 Vermont Avenue, Washington, DC 20425; phone 202-376-8177.

Equal Employment Opportunity Commission, 2401 E St., NW, Washington, DC 20506; phone 202-634-6930.

For complaints about discrimination in lending practices by financial and retail institutions based on race, color, religion, national origin, sex, marital status, age, or receipt of public assistance, contact the Housing and Credit Section, Civil Rights Division, Justice Department, Washington, DC 20530; phone 202-633-4734. (Also see HOUSING)

DRUGS AND COSMETICS

Consumer Inquiry Section, Food and Drug Administration, 5600 Fishers Lane, Rockville, MD 20852; phone 301-443-3170.

EDUCATION GRANTS AND LOANS

Office of Public Affairs, Office of Education, Washington, DC 20202; phone toll free 1-800-333-4636.

Provides general information about financial assistance for educational expenses.

ELDERLY

Administration on Aging, Washington, DC 20201; phone 202-245-0724.

EMPLOYMENT AND JOB TRAINING

Since nearly all employment and training programs are

handled at the state or local levels, check your phone directory under your state government for the Employment Service or under your local government for the mayor's office. If you cannot reach these sources, you can obtain general information by writing to the Employment and Training Administration, Department of Labor, Washington, DC 20213; phone 202-376-6905.

ENERGY

Director, Office of Consumer Affairs, Department of Energy, Washington, DC 20585; phone 202-252-5141.

ENERGY EFFICIENCY

Information Office, National Bureau of Standards, Washington, DC 20234; phone 301-975-2000.

ENVIRONMENT

Office of Public Awareness, Environmental Protection Agency, Washington, DC 20460; phone 202-382-2090.

FEDERAL JOB INFORMATION

Check for the Federal Job Information Center under the U.S. Government in your phone directory. If there is no listing, call toll-free directory assistance at **800-555-1212,** and ask for the number of the Federal Job Information Center in your state. In the Washington, DC metropolitan area contact the Civil Service Commission, 1900 E St., NW, Washington, DC 20415; phone 202-737-9616.

FEDERAL REGULATIONS

For information on Federal regulations and proposals, the Office of the Federal Register (OFR) is offering, among other services, recorded "Dial-a-Reg" phone messages. Dial-a-Reg gives advance information on significant documents to be published in the *Federal Register* the following work day. The service is currently available in three cities: Washington, DC telephone 202-523-5022; Chicago telephone 312-663-0084; and Los Angeles telephone 213-688-6694.

FEDERAL TAX INFORMATION

Call toll-free, **1-800-424-1040** to get tax information.

Operated by the Internal Revenue Service. Provides assistance on Federal income tax questions.

FIREARMS
(See ALCOHOL)

FISH GRADING
National Marine Fisheries Service, Department of Commerce, Washington, DC 20235; phone 202-634-7458.

FISH AND WILDLIFE
Fish and Wildlife Service, Office of Public Affairs, Washington, DC 20240; phone 202-343-5634.

FLOOD INSURANCE
National Flood Insurance, Department of Housing and Urban Development, Washington, DC 20410; toll free hotline **800-638-6580**. In Washington, DC call 755-9096.

Provides information on the Federal Government's program to provide low cost flood insurance in hazardous areas.

FOOD
Assistant Secretary for Food and Consumer Services, U.S. Department of Agriculture, Washington, DC 20250; phone 202-447-4623.

Consumer Inquiry Section, Food and Drug Administration, 5600 Fishers Lane, Rockville, MD 20852; phone 301-443-3170.

FOOD STAMPS
Provides information on the Food Stamp program such as eligibility requirements and benefits available. Each state has a toll-free telephone number. To get the number for your state, call toll-free, **1-800-555-1212** and ask for the toll-free Food Stamp number for your state.

FRAUD
Director, Bureau of Consumer Protection, Federal Trade Commission, Washington, DC 20580; phone 202-326-2222.

HANDICAPPED
Director, Division of Public Information, Office of

Human Development Services, Department of Health and Human Services, Washington, DC 20201; phone 202-245-2890.

HEALTH INFORMATION CLEARING HOUSE

This toll free hotline provides information on health related subjects. They can answer specific health questions and send you helpful information. Federally-funded program. Call toll free **1-800-336-4797**. In Washington, D.C. area phone 301-565-4167.

HOUSING

Department of Housing and Urban Development, Division of Consumer Complaints, Washington, DC 20410; phone 202-755-5353.

For complaints about housing discrimination call the housing discrimination hotline **1-800-424-8590**. In Washington, DC call 755-5490.

IMMIGRATION AND NATURALIZATION

Information Services, Immigration and Naturalization Service, 425 Eye St., NW, Washington, DC 20536; phone 202-648-1003.

INDIAN ARTS AND CRAFTS

Indian Arts and Crafts Board, Washington, DC 20240; phone 202-343-2773.

JOB SAFETY

Office of Information, Occupational Safety and Health Administration (OSHA), Department of Labor, Washington, DC 20210; call toll free **1-800-648-1003**.

Provides information to workers about OSHA activities. Also accepts reports about work-related accidents and dangerous working conditions.

MAIL SERVICE

Check with your local postmaster or contact the Consumer Advocate, U.S. Postal Service, Room 5920, Washington, DC 20260; phone 202-245-4514.

MAPS

Public Inquiries Office, Geological Survey, National Center, Reston, VA 22092; phone 703-648-4000.

MEDICAID/MEDICARE

Health Care Financing Administration, Department of Health, Education and Welfare, Washington, DC 20201; phone 202-245-0312.

MEDICAL RESEARCH

Division of Public Information, National Institutes of Health, 9000 Rockville Pike, Bethesda, MD 20014; phone 301-496-5787.

Center for Disease Control, Attention: Public Inquiries, Atlanta, GA 30333; phone 404-639-3534.

MENTAL ILLNESS

(See ALCOHOLISM, DRUG ABUSE AND MENTAL ILLNESS)

METRIC INFORMATION

(See ENERGY EFFICIENCY, National Bureau of Standards)

MOVING

Interstate Commerce Commission; Washington, DC 20423; phone 202-275-7849.

Accepts complaints from consumers on interstate moving of household goods. Also answers questions on train and bus passenger problems and common carrier rates. Provides information to independent truckers on ways to enter the independent trucking business.

PARKS AND RECREATION AREAS

National Forests

Forest Service, U.S. Department of Agriculture, Washington, DC 20250; phone 202-447-3957.

National Parks and Historic Sites

National Park Service, Washington, DC 20240; phone 202-343-4747.

Recreation Areas on Army Corps of Engineers Project Sites

Recreation Resource Management Branch (CWO-R), Army Corps of Engineers, Washington, DC 20314; phone 202-693-7177.

Other Recreation Areas

Office of Public Affairs, Department of the Interior, Washington, DC 20240; phone 202-343-3171.

PASSPORTS

For passport information, check with your local post office or contact the Passport Office, Department of State, 1425 K St., NW, Washington, DC 20524; phone 202-523-1355.

PATENTS AND TRADEMARKS

Patents

Commissioner, Patent Office, Department of Commerce, Washington, DC 20231; phone 703-557-3080.

Trademarks

Commissioner, Trademark Office, Department of Commerce, Washington, DC 20231; phone 703-557-3268.

PEACE CORPS

Provides information about volunteer opportunities in foreign countries. Call toll-free **1-800-424-8580**. In Washington, DC call 254-7346.

PENSIONS

Office of Communications, Pension Benefit Guaranty Corporation, 2020 K St., NW, Washington, DC 20006; phone 202-778-8800.

Labor Management Standards Administration, Department of Labor, Washington, DC 20210; phone 202-523-8776.

PHYSICAL FITNESS/SPORTS

President's Council on Physical Fitness and Sports, 400

6th St., SW, Washington, DC 20201; phone 202-272-3421.

PRODUCT SAFETY

Consumer Product Safety Commission, Consumer Services Branch, Washington, DC 20207; toll-free hotline **1-800-638-2772**. In Maryland call **1-800-492-8104**.

Receives reports and inquiries relating to hazardous manufactured products. Also assists consumers in evaluating safety of products on sale to the public.

RADIO AND TELEVISION BROADCASTING/ INTERFERENCE

Consumer Assistance Office, Federal Communications Commission, Washington, DC 20554; phone 202-632-7000.

SECOND OPINION SURGICAL HOTLINE

This hotline answers your questions and provides referrals to a doctor who will give you a second (or third) opinion. Free information is also available. **1-800-638-6833**. In Maryland call **1-800-492-6603**.

SMOKING

Office on Smoking and Health, 12420 Parklawn Dr., Room 158, Park Bldg., Rockville, MD 20852; phone 301-443-1575.

SOCIAL SECURITY

Social Security Administration toll free hotline **1-800-234-5772**. Write: Headquarters, Social Security Administration, 6401 Security Blvd., Baltimore, MD 21235.

Provides information on Social Security retirement, disability and death benefits, including medicare, hospital and medical coverage.

SOLAR HEATING

National Solar Heating and Cooling Information Center, P.O. Box 1607, Rockville, MD 20850; toll free hotline is **1-800-523-2929**.

Provides information on the commercial availability of solar installations for heating and cooling.

How to Collect Big $$$ from Uncle Sam

STOCKS AND BONDS

Consumer Liaison Office, Securities and Exchange Commission, Washington, DC 20549; phone 202-272-7440.

TAXES

The Internal Revenue Service (IRS) toll-free tax information number is **1-800-424-1040.**

TRAIN TRAVEL

AMTRAK (National Railroad Passenger Corp.). For consumer problems first try to contact a local AMTRAK consumer relations office listed in your phone directory. If there is not an office near you contact AMTRAK, Office of Consumer Relations, P.O. Box 2709, Washington, DC 20013; phone 202-383-2121.

TRAVEL INFORMATION

U.S. Travel Service, Department of Commerce, Washington, DC 20230; phone 202-377-4553.

VENEREAL DISEASE

VD toll free hotline **1-800-227-8922.**

Provides confidential and anonymous free information on all aspects of sexually-transmitted diseases. Also provides free consultation and referral information if requested.

VETERANS' INFORMATION

The Veterans Administration has toll-free numbers in all 50 states. Check your local phone directory, or call **1-800-555-1212** for toll-free directory assistance. For problems that can't be handled through local offices, write Veterans Administration, 810 Vermont Avenue, NW, Washington, DC 20420.

Provides information to Veterans and their dependents about the benefits available, including GI loans, education, medical care, and unemployment.

VISTA

Provides information about volunteer opportunities in

the United States. Call toll-free **1-800-424-8580.** In Washington, DC call 254-7346.

WAGES AND WORKING CONDITIONS
Employment Standards Administration, Department of Labor, Washington, DC 20210; phone 202-523-8743.

WARRANTIES
For a problem involving the failure of a seller to honor a warranty, contact the Division of Special Statutes, Federal Trade Commission, Washington, DC 20580; phone 202-326-2222. Or you may contact the FTC regional office nearest you. They are listed in your telephone directory under U.S. Government.

List of Independent Organizations by Subject

CHASE STUDENT LOANS
This toll free number puts you in contact with the student loan department of the Chase Manhatten Bank in New York. They can answer questions on college financial assistance or send you a free brochure. **1-800-645-8246.** In New York call **1-800-645-7203.**

CHILD ABUSE HOTLINE
If you're abusing your children or are on the verge of violence, you can call this toll-free number for help. Crisis counseling over the phone is available. **1-800-422-4453.**

COCAINE USERS HOTLINE
Hotline operators provide information on coping with drug related problems. The line is open to users and concerned relatives and friends. They can refer abusers to professional help. **1-800-COCAINE.**

MISSING CHILDREN HOTLINE
Operated by Child Find, Inc. This number can be used by missing children or anyone else who has information on the whereabouts of missing children. **1-800-843-5678.**

PARENTS WITHOUT PARTNERS

This organization can provide helpful information on how single parents can successfully raise children. It also gives single parents an opportunity to meet other single parents. Call toll-free **1-800-638-8078**. In Maryland call 301-654-8850.

RUNAWAY CHILDREN HOTLINE

The National Runaway Hotline; toll-free **1-800-621-4000**. In Illinois call **1-800-972-6004**.

Provides advice to parents of runaway children on a 24-hour basis. Calls are confidential.

The state of Texas operates a 24-hour message relay service to accept calls from runaways and forward messages to parents. Also provides counseling and confidential referral information on medical assistance, shelter, and other services. Call toll-free **1-800-231-6946**. In Texas call **1-800-392-3352**.

List of Federal Information Centers

ALABAMA
Birmingham 205-322-8591
Mobile 205-438-1421

ALASKA
Anchorage 907-271-3650

ARIZONA
Phoenix 602-261-3313

ARKANSAS
Little Rock 501-378-6177

CALIFORNIA
Los Angeles 213-894-3800
Sacramento 916-978-4010
San Diego 619-557-6030
San Francisco .. 415-556-6600
Santa Ana 714-836-2386

COLORADO
Colorado Springs. 303-471-9491
Denver 303-844-6575
Pueblo 303-544-9523

CONNECTICUT
Hartford 203-527-2617
New Haven 203-624-4720

FLORIDA
Fort Lauderdale 305-522-8531
Jacksonville 904-354-4756
Miami 305-536-4155
Orlando 305-422-1800
St. Petersburg .. 813-893-3495
Tampa 813-229-7911
West Palm Beach 305-833-7566

GEORGIA
Atlanta 404-331-6891

HAWAII
Honolulu 808-541-1365

ILLINOIS
Chicago 312-353-4242

INDIANA
Gary 219-883-4110
Indianapolis 317-269-7373

Epilogue — Where to Get Help

IOWA
    All locations ... 800-532-1556

KANSAS
    All locations ... 800-432-2934

KENTUCKY
    Louisville 502-582-6261

LOUISIANA
    New Orleans ... 504-589-6696

MARYLAND
    Baltimore 301-962-4980

MASSACHUSETTS
    Boston 617-565-8121

MICHIGAN
    Detroit 313-226-7016
    Grand Rapids .. 616-451-2628

MINNESOTA
    Minneapolis 612-349-5333

MISSOURI
    St. Louis 314-425-4106
    Other locations . 800-392-7711

NEBRASKA
    Omaha 402-221-3353
    Other locations . 800-642-8383

NEW JERSEY
    Newark 201-645-3600
    Trenton........ 609-396-4400

NEW MEXICO
    Albuquerque ... 505-766-3091

NEW YORK
    Albany 518-463-4421
    Buffalo 716-846-4010
    New York 212-264-4464
    Rochester 716-546-5075
    Syracuse 315-476-8545

NORTH CAROLINA
    Charlotte 704-376-3600

OHIO
    Akron 216-375-5638
    Cincinnati...... 513-684-2801
    Cleveland 216-522-4040
    Columbus...... 614-221-1014
    Dayton 513-223-7377
    Toledo 419-241-3223

OKLAHOMA
    Oklahoma City . 405-231-4868
    Tulsa 918-584-4193

OREGON
    Portland 503-221-2222

PENNSYLVANIA
    Philadelphia 215-597-7042
    Pittsburgh 412-644-3456

RHODE ISLAND
    Providence 401-331-5565

TENNESSEE
    Chattanooga ... 615-265-8231
    Memphis 901-521-3285
    Nashville....... 615-242-5056

TEXAS
    Austin 512-472-5494
    Dallas 214-767-8585
    Fort Worth 817-334-3624
    Houston 713-229-2552
    San Antonio ... 512-224-4471

UTAH
    Salt Lake City . 801-524-5353

VIRGINIA
    Norfolk........ 804-441-3101
    Richmond 804-643-4928
    Roanoke....... 703-982-8591

WASHINGTON
    Seattle......... 206-442-0570
    Tacoma........ 206-383-5230

WISCONSIN
    Milwaukee 414-271-2273

SOCIAL SECURITY ADMINISTRATION

Request for Earnings and Benefit Estimate Statement

To receive a free statement of your earnings covered by Social Security and your estimated future benefits, all you need to do is fill out this form. Please print or type your answers. When you have completed the form, fold it and mail it to us.

1. Name shown on your Social Security card:

   First   Middle Initial   Last

2. Your Social Security number as shown on your card:

   ☐☐☐ - ☐☐ - ☐☐☐☐

3. Your date of birth: Month   Day   Year

4. Other Social Security numbers you may have used:

   ☐☐☐ - ☐☐ - ☐☐☐☐
   ☐☐☐ - ☐☐ - ☐☐☐☐

5. Your Sex: ☐ Male ☐ Female

6. Other names you have used (including a maiden name):

7. Show your actual earnings for last year and your estimated earnings for this year. Include only wages and/or net self-employment income subject to Social Security tax.

   A. Last year's actual earnings:
      $ ☐☐☐,☐☐☐.☐0☐0
        Dollars only

   B. This year's estimated earnings:
      $ ☐☐☐,☐☐☐.☐0☐0
        Dollars only

8. Show the age at which you plan to retire: _____

Form SSA-7004-PC-OP2 (6/88) DESTROY PRIOR EDITIONS

9. Below, show an amount which you think best represents your future average yearly earnings between now and when you plan to retire. The amount should be a yearly average, not your total future lifetime earnings. Only show earnings subject to Social Security tax.

   Most people should enter the same amount as this year's estimated earnings (the amount shown in 7B). The reason for this is that we will show your retirement benefit estimate in today's dollars, but adjusted to account for average wage growth in the national economy.

   However, if you expect to earn significantly more or less in the future than what you currently earn because of promotions, a job change, part-time work, or an absence from the work force, enter the amount in today's dollars that will most closely reflect your future average yearly earnings. Do not add in cost-of-living, performance, or scheduled pay increases or bonuses.

   Your future average yearly earnings:

   $ ☐☐☐,☐☐☐.☐0☐0
     Dollars only

10. Address where you want us to send the statement:

    _____
    Name

    _____
    Street Address (Include Apt. No., P.O. Box, or Rural Route)

    _____
    City   State   Zip Code

I am asking for information about my own Social Security record or the record of a person I am authorized to represent. I understand that if I deliberately request information under false pretenses I may be guilty of a federal crime and could be fined and/or imprisoned. I authorize you to send the statement of my earnings and benefit estimates to me or my representative through a contractor.

▲

Please sign your name (Do not print)

_____

Date _____ (Area Code) Daytime Telephone No.

ABOUT THE PRIVACY ACT
Social Security is allowed to collect the facts on this form under Section 205 of the Social Security Act. We need them to quickly identify your record and prepare the earnings statement you asked us for. Giving us these facts is voluntary. However, without them we may not be able to give you an earnings and benefit estimate statement. Neither the Social Security Administration nor its contractor will use the information for any other purpose.

SP

Mail This Form To: Social Security Administration
Salinas Data Operations Center
100 E. Alvin Drive
Salinas, CA   93906

315

SOCIAL SECURITY ADMINISTRATION

Request for Earnings and Benefit Estimate Statement

To receive a free statement of your earnings covered by Social Security and your estimated future benefits, all you need to do is fill out this form. Please print or type your answers. When you have completed the form, fold it and mail it to us.

1. Name shown on your Social Security card:

   First ___ Middle Initial ___ Last

2. Your Social Security number as shown on your card:

   ☐☐☐ - ☐☐ - ☐☐☐☐

3. Your date of birth:

   Month ___ Day ___ Year

4. Other Social Security numbers you may have used:

   ☐☐☐ - ☐☐ - ☐☐☐☐
   ☐☐☐ - ☐☐ - ☐☐☐☐

5. Your Sex: ☐ Male ☐ Female

6. Other names you have used (including a maiden name):

   ___

7. Show your actual earnings for last year and your estimated earnings for this year. Include only wages and/or net self-employment income subject to Social Security tax.

   A. Last year's actual earnings:

   $ ☐☐☐ , ☐☐☐ . ☐ ☐
   Dollars only

   B. This year's estimated earnings:

   $ ☐☐☐ , ☐☐☐ . ☐ ☐
   Dollars only

8. Show the age at which you plan to retire: ___

9. Below, show an amount which you think best represents your future average yearly earnings between now and when you plan to retire. The amount should be a yearly average, not your total future lifetime earnings. Only show earnings subject to Social Security tax.

   Most people should enter the same amount as this year's estimated earnings (the amount shown in 7B). The reason for this is that we will show your retirement benefit estimate in today's dollars, but adjusted to account for average wage growth in the national economy.

   However, if you expect to earn significantly more or less in the future than what you currently earn because of promotions, a job change, part-time work, or an absence from the work force, enter the amount in today's dollars that will most closely reflect your future average yearly earnings. Do not add in cost-of-living, performance, or scheduled pay increases or bonuses.

   Your future average yearly earnings:

   $ ☐☐☐ , ☐☐☐ . ☐ ☐
   Dollars only

10. Address where you want us to send the statement:

   Name ___

   Street Address (Include Apt. No., P.O. Box, or Rural Route) ___

   City ___ State ___ Zip Code ___

   I am asking for information about my own Social Security record or the record of a person I am authorized to represent. I understand that if I deliberately request information under false pretenses I may be guilty of a federal crime and could be fined and/or imprisoned. I authorize you to send the statement of my earnings and benefit estimates to me or my representative through a contractor.

   Please sign your name (Do not print)

   ▲

   Date ___ (Area Code) Daytime Telephone No. ___

   SP

Form SSA-7004-PC-OP2 (6/88) DESTROY PRIOR EDITIONS

Mail This Form To: Social Security Administration
Salinas Data Operations Center
100 E. Alvin Drive
Salinas, CA 93906

SOCIAL SECURITY ADMINISTRATION

Request for Earnings and Benefit Estimate Statement

To receive a free statement of your earnings covered by Social Security and your estimated future benefits, all you need to do is fill out this form. Please print or type your answers. When you have completed the form, fold it and mail it to us.

1. Name shown on your Social Security card:

   First   Middle Initial   Last

2. Your Social Security number as shown on your card:

   ☐☐☐ - ☐☐ - ☐☐☐☐

3. Your date of birth:
   Month   Day   Year

4. Other Social Security numbers you may have used:

   ☐☐☐ - ☐☐ - ☐☐☐☐
   ☐☐☐ - ☐☐ - ☐☐☐☐

5. Your Sex: ☐ Male ☐ Female

6. Other names you have used (including a maiden name):

7. Show your actual earnings for last year and your estimated earnings for this year. Include only wages and/or net self-employment income subject to Social Security tax.

   A. Last year's actual earnings:
      $ ☐☐☐ , ☐☐☐ . ☐ ☐
        Dollars only

   B. This year's estimated earnings:
      $ ☐☐☐ , ☐☐☐ . ☐ ☐
        Dollars only

8. Show the age at which you plan to retire: _____

9. Below, show an amount which you think best represents your future average yearly earnings between now and when you plan to retire. The amount should be a yearly average, not your total future lifetime earnings. Only show earnings subject to Social Security tax.

   Most people should enter the same amount as this year's estimated earnings (the amount shown in 7B). The reason for this is that we will show your retirement benefit estimate in today's dollars, but adjusted to account for average wage growth in the national economy.

   However, if you expect to earn significantly more or less in the future than what you currently earn because of promotions, a job change, part-time work, or an absence from the work force, enter the amount in today's dollars that will most closely reflect your future average yearly earnings. Do not add in cost-of-living, performance, or scheduled pay increases or bonuses.

   Your future average yearly earnings:

   $ ☐☐☐ , ☐☐☐ . ☐ ☐
     Dollars only

10. Address where you want us to send the statement:

   Name

   Street Address (Include Apt. No., P.O. Box, or Rural Route)

   City   State   Zip Code

   I am asking for information about my own Social Security record or the record of a person I am authorized to represent. I understand that if I deliberately request information under false pretenses I may be guilty of a federal crime and could be fined and/or imprisoned. I authorize you to send the statement of my earnings and benefit estimates to me or my representative through a contractor.

   Please sign your name (Do not print)

   ▲

   Date _____ (Area Code) Daytime Telephone No.

   ABOUT THE PRIVACY ACT
   Social Security is allowed to collect the facts on this form under Section 205 of the Social Security Act. We need them to quickly identify your record and prepare the earnings statement you asked us for. Giving us these facts is voluntary. However, without them we may not be able to give you an earnings and benefit estimate statement. Neither the Social Security Administration nor its contractor will use the information for any other purpose.

   ☐ SP

Form SSA-7004-PC-OP2 (6/88) DESTROY PRIOR EDITIONS

Mail This Form To: Social Security Administration
Salinas Data Operations Center
100 E. Alvin Drive
Salinas, CA   93906

NOTES

INDEX

To order additional copies
of this book write:

R. Emil Neuman
Box 2344
Leucadia, CA 92024